PTSD/Borderlines in Therapy

By the same author

The Challenge of the Borderline Patient
The Reality of Mental Illness (with Martin Roth)

A NORTON PROFESSIONAL BOOK

PTSD/Borderlines in Therapy

FINDING THE BALANCE

Jerome Kroll, M.D.

Department of Psychiatry
University of Minnesota Medical School

W. W. NORTON & COMPANY, INC. • NEW YORK • LONDON

The text of this book was composed in 10/12 English Times.
Composition by Bytheway Typesetting Services, Inc. Manufacturing
by Haddon Craftsmen.

Library of Congress Cataloging-in-Publication Data

Kroll, Jerome.
  PTSD/Borderlines in therapy : finding the balance / Jerome Kroll.
    p.   cm.
  "A Norton professional book."
  Includes bibliographical references and index.
  ISBN 0-393-70157-3
    1. Borderline personality disorder—Treatment.   2. Post-traumatic
stress disorder—Treatment.   3. Adult child sexual abuse victims—
Rehabilitation.   4. Psychotherapy.   I. Title.
    [DNLM: 1. Stress Disorders, Post-Traumatic—therapy.   2. Child
Abuse, Sexual—complications.   3. Borderline Personality Disorder—
in adulthood.   4. Borderline Personality Disorder—therapy.
5. Psychotherapy—methods.   WM 170 K93p 1993]
RC569.5.B67K767   1993
616.85'8520651—dc20
DNLM/DLC   93-6841 CIP
for Library of Congress

W. W. Norton & Company, Inc., 500 Fifth Avenue, New York, N.Y. 10110

W. W. Norton & Company, Ltd., 10 Coptic Street, London WC1A 1PU

2   3   4   5   6   7   8   9   0

To my mother and father,
for the gifts of a gentle environment

Contents

Acknowledgments   ix
Introduction   xi

SECTION I: THEORY, RESEARCH, AND PRACTICE

Introduction   3
  1. Disconcerting Data: Seven Plus One Pieces of Evidence   9
  2. Childhood and Adolescent Sexual Abuse   30
  3. Post-Traumatic Stress Disorder and Borderline
     Personality Disorder: Are They the Same?   57
  4. Self-Injurious Behavior: Cross-Cultural and
     Historical Aspects   79

SECTION II: PSYCHOTHERAPY GOALS
AND THE THERAPEUTIC ALLIANCE

Introduction   101
  5. Gratification of Needs   110
  6. Replaying Old Patterns and Traumas   154

SECTION III: SPECIAL CONSIDERATIONS
IN THE THERAPY OF ABUSE VICTIMS

Introduction   179
  7. Coming to Terms with the Abuse of the Past   184
  8. How the Past Controls the Present   207
  9. How the Past Shapes the Transference   226
 10. Countertransference Issues   240
 11. Concluding Remarks   248

Bibliography   253
Index   263

Acknowledgments

Life has both changed and not changed. I am still deeply indebted to my patients, some old and some new, who persevere with me in the usually painful process of psychotherapy. If only we could translate theory into therapy as easily as putting words on a page. I also continue to gain enormously from my colleagues at the university and elsewhere, especially the staff of dedicated therapists and workers at the Community-University Health Care Center. Working there has been a privileged experience.

Long discussions about psychotherapy in general, and details of this text in particular, with Larry Greenberg, M.D., in the department of psychiatry at the University of Minnesota, and Jeremy Kisch, Ph.D., at the Community Health Care Plan in New Haven have enriched me immeasurably, and even longer discussions with Bernard Bachrach, Ph.D., in the department of history at the University of Minnesota have helped to keep me methodologically sound. Susan Barrows Munro, senior editor and now vice-president at W.W. Norton & Company, has, once again, been indispensable in her encouragement, patience, and literary skills. I would like to thank Janet Polich for her secretarial and computorial skills.

My love and gratitude, as always, goes to my wife, children and family, who collectively and individually have endured and supported me through all the travails of birthing this manuscript and much else.

Introduction

The great majority of borderline patients seen in psychotherapy are treated on an outpatient basis by licensed social workers, psychologists, and nurse-clinicians trained at a masters level, and by a smaller number of doctoral-trained clinical and counseling psychologists, and psychiatrists. Increasingly, these practitioners have not been educated in a strong psychodynamic tradition. The great majority of borderline patients in therapy are not treated by psychoanalysts, nor are they treated by psychotherapists with intensive psychoanalytic training and experience. Yet the prevailing model for treatment of borderlines is a psychoanalytic one, and such has been the persuasiveness with which this model has been taught in formal coursework and field placement during training that most practicing psychotherapists, although trained and supervised in only the rudiments of psychodynamic psychotherapy, have felt a compelling moral obligation to conform their therapeutic endeavors and frame of reference to the psychoanalytic model. The result has often been at best an ineffective, and at worst a regressive therapeutic experience for the patient and a demoralizing and humiliating or angering experience for the therapist.

The therapist, rather than recognizing that the psychodynamic theory explaining borderline personality is deficient and the therapy for borderlines derived from such theory misapplied and inappropriate, especially in the given context of once-a-week outpatient therapy, instead blames himself/herself for the inadequacies and inherent limitations of that particular borderline model. The convergence of a specialized technique and an unspecialized (general) practitioner makes for a very unfortunate combination.

The convention within psychotherapy has been that models of treatment informed by psychoanalytic theory are best, and that other models are, putting it politely, less best. Thus, Kernberg, in his influential 1984 book, states: "Here I will only say that supportive therapy is usually appropriate as a treatment of last resort — that is, when other modes must be ruled out" (p. 151). Since the dominant theorists of psychotherapy have, until very recently, been psychoanalytic in outlook, those practitioners without psychoanalytic training, who comprise the majority of psychotherapists in this country, and especially those with less than doctoral training, have been infused with a sense of gratitude that they have at least been afforded a glimpse of orthodox knowledge to strive toward and imitate in their practice, mingled with a sense of inferiority about their marginal relationship to psychoanalytic principles. The majority of psychotherapists in this country, thus labeled as practitioners of a "lesser" therapy, have struggled to understand the world of therapy from a psychoanalytic perspective, or at least to convey a sense of understanding by using the psychoanalytic vocabulary.

It is as if Bulgarian cooking were suddenly to come into vogue and, to make matters worse, all cookbooks started to be published in Bulgarian. Since most of the cooks in our country do not speak Bulgarian, a variety of primers, dictionaries, short courses, and compromise terminology would have to be developed to keep all the cooks, especially those without Escoffier training, from being left out of the kitchen. We would still get boiled potatoes.

It must be emphasized that my characterization of those therapists who are treating borderline patients as being primarily masters-level practitioners is not a pejorative value judgment, but only a description of the demographics of psychotherapists and the realities of psychotherapy training in North America. It is important to examine some of the implications of such a juxtaposition of actual training and clinical skills with expectations of therapeutic technique. The first is that most therapists who are treating borderlines have at best a relatively superficial knowledge of psychoanalytic theory and techniques. In a crowded two-year masters degree curriculum encompassing lectures as diverse as personality theory, group therapy, and understanding county bureaucracies, and with clinical placements in which perhaps three to six hours a week is spent doing hands-on psychotherapy, not very much time can be devoted to the refinements or even the basics of psychodynamic theory and therapy. The second implication is that, because of the intellectual attractiveness and persuasiveness of psychoanalytic teachings in the curriculum of mental health professional programs, the therapists are stuck trying to use a model and a vocabulary in which they are not well trained and for which there has been very little demonstrated effectiveness, especially when applied to the treatment of borderlines. The third is that, since the psychoanalytic model is itself of little practical value in helping a therapist work with impulsive, self-destructive, substance-abusing, dissociating borderline patients, most therapists of necessity are forced to proceed without benefit of a useful model in trying to offer their borderline patients a modicum of support, insight, and survivability.

In essence, the therapists are flying by the seats of their pants/ skirts, drawing upon their own common sense and humanity, life experiences, and the bits and pieces of various other theories and techniques that they have picked up along the way. The therapists recognize this and, being ethical professionals, are somewhat uncomfortable both about what is (or is not) transpiring in the therapy room and about their frequent inability to slow down the borderline's self-destructive life-style. They correctly perceive that the patients are always one step ahead of what the therapist has been able to figure out based on last week's session. In compensation, the therapist can take refuge in psychodynamic theory to explain why the patient is being so impossible, such as the patient is unable or unwilling to enter into a therapeutic alliance with the reasonable therapist, or the patient is employing the primitive defense of projective identification. But adherence to a remote and unassailable theory and to a system of techniques that fails to offer practical help for the course of therapy cannot be sustained forever; it anticipates its own collapse.

Are there any answers to this quandary? Yes and no. The first approximation of an answer is that there is no answer. There are many partial answers or, better yet, many thoughtful approaches that permit partial answers, but there is no single answer to the dilemmas and pitfalls that crop up in treating borderlines or any other type of patients. There are ambiguities that arise in therapy, and multiple levels of communication and meaning between patient and therapist, many of which can never be fully clarified. There are mysteries and distorted memories from childhood, such that one can never gain full understanding of what the experience of childhood was like and of how the events of the past have shaped the present. Finally, there have often been damages done in childhood and adolescence that have been so distorting of future development, as well as responses and accommodations to these traumas that have been so integrated into the adult personality, that it is unlikely that therapy can ever fully undo their effects.

It is particularly in relationship to those borderlines who have experienced childhood and adolescent sexual abuse that the psychoanalytic formulations about etiology and treatment are least helpful in providing a useful working model for the practitioner. While the linkages between BPD and childhood abuse are not nearly as simple and direct as some recent workers would imply, there is compelling evidence that specific types of traumatic childhood and adolescent events play an important role in the development of BPD. Approaches to the care and treatment of this group of patients that do not take cognizance of the traumatic environmental forces that shape the developing personality miss a central feature of borderlines that daily confronts the psychotherapist.

In view of this, the second approximation to an answer to the therapeutic quandary posed earlier about working with borderlines is that even partial answers have not been forthcoming because the wrong questions, based upon the wrong theories, have been asked. The critical questions to be asked, in the face of the evidence linking BPD to childhood abuse, are: (1) How are we to understand the complex role of sexual abuse in the etiology of borderlines without losing sight both of the broader context in which abuse occurs and the many ameliorating and exacerbating factors which contribute to the total picture, and (2) how are we to integrate these understandings into a coherent and practical approach to the treatment of that hybrid entity which we shall refer to as PTSD/borderline?

In the presence of the many ambiguities that we have here regarding the complex interrelationships between childhood abuse experiences, formation of self-destructive personality styles, and subsequent psychotherapy for these problems, what would be helpful is the development of a tentative working model that is useful without straitjacketing the practitioner or foreclosing the opportunity for new perspectives. The model developed in this book is designed to be a pragmatic one, linking a modest theory of etiology to clinical findings and thence to patterns and difficulties which practitioners have encountered in therapy.

The PTSD/borderline linkage obligates us to reappraise the core problems that patients live with and bring to therapy. We are no longer speaking of depressive-spectrum illnesses gone awry or of problems stemming from presumed separation/individuation difficulties or from a putatively pathological predominance of pregenital aggression, but, rather, of ongoing, intrusive symptoms and maladaptive personality styles related to early traumatic experiences.

PTSD/BORDERLINE AS A DISORDER OF
THE STREAM OF CONSCIOUSNESS

The PTSD/borderline person suffers first and foremost from a disorder of the stream of consciousness. More specifically, the PTSD/borderline person suffers from the inability to turn off a stream of consciousness that has become its own enemy, comprised of actual memories of traumatic events, distorted and fragmented memories, intrusive imageries and flashbacks, dissociated memories, unwelcome somatic sensations, negative self-commentaries running like a tickertape through the mind, fantasied and feared elaborations from childhood of the abuse experiences, and concomitant strongly dysphoric moods of anxiety and anger. Much that the adult PTSD/borderline does, in and out of therapy, is a response to, or an attempt to terminate or modify, the intolerable presence of this stream of consciousness.

The two basic patterns of self-destructive behaviors in PTSD/borderlines that pose the greatest challenges to their psychotherapy stem from the agonizing nature of their ongoing stream of consciousness. These interacting patterns center, first, around the destructive pursuit of gratification of needs, and second, on the repeated playing out in the present time of old hurtful interactions and relationships. Both patterns have been shaped by the distortions caused by the larger matrix that surrounded the abuse experiences, and continue to dominate PTSD/borderlines' perceptions and expectations of themselves and their surroundings.

Having outlined a model with which to organize our thinking about the types of problems that PTSD/borderlines have in general and bring to therapy, I wish to back off a little and examine the limitations inherent in model-building, even when one stays with the clinical evidence as closely as possible. My major concern is that we not slip into an overly simplistic model that identifies all PTSD/borderline issues with the trauma narrowly defined. After all, not all traumatized children develop the adult PTSD/borderline picture, especially the self-destructive patterns that characteristically involve repeatedly pulling others into their interpersonal entanglements.

The philosopher Isaiah Berlin, in an essay entitled "The Hedgehog and the Fox" (1986), divided all humanity into two basic types: those committed to the search for a single, all-embracing Truth (hedgehogs), and those attentive to many smaller truths (foxes). Berlin characterized Western civilization as consisting primarily of foxes yearning to be hedgehogs. Most of us are too firmly entrenched in empiricism and scientific skepticism to believe that there are Truths (or, worse yet, a universal Truth) out there waiting to be discovered, but we nevertheless admire and appreciate those who seek and especially those who claim to have found such "grand" generalizations. There is a compelling elegance to any unifying theory; it appeals to our need for causal explanation and systematization of the complexities of life that otherwise appear confusing and incomprehensible. We are in conflict ourselves about the tension between *knowing* and *doubting*, often alternating between ignoring small facts and details that do not fit with the big picture and at other times rejecting the big picture because there is just too much that does not conform. There is no inherent superiority to either hedgehogs or foxes, although glory usually accrues to the Hedgehog, the grand system builder. Rather, the question of which one each of us will be seems to come down to one of basic temperament and intellectual focus rather than deliberate choice.

This book is firmly in the fox tradition, adhering to the belief that the best we can do is approach small truths with a series of approximations. But this position has to be tempered with the realization that generalization, and even its poor relation, categorization, are essential to life at all levels, such as, for example, distinguishing nourishment from poison, friend from enemy, both very difficult tasks. Thus, generalizations are not only possible, even to a fox, but indeed necessary at a practical level, whether the activity is living life or doing therapy. The difference between a hedgehog and a fox, then, must finally come down to the attitude about what may be known about the world: The fox is suspicious even of his own small generalizations and guiding principles, while the hedgehog has more of an intuitive confidence that things fit together despite seemingly minor inconsistencies and discrepancies.

To apply this discussion to a consideration of models of psychotherapy with borderlines, the following statements can be made, which will then need to be expanded and examined throughout the book. First, there is no single Truth about the etiology of borderlines. The older theory that explained the development of the borderline personality structure as a failure to negotiate successfully the early separation/individuation phase of childhood has to be abandoned as a unifying theory because it has not been supported by the evidence. It is, for some, a felicitous theory that assists the conduct of therapy (i.e., it gives the therapist confidence that he/she knows what is going on), but it is untested, improbable in its breadth, explains only a small portion of borderline psychopathology, and has limited applicability to the practical problems encountered in therapy.

In a similar vein, a skeptical attitude in general about extending the scope of observations supporting the PTSD/borderline hypothesis into a grand theory forces me to emphasize that I am not suggesting that childhood abuse causes an intolerable stream of consciousness which causes repetitive self-destructive patterns of personal and interpersonal behaviors. Such a formulation is not a satisfactory unifying theory of borderlines. The matter of causality in psychiatry is complex, raising fundamental questions about what we mean by concepts such as "borderline," rather than calling for a premature closure of very important philosophical and clinical considerations. Examining the many questions, most without good answers, about the relationship between childhood abuse and borderline response constitutes the subject matter of this book.

I make this point here because there has been a tendency recently among single-issue schools of therapy to attribute all borderline problems to childhood abuse and, correspondingly, to design all therapies around a combined catharsis/victimology focus. I will comment on these problems later, but wish to return at this point to the discussion about what types of generalizations a philosophical fox, utilizing psychodynamic principles, can make about borderlines.

The most significant contribution of psychodynamic theory to the psychotherapy of borderlines consists not in the dubious explanations of the etiology of borderlines, but rather in a methodological approach to understanding what it is that happens in psychotherapy, not just with borderlines, but generically, with all patients. The full details of what caused PTSD/borderlines to become the way they are may or may not be unraveled in psychotherapy; it is the interaction between therapist and patient that will determine whether therapy will be helpful, and that will even define what is to be considered "helpful" in the first place.

Finally, what the psychotherapist needs from psychodynamic theory is not a theory of borderlines, but rather a theory and an approach to therapy. There are no secret techniques, no special knowledge, no obfuscating vocabulary that are essential to treating PTSD/borderlines. In a naive sense, PTSD/borderlines are just like you and me, only more so. The problems they have with cognitive confusions, with conflicts over dependency and vulnerability, with their impulsivity and despair, their sense of inadequacy and damage, and their trouble in tolerating an unending unpleasant stream of consciousness or inner monologue, are no different in character from what we all face. Most of us get into less difficulties than PTSD/borderlines in solving our problems and getting along in life, but then again, most of us have not been so traumatized in childhood. The differences in how we respond to life's challenges appear to be one of degree, not of absolutes. This is not false humility or melodramatic assertions of "I, too, know what it is to suffer," but only the acknowledgment that we share a common humanity and, with it, a range of attitudes and responses to the travails of life's journey. This is as much of a generalization as a fox can tolerate.

Without trivializing the intensity or absolutely horrific nature of many patients' childhood abuse experiences, there is a sense in which all of life is a response to a series of traumas, most of them minor and manageable. It is only when the stresses are blatantly identifiable and exceptionally noxious relative to a person's capacity to assimilate that we recognize how stress can be overwhelming. Recognition of a PTSD syndrome, however, does not eliminate the need to evaluate how much of the response is attributable to the nature of the stress and how much to the nature of the responder.

If the therapy of borderlines is, in principle, no different from the therapy of other types of patients, then what we need to do is examine the essentials of psychotherapy and shape them to the particular assortment and intensity of problems and life experiences that bring PTSD/borderlines to therapy. It is precisely here that the psychodynamic model of psychotherapy is relevant—not to provide us with a bad theory about borderlines, but to provide the tools and concepts of how to understand and conduct psychotherapy. The concepts of psychological defenses, of a dynamic unconscious that disguises and distorts one's perceptions and motivations, of treatment resistance, transference, and countertransference are what the psychodynamic model has to offer. Unless one utilizes a strictly cognitive-behavioral model, which intentionally ignores issues of motivation and conflict, then a psychodynamic model of psychotherapy provides the best guide for understanding and intervening into the kinds of problems that borderlines present in psychotherapy. This is so not because of what a psychodynamic model tells us about borderlines, but because of what it tells us about the conduct of therapy. The patient does not behave certain ways in therapy because he/she is a borderline; rather, the patient is a borderline because of the way he/she behaves in therapy (and elsewhere). The therapist has to understand therapy; the borderline stuff will take care of itself.

Perhaps a brief clinical example will help. The patient is a 32-year-old woman who has been verbally beating up on her therapist for months for being uncaring and aloof. Objectively, this accusation does not fit the facts. The therapist has been caring, almost heroically available, and frequently reassuring to the patient that she (the therapist) cares. The patient brings a small basket of homegrown tomatoes to the therapist on an appointment before Labor Day. The therapist accepts the gift and thanks the patient. The therapist judges that exploration of the significance or meaning of the gift would not be a good idea at that time. The following day, the patient calls the office receptionist and asks to speak to the therapist. The receptionist states that the therapist will have to call back later because she is in session at that moment. The receptionist then casually and naively, but with good intentions, mentions to the patient that she had had a tomato, comments on how good it was, and thanks the patient. When the therapist calls the patient back later, the patient angrily berates the therapist for not caring about her (the patient), since she had given the gift of tomatoes away to others. The patient states that she had not given the basket of tomatoes to the therapist to have them given away to office personnel (even though the receptionist is ostensibly on good terms with this patient). The therapist, annoyed and caught by surprise at one more unanticipated attack, explains to the patient that the tomatoes were very good indeed, that she does care for the patient, and that for that reason she wanted to share the

patient's tomatoes with others. The patient is unmollified; if anything, the condescending answer makes her angrier and she hangs
up the telephone, threatening suicide again.

This particular example could be multiplied a hundred times with
this particular patient. Part of the reason that the therapist responded to the patient on the telephone as she did is that she views
the patient as a fragile borderline and has been trying, unsuccessfully, to cultivate a positive transference and a holding/soothing
environment. The therapist feels unable to make a direct transference interpretation for several reasons. One reason is that the patient
has told the therapist very little about her life experiences, such
as family-of-origin issues and the nature of previous relationships,
although there have been obscure hints of childhood abuse that are
covered over when approached. Most of the patient's verbalizations
have been attacks alternating with pleadings directed to the therapist.
The therapist does not have available sufficient factual content to
link these kind of accusations to past relationships and experiences.
Also, the therapist knows that a generic transference interpretation
("You can't be this angry at me just for giving away a tomato;
something else must be going on; I must be a substitute for someone
else") will only be met with renewed scorn. The therapist knows
that the process of therapy has not established a basis for such an
interpretation even to be heard, let alone considered.

But surely there must be responses available to the therapist other
than the endless and futile reassurances that she cares for the patient.
The responses can either address the content of what the patient is
saying, such as: "When you give me a gift, don't tell me what I may
do with it," or, "You are applying the wrong test to determine if I
care for you or not," or, "You seem to have some problems about
gift-giving; shall we talk about it?" Or the therapist can address the
process of what is happening on the telephone, such as: "Is that
what you called me up to tell me?" or, "You are once again demanding that I behave in conformity with your hidden wishes," or, more
simply, "The issue is control," or, again, "The issue is not whether I
have to eat all your tomatoes myself to prove that I care for you,
but what is going on between us right now."

I am not necessarily suggesting that any one of my responses is
the proper one, or that any particular response at that time could
have had a therapeutic effect then. The issue, rather, is that what is

needed to guide a response to this kind of prototypal borderline attack is not a theory of borderlines, but a theory about therapy that assists the therapist in analyzing the interaction (not the patient) at the moment, in providing some guidelines for the type of response he/she may wish to make, and in establishing a basis for what will occur between patient and therapist in therapy.

Such a focus on fundamental principles of psychotherapy must be maintained, whatever the special circumstances or diagnostic category of the patient. The rules of psychotherapy do not change when working with borderlines who have experienced childhood abuse. If anything, there seem to be certain sequelae to childhood abuse which call for even closer adherence to basic rules of psychotherapy, while still encouraging flexibility within the safety of these basic principles. For example, the knowledge that patients who were abused in childhood will inevitably have boundary issues mandates that a therapist pay extra attention to boundary problems in therapy. It is from the juxtaposition of the special features of PTSD/borderline patients and the particular problems that occur in the psychotherapies of such patients that the discussions in this book will develop.

PTSD/Borderlines in Therapy

SECTION I

Theory, Research, and Practice

INTRODUCTION

It is somewhat traditional to think of the field of medicine as embracing two worlds, one being the science that underlies medical theory and practice and the other being the art of healing. The degree to which the art of healing leans upon the science of medicine in the different subdisciplines of medicine varies greatly within our own society. The optimal admixture of the two is a matter of controversy, with some favoring the relentless increase of a scientific influence upon the practice of medicine, and others lamenting what they perceive as the loss of a humanistic perspective accompanying the increased reliance on medical technology.

In the field of psychiatry and psychology, there has been a tendency for the scientific and healing perspectives to develop distinct languages, such that an integrative discourse becomes more difficult. This divergence between technical science and healing art has been especially evident in the field of psychotherapy, defined here as those techniques of healing through the exchange of conversation. It has been a field in which theories flourish in the absence of empirical grounding, idiosyncratic schools of practice centered around charismatic figures rise and fall in the absence of any well-thought-out, systematic, or even intelligible theory, and the possibility of a scientific foundation to the development or investigation of therapeutic endeavors is denied, either on practical grounds that such studies are infeasible because of the many variables involved that affect therapeutic process and outcome, or on philosophical grounds that meaningfulness and human happiness and misery, by the very nature of subjective phenomena, are inaccessible to scientific study.

These objections notwithstanding, there have, in fact, been many excellent studies of psychotherapy recently, but these appear to have made little impact on the day-to-day practice of psychotherapy. This is especially the case as the descriptions and standards of what constitute the requisite training and knowledge base of a psychotherapist

broaden and stretch to include bachelor-degree human service workers, pastoral counselors with and without formal training in psychology or psychotherapy, sex-addiction therapists, holistic nutrition
therapists, followers of religious-type cults and sects, and many others who have a message to convey or see a lucrative market. Since
introspection and social conversation, the putative components of
psychotherapeutic technique, are ubiquitous to the human species,
each person feels uniquely qualified to render an expert opinion as
to what it is that troubles humankind and what should be done to
correct it.

Although government may limit somewhat the freedom of action
of unlicensed therapists precisely by establishing basic licensure requirements (such as minimal training and a formal apprenticeship)
and standards of practice necessary to hang out a shingle or advertise
oneself as a psychotherapist, or to collect fees from government and
third-party carriers, such regulations do not prevent a panoply of
"psychotherapists" from carrying on their counseling business as
usual, uninfluenced by whatever scientific developments may come
to light that have relevance to mental illness and psychotherapy.

The practice of psychotherapy by licensed practitioners is undergoing change, but this appears to be brought about more by the
influence of social and economic factors extrinsic to psychotherapy
itself than from the development of new theory, the analysis of
difficult issues in the practice of psychotherapy, or research findings
about the process or outcome of therapy. The most obvious factors
forcing changes in the conduct of psychotherapy are the managed
care programs and economically-driven governmental and private
insurance company policies regarding reimbursement of psychotherapy. Theories and techniques of short-term psychotherapy have pro-
liferated and gained new respectability under the impetus of financial
constraints upon the practice of psychotherapy. In parallel, econom-
ically inspired research has demonstrated that short-term therapy
serves the needs of patients (and society) at least as well as long-term
therapy does. One additional factor brought about by governmental
and third-party carrier regulation of psychotherapy that may contribute to changes in the nature of therapy has been the increasing
load of paper requirements for written treatment plans and prior
authorizations, complete with lists of goals, interventions, and dates
for completion. Although it is uncertain to what degree the answers

provided to insurance carriers have any relationship to the actual therapy, it is possible that the paper requirement, with the teeth of a review board behind it, may in fact bring about some reappraisal of the progress, or lack thereof, of a course of therapy by the psychotherapist.

As an aside, it is interesting to see how particular constructs, which remain fairly controversial within the field, can find their way into insurance forms, as if the meaning of a term and what it refers to are entirely clear. I recently had to fill out a form requesting prior authorization for an additional six sessions for the treatment of an elderly gentleman whom I was treating monthly, primarily with antidepressant medications but also with supportive counseling, for a depression. On the third and last page of the form, I encountered the question, "What is the nature of the therapeutic alliance between you and the patient?" Now, what is one to do with such a question? How did it find its way onto the page of a prior authorization form? As will be discussed later, major disagreement exists as to what, if anything, the therapeutic alliance is, how it operates, what ought one to do, if anything, to promote it, and what one ought to do when it has gone awry. But there it is, come to life on a printed page, and if I do not take it seriously and answer it correctly, as judged by someone in an insurance office, my patient will not receive reimbursement for my bill. Surely that, more than anything else, would disrupt our therapeutic alliance.

A second social factor importantly affecting the conduct of psychotherapy is the proliferation of lawsuits against psychotherapists for unethical or substandard practice. While gross deviations from ethical and competent practice are relatively easy to define and recognize, the anxiety and paranoia consequent upon our shared vulnerability to allegations of wrongdoing in psychotherapy have resulted in a shift toward regimentation, closure, and petrification of complex therapeutic issues on the basis of fear rather than facts or good judgment. For example, a therapist working with a chronically suicidal outpatient was criticized by a review board, when a crisis arose necessitating brief rehospitalization, for not having contracted with the patient that he (the patient) not commit suicide. Along with the annoyance at criticism by a review board, the therapist must now be concerned that, if the patient does suicide, he will be liable to a tort action for having neglected to contract with the patient. But what is the basis for believing that contracting with a suicidal patient is an effective rather than a fruitless or even damaging psychotherapeutic intervention? Are there research data here? I personally am very skeptical about the place of contracting in psychotherapy, especially in outpatient therapy, but surely, if one thinks it valuable, that is a determination that must be made on an individual situation-to-situation basis. Yet, the risk of censure by a reviewing body and concern regarding a lawsuit may well push many therapists into contracting with their patients, even when they think it is ill-advised. Interestingly enough, I have recently consulted on a case in which a hospitalized patient committed suicide after signing a no-suicide contract, and the hospital, nursing staff, and psychiatrist are being sued for relying on the merit of a depressed person's promise.

The point about the absence of outcome data regarding the value of no-suicide contracts with patients highlights the difficulty of determining what the proper role of research findings should or could be in guiding the details of specific interchanges between patient and therapist at any given moment. As another example, when a patient in therapy says, "I don't now why you bother spending time with someone like me," there are no studies that inform the therapist whether it is better to respond supportively to the self-denigrating content, such as, "Because you are a worthwhile person," or to respond exploratively to the content, such as, "Why do you put yourself down?" or to ignore the comment entirely and proceed onto other matters, or to respond to the process, such as "What is the significance of your making that statement to me, your therapist?" or to respond to the process with an interpretation or confrontation, "You are playing the role of the undeserving person again," or, worse yet, "What you really mean is that you are not getting enough of my time."

The response that a therapist will make may depend upon the therapist's theory of character formation and theory of therapy, and upon the therapist's personality, mood state at the moment, appraisal of the needs of this patient, personal feelings about the patient, timing of the patient's statement within the therapy session and within the overall course of therapy, and many other factors, but the one thing that the therapist cannot do is fall back upon research studies that will guide the specific form of the response, because such studies do not exist.

If scientific findings and psychotherapy research cannot be of assistance at such a moment in helping the therapist decide upon a specific reply to a patient, in what way can science contribute to the art of psychotherapy? Research can be helpful in informing the therapist about the general characteristics, course, and outcome of patients similar to the one under consideration, and can provide a knowledge base from which intelligent decisions can be made, even if this knowledge base will not directly assist the choice of wording, or even the particular modality (supportive or exploratory, process or content), at any given moment. For example, knowledge that several borderline follow-up studies have demonstrated that wrist-cutters have very low suicide rates should have some impact on how a therapist responds to an outpatient borderline wrist-cutter. It should not, however, dictate treatment decisions; a therapist cannot conclude by the use of statistics that it is safe not to hospitalize this particular borderline patient at this particular time, but the research statistics should at least enter into the equation, along with many other factors, of deciding what to do in response to the latest episode of wrist-cutting. It may even be that wrist-cutters have a low rate of suicide precisely because their wrist-cutting has resulted in hospitalizations, and the hospitalizations have helped prevent suicide, but we do not know if this hypothesis is correct.

Given this orientation that the findings of clinical studies can be important to the psychotherapist, both in terms of providing some data base and in helping to clarify conceptual confusions, the four chapters comprising this first section will explore three interrelated issues.

Chapter 1 will examine eight pieces of data, so to speak, that have relevance to the conduct of psychotherapy of borderlines in general.

Chapter 2 will review the major findings on the correlations between childhood and adolescent physical and sexual abuse and adult psychiatric problems, most specifically, borderline personality disorder.

Chapter 3 is of a more conceptual nature, and tackles the question, given the findings discussed in Chapter 2, of whether the disturbances that appear to follow upon childhood and adolescent abuses might more properly be considered as post-traumatic stress responses rather than as borderline personality disorder. Such a consideration raises theoretical issues as to the nature and status of personality disorders in general, the role of traumatic events in character development as opposed to symptom formation, and the importance of social attitudes in the process of forming a psychiatric diagnostic system. Important consequences ensue, in therapy and in general outlook, from the "decision" to consider a particular behavioral pattern as characterological versus reactive to stress. Whether these consequences should influence the diagnostic process is itself an important and fascinating question, to which scientific principles and personal and social values may each make different contributions.

Chapter 4, written in collaboration with the medieval historian Bernard Bachrach, picks up on the question of cultural influences of symptom choice. How does it come about that persons in our culture with PTSD resulting from childhood sexual abuse develop dissociative episodes and self-injurious behaviors? What is the role of self-injurious behaviors in our society, as compared to other societies? Some similarities and differences between our own and medieval European responses to self-injurious behaviors are discussed in this chapter as a way of gaining perspective on our own ambivalent attitudes toward PTSD/borderlines.

1

Disconcerting Data: Seven Plus One Pieces of Evidence

If we examine the important factors that have brought about changes in the ways psychotherapy is conducted in this country, it seems that the major influences in recent years have been extrinsic and, in large part, unwelcome, to the basic theoretical systems and professional approaches of most psychotherapists. The extrinsic factors have stemmed from economic pressures to shorten the course of psychotherapy in order to reduce the overall expenditures of providing health care. Intellectual and theoretical legitimization to the economic basis for altering the nature of psychotherapy in the 1980s and 1990s has been provided by the failure of psychotherapists to demonstrate convincingly an increased benefit of long-term therapy commensurate with the increased costs of long-term therapy, combined with the clear demonstration that a small segment of mental health service utilizers — not necessarily the sickest ones either — account for the overwhelming majority of mental health services and costs.

Economic factors have overshadowed basic science and clinical research findings in influencing changes in how psychotherapy is conducted. It is likely that, without third-party intrusion and mandates regarding which types and durations of therapy will qualify for reimbursement, most therapists would continue to practice the type of psychotherapy in which they were trained in graduate school. Propelled by the impetus of economic forces, however, even traditional fields of psychotherapy, with some exceptions, have modified their therapeutic approaches to take into account the research and clinical findings of the efficacy of pharmacological treatment in some areas of practice.

For example, three to four decades ago the primary modality recommended for treating depression, especially of the mild to mod-

9

erate sort, was exploratory psychotherapy. When antidepressant medication or ECT was used for treating depression, no attempt was made to accommodate the successes of these somatic modalities into the prevailing psychodynamic theories that depression was caused by conflicts about anger and loss. The theoretical position regarding the etiology of depression remained unchanged. Today the primary modality for treating depression, even of the mild to moderate sort, is antidepressant medication. This is true not only for psychiatrists, but also for psychologists and social workers, who increasingly team up with psychiatrists to provide a combination of psychotherapy or counseling and antidepressant medications for their patients. A faction within professional psychology is advocating training of psychologists in psychopharmacology, indicating an endorsement by this group of psychologists of the central importance of somatic modalities in the treatment of depression and other mental illnesses.

In essence, we are seeing the reciprocal influences of economic factors and scientific progress upon the ways psychotherapy is conducted. Each sector (insurance carriers and managed care organizations; scientific establishment) has endorsed and used the other sector to push through a new paradigm of what mental disorders are and how they should be treated. The earlier, and still ongoing, attempt to define the borderline disorders as affective spectrum conditions carried with it the clear implication that the proper primary treatment, and therefore the treatment that would be reimbursed, would be pharmacological rather than psychological.

Compared to the impressive developments within the field of psychopharmacology in the past three decades, there have been only very modest advances in theory or techniques of psychotherapy. The most notable developments have been in the areas of brief psychotherapy and the cognitive-behavioral therapies, both well-suited to the budgetary constraints of third-party reimbursers. In general, however, the traditional notion of open-ended, weekly or biweekly, exploratory psychotherapy of nonpsychotic emotional disorders, in which the patient-therapist relationship is of paramount importance, has been little affected by progress in the neurosciences, even if in practice psychotherapists have reluctantly adapted to the guidelines mandated by the insurance carriers. An example of accommodation to the expediency imposed by third-party carriers is the relative ease with which therapists and patients presently part company once a patient's health insurance has been changed, a disruption of the therapeutic relationship that would have been practically unthinkable, as bordering on the unethical, three decades ago, but which is accepted as commonplace now.

The conservatism of how therapists practice therapy has been most clearly demonstrated in the resistance to biological inroads with regard to the models of psychotherapy applied to the treatment of the character disorders as compared to, for example, treatment of the depressions. Undoubtedly, this reflects the many areas of uncertainty and disagreement as to the nature and status of personality disorders in relation to the other psychiatric entities, as well as the paucity of clinical pharmacological approaches equivalent in effectiveness to those for schizophrenia and the affective disorders (Soloff, 1992). Our major difficulties in deciding what are and are not personality disorders, who has them, and in what ways persons with personality disorders differ from those without such disorders are reflected in a lack of understanding of how best to treat such persons. The therapist is left to fall back upon his or her intuitions, personal therapeutic style, and often, the hope that sufficient demonstration of concern and warmth will carry the patient through difficult times.

As often happens when the causes and cures of a condition are uncertain, we see the proliferation of ingeniously faddish therapies in which isolated aspects of the borderline symptom picture become emphasized. Driven by market forces, a deluge of psychological therapies have developed to cater to newly appreciated and narrowly focused "borderline" symptoms (sexual addiction, codependency, dissociation, bulimia, multiple personality), thereby ensuring economic survival to mental health providers and treatment accessibility to borderlines under changing rules and restrictions.

USEFUL EVIDENCE

Although there is no body of knowledge that dictates what the optimal therapy of borderline patients might be, there is, nevertheless, an accumulation of circumscribed findings about the life course of borderlines and their experiences in psychotherapy that therapists can use in framing their individual approach to particular patients. I would emphasize that statistical information from clinical studies can only provide part of a framework for working with borderline patients. It is my thought that, in actuality, the moment-to-moment give-and-take process of psychotherapy, as a conversation between two individuals, is most influenced by the personal characteristics, value systems, and life histories of each of the participants in the therapeutic endeavor, and accounts for the relatively unchanging nature of most therapist's verbal (and nonverbal) exchanges with their patients. The nature of such interactions will be examined in Section II of this book.

This chapter will examine seven pieces of evidence (and introduce an eighth) that ought to, or might, have some bearing upon the way therapists think about and conduct psychotherapy with borderline patients. They are presented as pieces of evidence, certainly not as facts. Some of the evidence is based upon only one or two studies from a single group of investigators. Generalization from such limited data is hazardous; yet the studies seem to get at larger considerations which therapists at times intuitively know and certainly ponder, as they struggle to find meaning and purpose in the course of doing psychotherapy. The seven pieces of evidence do not allow the construction of a grand theory of borderline therapy, but should provide some balance, perspective, and humility. The eighth piece is something else, both more controversial and more complex, thereby deserving and getting its own chapter.

The eight are as follows:

1. The effectiveness of psychotherapy with borderlines has not been demonstrated.
2. Fifty percent of borderlines quit therapy within six months.
3. Fifty percent of borderlines in successful therapy ("successful" as defined by their therapists) terminate therapy against the advice of their therapists.
4. Most borderlines improve around age 30.
5. About 8–15% of borderlines have suicided by 10–15-year follow-up.
6. Suicide in borderlines is correlated with antisocial personality, ongoing alcohol abuse, and depressions of an angry-hostile nature.
7. Suicide is negatively correlated with wrist-cutting.
8. About 70–80% of borderlines appear to have experienced some form of sexual and/or physical abuse in childhood.

*   *   *   *   *   *

1. The Effectiveness of Psychotherapy with Borderlines Has Not Been Demonstrated

Although there appears to be increasing interest in the use of pharmacological agents in the treatment of borderlines, it is generally assumed by borderline patients and their therapists that what they need, and what would be most helpful, is psychotherapy, especially long-term exploratory psychotherapy. There are no large-scale statistical studies of the efficacy of psychotherapy with borderlines, but what information we have, derived primarily from a few long-term follow-up projects, fails to demonstrate an advantage or even an impressive track record for intensive, psychodynamic psychotherapy. In general, the studies of McGlashan (1986) from Chestnut Lodge and Stone (1990) from New York State Psychiatric Institute (NYSPI) have shown that some borderline patients do extremely well, whether they have received intensive therapy, supportive therapy, or hardly any therapy in the years following discharge from the index hospitalization, while others do very poorly, again with no seeming relationship to the type or amount of therapy received.

Stone (1990) compared the outcome of borderline patients treated at NYSPI by the "best" or "worst" therapists (as rated at the time by their psychotherapy supervisors) and was unable to demonstrate a better outcome on follow-up in the group of patients treated by the "best" therapists. Stone correctly points out the many methodological pitfalls in trying to rate therapists, since we do not know that the traits or attitudes we value are the ones that really make a difference in therapy. Nevertheless, he wanted to address the argument that therapeutic benefit is difficult to demonstrate because suitable and unsuitable therapy patients and good and bad therapists cancel each other out when results are averaged. Stone concludes that some patients appeared to benefit from expressive therapy and some from supportive therapy, but that one could not predict such results either from patient or therapist characteristics, nor did his data demonstrate that those who received therapy of any kind did better than those who received little or no therapy following discharge from the index hospitalization.

Wallerstein's (1986) report of the results of the Menninger psychotherapy project similarly showed that experienced clinicians and researchers could not predict from patient characteristics and psychopathology prior to the onset of therapy just which patients would do well in which kind of psychotherapy. There were surprises in both directions; predictions of a good outcome with psychoanalytic psychotherapy often proved to be wrong, and predictions of poor outcomes equally often were incorrect. Furthermore, supportive psychotherapy, assumed to be a less ambitious and less effective psychotherapy reserved for those too ego-deficient to tolerate intensive psychotherapy, proved to be at least as effective on follow-up as intensive therapy, with these "sicker" patients, who therefore had been selected for supportive therapy, doing as well on follow-up as the "healthier" patients, who had been selected for exploratory therapy.

The finding that patient characteristics, essentially how disturbed the borderline looks at the beginning of therapy, do not predict outcome was corroborated indirectly by Gunderson's group (1989) in a study that found that hospitalized borderlines who dropped out of psychotherapy were healthier on some baseline measures than those who continued in therapy. Mohl et al. (1989), in a study of psychotherapy refusers (not necessarily borderlines, but with about half the patients having an Axis II diagnosis) at a university clinic, found no differences in severity of symptoms between those who began and those who refused psychotherapy after being accepted into a psychotherapy program. Mohl et al. hypothesize that the patient-screener interaction that occurred prior to the start of therapy, rather than patient variables, may be the critical factor in influencing therapy refusal.

Two recent studies have reported favorable outcome results in the psychotherapy of borderlines. Interestingly, each treatment program utilized completely different technical approaches from the other. Stevenson and Meares (1992) reported on a one-year program of twice-weekly psychodynamic therapy, based upon a psychology of self, of 30 borderline patients in Australia. Diagnoses utilized DSM-III and DIB criteria rated by three independent psychiatrists. Severity of symptoms and level of functioning were rated for the year prior to entry into the treatment program and the year following completion of the 12-month course of therapy. The patients showed significant symptomatic and behavioral improvement, with 30% no longer fulfilling DSM-III criteria for BPD. No control group was used; each patient served as his/her own control, using pretreatment scores. The authors point out that this was a fairly dysfunctional group, with many previous failures of inpatient and outpatient treatment. Almost 80% were on some form of public assistance prior to the treatment program. No antidepressants or antipsychotic medications were used. What makes this study particularly intriguing is that the therapists were all relatively inexperienced trainees (psychiatric residents, registered nurses, psychologists) who were closely supervised by senior therapists who adhered to a consistent treatment model and mode of supervision. Perhaps this is an ideal treatment team: inexperienced but enthusiastic therapists and experienced but more reflective supervisors.

Linehan et al. (1991) reported the results of a randomized one-year clinical study of parasuicidal borderline women, comparing a cognitive-behaviorally based program of individual and group therapy sessions to a "treatment as usual" group. The group treated with the cognitive-behavioral regimen (termed Dialectical Behavior Therapy, or DBT) showed a significantly greater reduction in frequency and medical risk of parasuicidal behaviors, lower one-year therapy dropout rates, and less inpatient hospital days. These treatment effects occurred despite absence of significant changes in patients' reports on measures of depression, hopelessness, suicidal ideation, or reasons for living.

Despite important differences in underlying theory and technical style between Linehan's and Stevenson and Meares' treatment approaches, what the two studies have in common is that the therapists were instructed in their respective techniques and received close supervision throughout the duration of the one-year treatment programs. The good clinical outcome of these two studies is somewhat at variance with a meta-analysis of 11 outcome studies of various kinds of brief dynamic therapy, all of which utilized specific treatment regimens based upon training manual or guides. The meta-analysis, reported by Crits-Christoph (1992), concluded that the brief dynamic therapies were superior to waiting-list conditions (presumably, no therapy), but only slightly superior to nonpsychiatric treatment (e.g., self-help groups, chemical dependency counseling), and equal in effectiveness to other forms of psychotherapy and to medication. Crits-Christoph comments that the generalizability of outcome results from therapy adhering to fairly rigid protocols to the efficacy of eclectic psychotherapy as it is ordinarily practiced is not clear. Only one of the 11 studies cited by Crits-Christoph involved borderline patients.

This is a curious situation, in which two therapy outcome studies of borderline patients utilizing manual-based therapy techniques and supervision demonstrated a clear superiority over "treatment as usual," while 11 other studies primarily with other types of patients failed to show superior outcomes for the protocol-based therapies. How are we to understand this? Although it is very clear that the studies are not directly comparable, and that even the use of treatment manual-based directions cannot prevent therapist variables from affecting outcome, the fact nevertheless remains that borderline patients, who are supposed to be more difficult to treat, showed improvement when treated by protocol-bound and closely supervised therapists, although the techniques used in the two protocol-based studies were very different from each other.

This point is underscored by Lambert (1989, p. 470), who concluded in his review of psychotherapy process and outcome research that, to date, research studies "have not demonstrated that the changes that follow psychotherapy are strongly related to the use of specific techniques." Lambert goes on to point out that, even with the use of treatment manuals to try to insure a high degree of conformity of technique and to minimize the variability between therapists, the qualities of individual therapists nevertheless appear to be very important factors in the success or failure of the psychotherapy.

What this suggests to me is that the treatment of borderline patients might be best done with supervision, even if the supervision is peer group supervision. In essence, since it is hard to avoid mistakes in working with borderline patients, and since these mistakes seem to lead to more problems in the therapy of borderlines than of other patients, the mere presence of a supervisor or peer review group might help keep the therapist on track and away from serious errors in the conduct of therapy. This does not provide a guarantee, of course, since a supervised therapist can always omit reporting relevant information to the supervisor or group, except when using audio or videotapes, as was the case in Stevenson and Meares' (1992) study. What I am suggesting is that therapy of borderlines done in isolation is at greater risk of disaster than therapy done in conjunction with discussion with other therapists, and that part of the reason for the successful outcomes of two very different techniques (cognitive-behavioral and self psychology) was the presence of a righting mechanism, a gyroscope, built into each program. In working with other types of patients who are less problematic in therapy, the presence of a supervisor is less critical, and therefore the other studies failed to demonstrate superior outcomes compared to control groups.

To summarize, it is an article of faith, anecdotal evidence, and professional commitment that borderlines need psychotherapy and that psychotherapy can help borderlines. These attitudes inform and guide the treatment of borderlines, despite the absence, until very recently, of any statistical evidence that psychotherapy helps and the considerable contrary, although equally anecdotal, evidence that many borderlines do poorly in therapy and may even become more symptomatic. Second, and perhaps this is the uncertainty that keeps the whole enterprise afloat, it is not possible to predict just from the severity of a borderline's symptoms whether that person will do well in the future, let alone whether psychotherapy, or which psychotherapy if any, will be helpful. It appears likely that the interaction within the first three or four sessions of psychotherapy can reasonably predict whether that particular psychotherapy with that particular therapist will have a positive outcome, but this appears to have as much to do with the qualities of the therapist and the compatibility of the match between patient and therapist as it has to do with patient characteristics.

Finally, we have to keep in mind that the very notion of borderline was in large part originally defined with the observation that certain patients became worse in psychotherapy. By the very concept of what we mean by "borderline," we can expect that psychotherapy will be a difficult, often unsuccessful, and at times deleterious enterprise. The shifting symptom picture of borderlines, which seems recently to involve a reciprocal interplay with therapists too eager to redefine the core borderline problems and discover the latest therapy, bears witness to this. Borderline symptoms shift back and forth between dissociative and multiple personality symptoms, self-injurious behaviors, bulimia, drug abuse, sexual addictions, and flashbacks. Clinics to serve these special problems spring up just as readily, sometimes even in helpful and eager anticipation of a new swing of the symptom-pendulum. The metamorphosis of symptoms and the proliferation of programs to treat these newly appreciated symptoms pose some very basic questions regarding the nature and core features of "borderline personality disorder" and the role of the psychotherapeutic industry in shaping the ways in which "borderline" persons express their very great distress. Many borderline patients, being very adaptive, readily take on new symptoms that they perceive will capture the interest of their therapists. This somewhat resembles the Scheherazade Syndrome, in which the beautiful lady must keep the emperor intrigued from session to session in order to preserve her head. We know how the story ends; after 1001 nights, the emperor cannot live without the beautiful and resourceful lady and so he marries her.

2. Fifty Percent of Borderlines Quit Therapy within Six Months

The interpretation of outcome data about psychotherapy is always hazardous because there are so many variables and so many loose concepts. Furthermore, any statements about the psychotherapy of borderlines ought to be viewed against a baseline of the experience of psychotherapy in other conditions. It might not be very meaningful that 50% of borderlines quit therapy in six months if this were the norm for all patients in therapy.

Second, all statistics reporting length of time in therapy demonstrate that there is a high attrition rate within the first four sessions, and even up to the first eight sessions of a psychotherapy, but that the dropout rate sharply falls (for patients of all diagnoses) for those who stay beyond four, or eight, sessions. Surveys of national utilization rates have shown that, of persons making a mental health visit (not always for the purpose of psychotherapy), about 25% do not come back for a second visit and another 25% attend fewer than four sessions. In Taube et al.'s (1988) national utilization survey, only 16% of patients made more than 24 visits, but they accounted for 57% of the total expenditures. In Howard et al.'s study (1989) at a psychodynamically oriented psychotherapy clinic in Chicago, the median number of visits for those who made more than four visits was 21, and for those who made more than eight visits was 28. The number of visits ranged from one to 207.

This latter point is underscored by Kisch (1992), who studied utilization rates for mental health services for the years 1986–89 in a large HMO in New Haven. Kisch points out that, although the average number of mental health sessions for individual users (for all purposes, not just psychotherapy) in any particular year was 5.6 and for all years was only 8.35, it would be a mistake to think that individuals at the fifth session will need only one or, at most, two additional sessions to close the case. In fact, the average number of sessions for individuals who have had five sessions will be 15.7 sessions. Individuals who have completed the fourteenth session will reach an average of 29.2 sessions.

The therapy experiences of borderlines have to be viewed against this background of mental health services in general. As indicated, data from national surveys include contact with mental health professionals for all reasons, not just requests for psychotherapy. In a study (Skodal, Buckley, & Charles, 1983) comparing therapy dropout rates of borderlines to schizophrenics and neurotics and/or other character disorders at a clinic in New York City, the borderlines had a dropout rate of 67% at six months, compared to rates of 40% for the neurotic/other personality disorder patients and 13% for the schizophrenic patients. The study was a small one; it is not clear whether one can generalize the findings to other clinics and regions of the country. Gunderson et al. (1989), in a study of 60 inpatient borderlines, similarly found a dropout rate from psychotherapy of 60% in six months. Six patients dropped out within the first week. The authors concluded that process variables, that is, factors reflecting the interactions taking place between patient and therapist within the early phase of therapy, more than patient pretreatment characteristics, appeared to explain the high dropout rate. In a separate study by Waldinger and Gunderson (1984) of successfully treated borderlines, experienced therapists reported that, of all their borderline patients, roughly half terminated within the first six months of therapy. By contrast, Winston et al.'s (1991) study of time-limited (40 sessions) psychotherapy for non-borderline, non-acting-out Axis II patients reported a dropout rate of only 18%, all of these occurring within the first six sessions. In Linehan et al.'s (1991) study of cognitive-behavioral therapy of self-injurious borderlines, about 50% of the borderline control group receiving therapy as usual dropped out of therapy within one year's time.

It would appear that the dropout rate of borderlines has to be compared to patients specifically requesting psychotherapy; the national utilization figures are presented to provide a broader perspective to the picture. Most borderline patients, when they drop out of therapy, seek therapy elsewhere. Dropping out may not show lack of motivation for therapy, but rather some failure of patient and therapist, for whatever reason, to work out an acceptable treatment relationship.

In presenting these incomplete pieces of data regarding therapy attrition in the context of this chapter, I am not directly concerned at this time in finding reasons why it happens or what to do about it. Since our focus ultimately is to examine the process of psychotherapy with borderlines, I am most interested in how the therapist's knowledge that borderlines frequently drop out of therapy, as well as the actual interactions within therapy which convey to the therapist that this particular patient is considering quitting therapy, influence the therapist's behavior in ways that either facilitate or compromise the progress of therapy. Is the high dropout rate a reflection of the therapist's failure to emphasize the positive transference and to create early in therapy a proper holding environment such that the patient can withstand the inevitable pains and deprivations of therapy? When does creating a positive environment slide into encouragement of regression and dependency in order to keep the patient in therapy? Should the patient's early expressions of anger be confronted directly as manifestations of negative transference that threaten to wreck the therapy, as Kernberg (1984; Selzer, Koenigsberg, & Kernberg, 1987) suggests, or soothed over as understandable expressions of abandonment anxiety or reflections of prior hurts, as Adler (1985) suggests?

There are no "correct" answers to these questions, nor is this chapter the place to reflect upon them. The essential point here is to think about whether high borderline dropout rates propel therapists into untherapeutic maneuvers in an attempt to keep the patient in therapy with the rationalization that, within reasonable and ethical behavior, it is best to help the patient get over the initial difficulties in therapy, whatever it takes, because the patient needs and will benefit from therapy if only he or she does not quit prematurely.

3. Fifty Percent of Borderline Patients in Successful Therapy, as Judged by Their Therapists, Quit Therapy Prematurely, as Judged by Their Therapists

What is the proper end point to therapy? The question touches upon a major theoretical and practical problem in the conduct of psychotherapy. Once again, the data are sparse, but probably reflect fairly common experience. The single study relating to this is by

Waldinger and Gunderson (1984), and the finding is incidental to the main interest of their study of successful therapeutic outcomes with borderline patients. In this study, experienced psychodynamic psychotherapists were asked to describe successful treatment cases of borderline patients. Of 78 cases reported by 11 therapists, 60% of patients who terminated treatment did so against their therapist's advice. Waldinger and Gunderson point out the many limitations to their study, including the absence of uniform diagnostic criteria and the inevitable biases of perspective by the therapists. Granted these limitations and that the data examined here reflect the judgment of the therapists involved and is by its very nature subjective, the fact remains that the therapists thought that the majority of their borderline patients, although doing well, should not have terminated therapy when they did. This is not a question of right or wrong, but of how one views the goals, purposes, and end points of therapy. If we were to generalize this observation, it is either that therapists have difficulty in letting go of their patients or that therapists think that borderline patients need more therapy than the patients think they do.

4. Most Borderline Patients Improve Toward Age 30

This has been one of the most consistent findings of the long-term follow-up studies of borderlines (Kroll, Carey, & Sines, 1985; McGlashan, 1986; Paris, Brown, & Nowlis, 1987; Plakun, 1991; Plakun, Burkhardt, & Muller, 1985; Stone, 1990). The issues are complex, definitions of "improvement" and "doing well" can be debated, and the variables influencing outcome are themselves interactive with each other. Nevertheless, the finding holds up that over 50% of fairly severe borderlines (those who required hospitalization) are doing well on 10–15-year follow-up. This is an impressive finding when one thinks of how symptomatic and self-destructive the borderline population was to begin with, and how desperately ill they appeared in their late teen years and early to mid twenties. The earlier viewpoint that a borderline condition carried a terrible prognosis was derived from the short-term follow-up studies which found the patients still in their twenties and still engaged in acting-out and self-destructive behaviors. As the long view came into sight, it became apparent that most borderlines settle down as they move into their fourth decade of life. It must be of some comfort to therapists, parents, and the borderlines themselves to know that the odds are in their favor. The positive outcome appears to occur independently of treatment, although this statement needs to be nuanced.

There are no satisfactory explanations for the long-term positive outcome findings. Negative outcome data are never difficult to explain. As indicated, the improvement cannot be attributed to treatment effect, which scatters equally between good and bad outcome. This does not mean that some persons are not helped with psychiatric treatment; it is very possible that the positive results of treatment are obscured when averaged in with the negative results. It is likely that many factors account for outcome results, with the role of chance or luck, i.e., factors extrinsic to the person's own plans or efforts perhaps playing a large part. But even here we cannot be sure that good luck, so to speak, does not require a person prepared to benefit from it.

It is also likely that those persons who showed borderline behaviors in their youth, but also were recognized to have underlying depressive or bipolar disorders, benefited from appropriate pharmacological treatment and were able in this way to drop out of the ranks of the borderline diagnosis. In fact, many borderlines drop out of the mental health system entirely and get on with their lives. We know of this indirectly because we see comparatively few psychiatric patients in their forties and fifties who have histories of borderline troubles. What has happened to the borderlines of yesteryear? The only answer is that most are doing well and no longer seeking psychiatric services.

My own thought is that maturation — quite literally central nervous system maturation, such as final myelination of the frontal and temporal lobe intracortical neurons occurring between ages 20 and 30 — accounts for a fair amount of the clinical improvement toward age 30. It is common knowledge that a certain number of dramatic antisocial and borderline traits "burn out" in the thirties; many of the young machos and hysterics of teenage years have joined the ranks of the relatively stable working majority by late twenties. Unlike personality traits relating to obsessionality and schizoidness, the impulsivity and grand theatrics of youth are often tempered with age.

On the other hand, optimism about borderlines should not be overstated; there remains considerable morbidity in terms of marginal functioning and ongoing emotional problems for an appreciable number of borderline patients. Although the statement sounds circular, those patients who do not improve by age 30 or so, probably representing a more severe form of the personality disorder in the first place or having been more severely traumatized in childhood, often go on to chronic disability. Nevertheless, the basic maxim has application to psychotherapy:

> Help the borderline stay alive
> To age 30 or 35.

5. About 8–15% of Borderlines Have Committed Suicide by 10–15-Year Follow-Up

The companion piece to the finding that over half the borderlines are doing well is that somewhere around 10% (8–15%) will have suicided within the 10–15 years following the index (not necessarily the first) hospitalization. The figures vary with the characteristics of different borderline populations, but it is unlikely that any new study will depart significantly from this finding. Although deaths of young adults are always a tragedy, the evidence that 8–15% of borderlines take their own lives can be restated either as, "only 8–15% of borderlines . . . " or, "as many as 8–15% of borderlines . . . commit suicide." If one considers that the borderline populations studied were practically defined at outset by self-destructive behaviors serious enough to necessitate hospitalization, then a suicide rate of only 8–15%, although certainly no basis for complacency, can be seen as providing some optimism and reassurance that most borderlines are amenable to treatment and/or spontaneous improvement and can have a fairly good outcome. After all, if a cancer follow-up program found that only 8–15% of cancer patients died of cancer (excluding unrelated causes) in 10–15 years, that would be considered a very acceptable mortality rate. This analogy can hold up only if one views borderline patients as having a serious psychiatric condition that is the equivalent of cancer for medical-surgical illnesses. On the other hand, if we consider the sanctity of each life, and view borderlines as having less than a predictably lethal condition, especially in light of the favorable prognosis for most borderlines, then a suicide rate of 8–15% is unacceptably high.

When we look at studies of psychiatric patients who have suicided to see what percentage are borderline, rather than at what percentage of borderlines have suicided, then the picture takes on a different perspective. In a Swedish study (Kullgren, 1988; Kullgren, Renberg, & Jacobsson, 1986) of suicides of patients in hospital or within six months of discharge, 16 of 134 (12%) patients who suicided met borderline criteria. In a second Swedish study (Runeson & Beskow, 1991), 19 of 58 (33%) suicides were borderline. Borderlines do not account for the majority of psychiatric patients who suicide; patients with severe depressions with prominent anxiety symptoms and schizophrenic patients have higher suicide rates.

Nevertheless, statistics are of small comfort to the therapist facing a particular borderline teenager or young adult who is threatening suicide at the moment. Will this patient be one of the 85–90% who do not suicide or one of the 10–15% who do? The major problem in suicide prevention in all conditions is that we have some very good evidence about what are the major risk factors, but are unable to translate this into predicting which individuals among the high-risk cohort will actually go on to suicide. This dilemma was elegantly demonstrated by the Iowa group (Goldstein et al., 1991) in a recent retrospective study testing the accuracy of suicide prediction factors in 1,906 patients with affective disorders, of whom 46 eventually suicided. In the authors' own words: "Although the list of potential predictors from which the present model was generated included nearly all of the demographic and clinical risk factors for suicide that have been reported consistently in the literature, the model failed to predict even one of the eventual suicides" (p. 421).

The clinical problem in dealing with suicide prediction with borderlines is particularly complicated by the likelihood that the vigorous short-term interventions (hospitalization, one-to-one nursing assignments, extra telephone calls and office visits) designed to prevent suicides often appear to undermine the long-term goals of decreasing self-injurious behaviors and interpersonal manipulations. By contrast, this is not the case, for example, with depressed patients without serious character pathology, whom one can hospitalize with the expectation of a fairly rapid decrease of preoccupation with suicide once the depression is adequately treated.

It would appear, then, that statistics do not aid prediction in individual cases; I would, however, contend that therapists have tended to ignore whatever information about risk factors in borderlines can be gleaned from the follow-up studies in regard to suicide. Therapists in general overhospitalize borderline patients and become overly involved in suicide discussions, safety plans, and suicide contracting. This is therapeutically counterproductive in the sense that getting caught up in the threats and acting-out of borderline patients reinforces further threats and acting-out. Recent writings about the treatment of borderlines have emphasized the risks of encouraging parasuicidal behaviors through overzealous involvement of the treatment team (Dawson, 1988; Hawton, 1990; Sederer & Thorbeck, 1986) and others have suggested that many borderlines do well with intermittent therapy of decreased intensity (Gabbard, 1989; Perry, 1989; Shay, 1987) or even with no therapy at all (Frances, Clarkin, & Perry, 1984). Linehan et al.'s study (1991) showed that a decrease in actual parasuicidal behavior in patients undergoing cognitive-behavioral therapy was not accompanied by a decrease in the borderline's thinking about suicide. The suicide statistics regarding borderlines provide some basis of confidence that, most of the time, the therapist can stop responding to suicidal talk with rescue attempts and get on with the business of therapy.

Of course, this "most of the time" phrase is my hedge, my sliding out of foolish predictions and categorical rules. There are times when the therapist must respond to the self-destructive threats of the suicidal borderline patient, and there is no blanket rule to discern this. It is possible that the suicide rate would be higher if therapists did not respond so directly and frequently to the borderline's threats, although there is no evidence to support this. It is certainly possible that the reason that self-mutilators, in the absence of other risk factors, have low suicide rates is that their cutting has obtained for them a sufficiently high level of expression of concern, such that they are sustained through the dangerous times. We do not know if this is the case, nor do the treatment data particularly support this, but it is a viable possibility. The opposite effect is also possible: that suicide attempts in this population are increased by expressions of concern. What we do know is that 85–90% of borderlines, most of whom have threatened suicide sufficiently seriously to be hospitalized several times, are alive 10–15 years later, and that over half of those still alive are doing well.

6. Suicide Is Correlated with Antisocial Personality, Alcohol Abuse, and Major Depressions

One critical issue in assessing risk of suicide and serious self harm in borderlines is the need to correlate factors associated with favorable and unfavorable outcomes. Stone's (1990) large follow-up study is our best source of information. Not surprisingly, borderlines who also have prominent antisocial traits, meaning that they are less likely to be amenable to therapy and more likely to be males and aggressive, have a higher suicide rate, as males in general are more prone to violent and completed suicide attempts. Females who have major affective illnesses and alcohol abuse are also at greater risk for suicide. Of the 181 borderline women in Stone's study, 24 were alcoholics, of whom 5 (21%) suicided. This linkage was also found in Fyer et al.'s study (1988) correlating major affective disorder and substance abuse with more serious suicide attempts in borderlines. Paris' (1990) work did not support this correlation.

We do not know whether alcoholism is a major direct contributor to suicide or a marker of a more severe borderline condition, such as evidence of genetic dispositions or of severe childhood sexual abuse. The implications of this particular finding, nevertheless, are fairly clear, even if the direction of causality is not. It is essential to target alcohol abuse as an important symptom, and to work to get the patient into a chemical dependency treatment program. Whatever the specific etiological role of alcohol, we do know that its use in borderlines interferes with social and interpersonal competence and is often directly associated with suicide attempts. In Stone's study (1990, p. 172), all the alcoholic borderlines who joined and remained with AA were doing well at the time of follow-up.

The issue of what to do with the depressions in borderlines is a more troublesome one. Notwithstanding a seeming imperative that the depression should be treated vigorously, in fact, the reactive nature of the depression in some borderlines and the evidence of clinical trials that many depressed borderlines are not helped by antidepressants (Soloff, 1992) gives one pause to thought. I am not suggesting that depression in borderlines ought not to be treated, but only wish to remind us that the presence of a borderline personality disorder both confounds the diagnosis and complicates the treatment of depression.

7. Suicide Is Negatively Correlated with Self-Mutilative Acts

Self-mutilative behaviors (usually wrist-cutting and burning), especially in the absence of a history of suicidal acts, predict very low suicide risk. In fact, in Stone's study, there were no suicides in this category. McGlashan (1986), too, found that self-mutilative behaviors correlate negatively with suicides. In Plakun's follow-up study (1991), a history of self-destructive actions prior to the index hospitalization did not correlate with any direction of outcome, and the presence of self-destructive acts during the index hospitalization correlated only with good intimate functioning in relationships and a higher achievement in marriage or a stable partnership. Again, the implications are fairly clear. Since wrist-cutting is a dramatic action which tends to mobilize outpatient therapists and inpatient staffs into a variety of rapid responses, such as hospitalization, seclusion room use, cancellation of passes, initiation or changes in medication, and general derailment of the course of therapy, it behooves therapists to reconsider their responses in light of the relatively favorable statistics correlating wrist-cutting behavior and low suicide risk.

8. The Majority of Borderline Patients Appear to Have Experienced Some Form of Sexual and/or Physical Abuse in Childhood

Unlike some of the other seven pieces of evidence, in which some of the studies were of limited scope and the conclusions to be drawn could be considered ambiguous, the evidence linking early abuse and borderline personality characteristics is robust and impressive. Yet, partially because of the almost overwhelming nature of the correlations, which suggest a clear cause-effect relationship between abuse and borderline personality disorder, it is all the more important that

we slow down and think over very carefully the theoretical and practical implications of this etiological hypothesis. This goes back to
my earlier discussion regarding hedgehogs (those who seek and find
Grand Theories) and foxes (those who are skeptical even of Large
Generalizations). It is too easy to get caught up in the bandwagon
mentality that proclaims a singular "Childhood abuse causes borderline symptoms, that's all there is to it" formula without examining
the details of how well the specific linkage holds up or of what might
be some modifying factors, contrary evidence, or major implications.

In essence, the rest of this book will be devoted to examining the
evidence and the issues raised by studies correlating childhood sexual
and physical abuse and borderline patterns. Since not all borderlines
have been abused in childhood and since not all abused children
develop borderline symptoms, there clearly must be additional specific contributory and protective factors present. Furthermore, as
we need to keep reminding ourselves, abuse almost always occurs in
a larger matrix of disturbed family relationships in which it would
be arbitrary to single out the specific abusive acts from the other
toxic factors. This is not to argue against the centrality of the impact
of severe abuse experiences in the development of post-traumatic
and borderline syndromes, but rather to keep a larger perspective in
sight. The major theoretical question raised by the abuse data concerns the very concept of borderline itself; if, in fact, the majority
of borderlines are displaying the effects of serious childhood sexual
abuse, might not all be better served by dropping the borderline
diagnosis and using the more specific post-traumatic term?

The important practical question is how the abuse data shall affect
therapeutic considerations of the PTSD/borderline patient, as I shall
refer to this group. A therapeutic approach that narrowly identifies
all problems in the adult victim of childhood abuse as understandable only within an abuse (PTSD) framework does a disservice to
the complexity of human development and the myriad creatively
destructive and constructive uses to which the abuse victim can put
such childhood experiences. Thus, for example, adult patterns of
entitlement would surely be colored by childhood abuse experiences,
but a therapist would have to deal with entitlement in the transference as a generic issue involving active fantasies on the patient's part,
rather than only as the understandable and thereby justified response

to childhood traumas. This point is elaborated in an excellent article by Haaken and Schlaps (1991) who, writing from a feminist psychoanalytic perspective, warn that "incest resolution therapy risks over-objectifying incest in that the incest becomes the unifying event around which the patient's symptomatology and difficulties are organized." The authors proceed to comment that "Pitfalls include overreliance on catharsis, neglect of specific developmental and object-relational factors, and countertransference reactions based on overidentificaton with the survivor" (p. 39).

The central links in the causal chain connecting childhood abuse and PTSD/borderline response are always the person's individuality, which is, of course, itself evolving out of, and influenced by, not just the abuse experiences, but genetic and constitutional factors and all else that has occurred in that individual's lifetime. Finally, the abuse experiences often occur in the larger context of family violence, neglect, boundary violations, and intergenerational confusions and role reversals of many sorts. These factors are more difficult to ascertain and recover, especially, as is always the case with our adolescent and adult patients, retrospectively. The next chapter will provide a critical review of the studies linking sexual abuse to the borderline disorder.

2

Childhood and Adolescent Sexual Abuse

The history of psychiatry is a history of unceasing swings of the theoretical pendulum explaining what causes mental illness and why people behave the way they do. Innovations in technology, new clinical insights, and imaginative theories of human development either propel the pendulum further in the direction it is already heading or pull it back to the opposite pole from where it had previously come. Breakthroughs in one category of the biological or social sciences tend to be generalized to other areas, sometimes fitting well, at other times poorly. At the same time that compelling evidence and arguments are being amassed to extend a theoretical claim for broader applicability, counterforces are beginning to document examples which argue against generalizing the newest findings into a broad theory. When Franz Kallman (1946) proposed that there is a very strong genetic component to schizophrenia, he was by and large ridiculed by proponents of the double-bind and schizophrenogenic mother theories of the etiology of schizophrenia. How could an illness with behaviors as variegated and complex as schizophrenia have a genetic or biochemical foundation? Arguments that appear compelling to one generation seem shallow and self-serving to the next. The speed with which new theories, purporting to explain all, appear and disappear, and the enthusiasm with which devotees wholeheartedly endorse explanatory systems which are compatible with their other beliefs and prejudices should at the least imbue us with a sense of modesty and cautiousness as we embark on an evaluation of the evidence relating to the latest etiological theory about borderlines.

The richness and diversity of borderline symptoms have made it an irresistible magnet for each new psychiatric system to claim dominion in explaining its causes and expertise in guiding its treatment.

30

During the brief lifetime of the formal recognition of borderline personality disorder as a specific condition, we have so far lived through three different theories purporting to explain what borderlines are and how they were made that way. All three theories are still active and in varying states of robustness. The first theory was the psychodynamic one, conceptualizing the borderline character in terms of developmental problems occurring primarily during the separation/individuation phase of young childhood. The second theory, reacting against the first, was the biological one, conceptualizing the borderline syndrome as primarily an atypical affective disorder, with mood instability and rejection-sensitive dysphoria as the core features responsible for the panoply of "borderline" behaviors. The third theory, similar to the first in that it focuses on adverse life experiences rather than endogenous biological factors as the major causes of borderline behaviors, conceptualizes borderline traits as an understandable response to childhood and adolescence sexual and physical abuse, and the borderline personality as the result of the warping effects of such early traumatic life experiences upon the developing and vulnerable child.

Yet BPD itself remains a construct, a way of looking at and organizing a staggering amount of observations, theories, anecdotes, irreplicable clinical experiences, and often contradictory research findings in a way that begins to make sense. When examining the evidence that borderlines have experienced sexual and physical abuse in their childhood and adolescence, the natural tendency is to infer from this evidence that such abuse was instrumental in bringing about the development of those personality traits that we have come to identify as "borderline." Such an inference redefines, to a large extent, the very notion of borderline into an understandable reaction to noxious early life experiences. This redefinition of the borderline concept, if accepted, has very important implications for prevention and treatment; it also enters into the larger controversy in developmental psychopathology about the role of adverse life experiences, as compared to genetic and biological factors, in the etiology of some of the personality disorders.

The examination of the linkage between childhood abuse and borderline etiology raises a two-part question. As in most scientific inquiries, a distinction must be made between (1) the evidence concerning the question at hand, which is taken up in this chapter, and (2) conclusions, or hypotheses, that can be drawn from the evidence, discussed in the next chapter. Evaluating the evidence itself involves scrutinizing the methodological soundness of the studies, including the credibility of the persons answering the questionnaires. While this is true for all psychiatric research, it is especially the case here, since inquiring about a person's childhood sexual abuse experiences is a subject in which emotions of both researchers and subjects run very high. Furthermore, any discussion of the etiological conclusions drawn from the data sets about childhood sexual abuse in border-lines must be cognizant of the base rates for sexual abuse in populations other than borderline. Finally, we need to keep in mind, even if out of sight, the definitions by which we decide what shall and shall not count as abuse, and the philosophic rules that we employ in determining what constitutes evidence and what is considered legitimate "proof" of causality.

In view of the above distinction between evidence and conclusions drawn from evidence, several cautionary notes must be elaborated as we review the studies inquiring into abuse in the life histories of psychiatric patients and others. The cautions involve, first, an appreciation of the very nature of the types of experiences under consideration, since such experiences appear to be able to affect one's ability and accuracy of recall of the events themselves and of the larger context in which they occurred. Given the immaturity of most of the victims at the time of the abuse, the traumatic nature of the abuse, the disturbed environmental matrix in which abuse usually occurs, and the layers of successive life experiences further colored by being filtered through the consciousness of an already traumatized child, it is not surprising that distortions, in the form of amnesias, partial and merged memories, and misperceptions of the significance of events, occur. In fact, much of the work in many therapy cases involves the attempt, as best as possible, to sort out distortions from accurate memories as part of coming to terms with the past. One critical problem, both in therapy and in research, arises in trying to distinguish what "really" happened from what is consciously remembered or comes to be remembered or is vaguely remembered or is suggested by a therapist.

It is not that we need to maintain that any person can ever recover a full memory of childhood, or that, psychologically, one can speak objectively of what "really" happened disengaged from the subjective sense of how the child experienced the event. To the child, the subjective experience of the event is the critical component of what "really" happened, and this can never be fully described or even appreciated. Nevertheless, in terms of making objective/scientific statements that such and such percentage of persons experienced childhood sexual abuse and, further, inferring from this statistic that childhood abuse experiences bring about the development of borderline traits, the investigator, and the reader, have to come to terms with the problems associated with distortions of recall of childhood memories (Claridge, 1992). This problem, and the one to follow, are addressed by almost every research article reviewed here, although there is never any full resolution.

The second cautionary note involves the possibility of deliberately false claims of having experienced sexual abuse in childhood. The question of how credible are the statements or denials of childhood abuse must always be raised. First of all, we know that, for a variety of reasons, there is considerable underreporting of abuse experiences. Patients, because of their own sense of shame and self-blame, protectiveness toward the perpetrator and the "cohesion" of the family, and their awareness of the hostility, rejection, disbelief, and prurient interest of others, are reluctant to reveal that they have been abused, even when they have fairly complete memory of the abuse.

On the other hand, there may at times be fabrications or exaggerated reports by suggestible persons caught up in the highly publicized epidemic of fascination with and suspiciousness of all adult-child relationships that carry a possibility of exploitation. The possibility that mental health professionals and extensive media coverage have convinced some borderline patients that there was sexual abuse when there was none is raised in much of the psychiatric literature, especially as a focused criticism of the sudden surge of cases of multiple personality disorder (Merskey, 1992).

Intentionally false claims of abuse have been motivated by revenge and extortion, as well as by transference reactions in therapy that have overwhelmed the patient's judgment of reality. Offensive as this thought may be, since it tends to discredit the legitimate claims of those who have been abused, the potential for false claims cannot be ignored in evaluating the evidence of adult statements about abuse in their childhood. Just as there are persons with Munchausen's syndrome who seek medical attention by feigning physical signs and symptoms, so too there are persons who, recognizing which topics intrigue the psychiatric profession and lead to further treatments, are more than willing to oblige. The problem is exacerbated by the zealousness of some mental health professionals, lawyers, and media figures who, often motivated by market forces (maintaining a full caseload, suing alleged perpetrators, selling newspapers and books and raising TV ratings, respectively), have added to the public hysteria about abuse. This is most unfortunate, since there are enough real predators and victimization in our society without adding an element of exaggeration and doubt to the problem.

There are no simple answers to this dilemma of credibility. Clearly, there is good evidence of underreporting. The studies of Briere and Zaidi (1989) in the setting of the Los Angeles emergency room and those of Jacobson et al. (1987) in Buffalo, New York, demonstrate a substantial increase in the reporting of sexual abuse histories when the patient is directly asked about abuse, compared to information disclosed in a routine psychiatric assessment that does not make specific inquiries about abuse, past or present. Such findings, of course, do not fully answer the charge that patients may merely be telling us what they think we want to hear, but recourse to such a conspiracy theory cannot stop at questioning just these particular pieces of life stories without throwing into doubt the veracity of anything at all that a psychiatric patient reports. I do not think that we are ready yet to replace a patient's narrative history with radiological exams and blood tests. Furthermore, abuse histories, especially those involving children and adolescents, are often validated by families and public agencies, as Herman and Schatzow (1987) have reported.

The third cautionary note moves from questioning the validity of the data to questioning what to make the data. This is the problem of how one goes about deriving inferences from the data that have been gathered. At issue, specifically, is the temptation of linear thinking, of concluding that there is a direct one-to-one causal relationship between childhood abuse and borderline traits and symptoms in adulthood. Is the line of reasoning as simple as "sexual abuse in childhood causes adolescents and adults to become borderlines"? As everyone is aware, not all borderlines have been abused, and not all abused children become borderline, so clearly, many more factors are involved. This is as we might expect, since the relationships between untoward life events and outcome are almost always very complex (Scarr, 1992). If the prevalence of sexual abuse of women is about 10–20% in the general population, 20–50% in the psychiatric population, and 50–80% in the borderline population, then it is misleading to speak of childhood sexual abuse as the specific cause of the borderline syndrome. We will return to this point in the next chapter, but it is raised here as a reminder against rushing to judgment.

Furthermore, with reference to complexities, sexual abuse, especially of an ongoing nature, almost always occurs in the context of a disturbed family environment that has already and will continue to exert its multiple influences on the development of the child in question. It makes no sense to speak of the abuse alone, independently of the family context, as the cause of the borderline outcome, anymore than to speak of the disturbed family constellation, independently of the sexual abuse, as the cause.

We do best to think in terms of Meehl's (1977) concept of strong and weak influences of psychological causation, rather than of specific etiology. The question of what causes borderline personality traits is not one that will yield an easy answer, either conceptually or empirically. Much more research, including prospective studies, will be necessary to unravel just some of the more powerful, let alone more subtle, causal connections between life events and personality outcome. It may turn out that a disturbed family constellation provides the background for borderline-type symptoms, but that specific types of abuse experiences are necessary (but not sufficient) to produce the full borderline picture of self-injurious behaviors, perceptions and scenarios of self as victim, dysphoric moods, and altered states of consciousness. It may also be that we are dealing with a threshold phenomenon, such that abuse experiences beyond a certain degree of horrendousness are alone sufficient to produce the borderline picture, but that lesser degrees of abuse in combination with other destructive factors in the absence of ameliorative factors can also produce the borderline picture. We do not know what mediating variables might serve to buffer or protect the abused child from deviant or pathological personality development (Garmezy, 1981; Garmezy, Masten, & Tellegen, 1984; Widom, 1991). We do not know the extent and specific mechanisms of the role of genetics, basic temperament, and neurologic integrity in making a borderline outcome more or less likely in abused children, but we do know that such factors cannot be ignored in any comprehensive etiological statement.

While on the topic of the etiology of borderline as a prelude to examining the data correlating childhood abuse and adult borderline outcome, we might do well to outline the requirements for an adequate theory of etiology. A theory of borderline etiology should be consistent with and account for, within the limitations of our knowledge, the following six considerations:

1. Clinical symptoms
2. Dimensional rather than categorical nature of the condition; in this case, there should be a correlation of severity of trauma to severity of adult symptoms, taking into account the possible presence of ameliorating factors
3. Sex ratio and other demographic features
4. Family history
5. Course
6. Response to treatment

We shall return to this list in the next chapter, but need to keep these requirements in mind as we sift through the many research studies examining the childhood and adolescent life experiences and family backgrounds of borderline patients.

EMPIRICAL STUDIES

There are two major approaches to investigating the prevalence of sexual abuse in our society and, specifically, the association between childhood sexual abuse and adult emotional problems and psychopathology. The first method is to define a population cohort and then survey this population for psychiatric symptoms and for a history of childhood abuse, using questionnaires that appear to provide the best balance between sensitivity to the types of questions being asked and comprehensiveness, reliability, and relevance to the information sought. The second method is to start with a population of identified victims of childhood abuse and then investigate their health status as adults. We shall first assess studies of cohorts that were not identified primarily as borderline, then at studies of borderline patients, third, at populations identified by self-injurious behaviors, and last, at studies of persons already identified as victims of childhood sexual abuse.

CHILDHOOD ABUSE IN NON-BORDERLINE PSYCHIATRIC POPULATIONS

As our awareness of the high incidence of childhood sexual abuse in our society in general grew (Finkelhor, 1986; Russell, 1986), and our denial lessened, the logical next step was to investigate the presence and impact of childhood abuse in different psychiatric populations, such as inpatients, outpatients, women and men patients, chronic psychotics, eating disordered patients, and other specific diagnostic categories (see Table 1). Furthermore, as initial answers came in regarding psychiatric consequences of childhood abuse, a so-called second generation (so-called because it is occurring all within a single decade) of studies developed special research instruments designed to focus upon some of the specific findings suggested by the initial series of studies.

Carmen, Rieker, and Mills (1984) did a chart review of all psychiatric inpatients discharged from hospital between January 1980 and June 1981. The age range of the patients was 12–88; 65% were women; 80% were white, 20% black. Of 188 charts complete enough for inclusion in the study, there was documentation of abuse in 88 (43%) patients sometime in their lives. Forty-two (53%) patients reported physical abuse alone, 15 (19%) sexual abuse alone, and 23 (29%) both types of abuse. There were 122 women in the study; 65 (53%) reported abuse, most beginning in their childhood. The lifetime prevalence rate for men was 23%. Patients with a history of abuse had a higher incidence of suicide attempts and assaultive behaviors. In this index hospitalization, these patients had longer lengths of stay; women patients with abuse histories were more self-destructive than non-abused women patients, and men patients with abuse histories were more aggressive than non-abused men patients. This study did not examine childhood abuse specifically. It did demonstrate, however, the high incidence of sexual and physical abuse across the lifetime of psychiatric patients and suggested that such life experiences influenced the types and severity of symptomatic behaviors seen in this group.

Beck and van der Kolk (1987) reviewed the records and inter-

TABLE 1

History of childhood and adolescent sexual abuse
in general psychiatric populatoins

AUTHOR	POPULATION	N	SEXUAL ABUSE
Carmen et al. (1984)	Female inpatients	122	65 (53%)
	Male inpatients	66	15 (23%)
Beck & van der Kolk (1987)	Female chronic psychotic	26	12 (46%)
Craine et al. (1988)	Female state hospital	105	54 (51%)
Morrison (1989)	Female somatization disorder	60	33 (55%)
	Female primary affective disorder	31	5 (16%)
Briere & Zaidi (1989)	Female ER (chart)	50	3 (6%)
	Female ER (interview)	50	35 (70%)
Chu & Dill (1990)	Female inpatient	98	35 (36%)
Waller (1991)	Female outpatient bulimics	67	27 (40%)
Brown &	Female inpatients	418	71 (17%)
Anderson (1991)	Male inpatients	601	25 (4%)
Surrey et al. (1990)	Female outpatients	101	40 (39%)
Swett et al. (1990)	Male outpatients	125	11–16 (9–13%)
Goff et al. (1991)	Male and female outpatients	61	15 (25%)
Jacobson et al. (1987)	Female inpatients	50	11 (22%)
	Male inpatients	50	8 (16%)
Palmer et al. (1992)	Female inpatients and outpatients	103	53 (51%)

viewed the staff of every chronically hospitalized (more than one year of continuous hospitalized) female patient on two wards of a Massachusetts state hospital. Of the 26 women who met the study criteria, 12 (46%) reported histories of childhood incest. There was corroborative evidence of sexual abuse in half the cases. While all 26 women in the study were actively psychotic, the patients with incest histories were, on average, younger in age, had more sexual delusions, affective symptoms, histories of substance abuse, and suspected organicity, and spent more time in the seclusion room. Interestingly, this group also was more likely to engage socially with the ward staff, but, as the authors point out, "their attempts at social contact were characterized by hyperarousal and agitation, disorganized thinking, and, in some cases, delusions." The majority of patients were given a diagnosis of chronic undifferentiated schizophrenia; only one received a diagnosis of borderline personality disorder. The import of these findings is to strengthen the case of childhood sexual abuse as a general risk factor that colors the particular symptomatology of whichever condition the patient has, a consideration that shows up time and again as we review the studies.

A second study of state hospital patients, one employing a more rigorous recruitment methodology, was reported by Craine et al. (1988). Using a table of random numbers, 12 female patients were selected from each of 9 of 11 Illinois state hospitals. There were 760 mentally ill women in these hospitals at the time of the study; thus the 105 women in the study represent 14% of the female state hospital population. Each patient was evaluated for childhood abuse (under age 18) using a structured one-hour interview. Fifty-four (51%) of the 105 patients were found to have been sexually abused in their childhood or adolescence. The reported mean age at first abuse was 10.5; mean duration of abuse period was 2.8 years. Thirty (56%) of the 54 abused women had not previously been identified as abuse victims, and 36 (66%) of the abused women at the time of the study met DSM-III criteria for post-traumatic stress disorder, although none had been diagnosed as such. Although a constellation of six symptoms (compulsive sexual behaviors, chemical dependency, sadomasochistic sexual fantasy, sexual identity issues, low energy and chronic fatigue, and loss of interest or enjoyment of sex) was seen only in the sexually abused patients, the study does not suggest that these patients were clinically more deteriorated or sicker than the non-abused patients. Confounding the specificity of any direct link-age of sexual abuse to particular symptoms or overall severity was the finding that half of the sexually abused patients had also been physically abused in their childhood or adolescence. This, too, is a constant finding that needs to be taken into account in any consider-ation of specific etiology of sexual abuse for borderline personality disorder.

A third study of the incidence of childhood abuse in chronic psy-chotic patients was reported by Goff et al. (1991). The study, con-ducted at a Boston community health center, interviewed outpatients who had been continuously or intermittently delusional or hallucina-tory, so that they required neuroleptic medication, for over one year. In recognition of more recent observations of the psychiatric se-quelae to childhood abuse, two research instruments designed to capture dissociative experiences were used. Of 85 patients invited to participate, 72 accepted, generating 61 usable data sets. Diagnoses were predominantly schizophrenia and schizoaffective disorder; there were eight patients with a borderline diagnosis. Twenty-one (34%) of the 61 patients were women. Childhood abuse was defined as abuse occurring before age 16. Twenty-seven (44%) of the 61 patients gave a history of childhood abuse: 12 (20%) physical abuse only; 4 (7%) sexual abuse only; 11 (18%) both types of abuse. Thus, 15 (25%) of 61 chronically psychotic patients reported sexual abuse (with or without concomitant physical abuse) occurring prior to age 16. Compared to patients who did not report abuse, the abused patients had an earlier age of onset of illness, more relapses, and higher scores on the dissociative research measures. Sexually abused patients tended to have higher dissociative scores than physically abused patients, but the differences were not statistically analyzed because the overlap between the two abused groups was so great. Once again, it is apparent that a history of childhood abuse is not limited to borderline patients, and that a large number of sexually abused children have also been physically abused. The dissociative findings will bear watching, since this cluster of symptoms is claimed to derive most specifically from childhood abuse experiences.

There have been several studies of general hospital psychiatric inpatient populations. Jacobson, Koehler, and Jones-Brown (1987), in a project designed primarily to examine whether clinicians inquire about assault histories and record the information in the patient's chart, assessed 100 inpatients at a university-affiliated hospital in Buffalo, New York, using a very detailed structured interview. There were 50 male and 50 female patients; approximately 60% were diagnosed as having either schizophrenia or an affective disorder. Childhood abuse was defined as major abuse (physical assault of kicking or hitting with fist or with a weapon; sexual assault involving forced genital contact) under age 16. Rates of childhood physical abuse were 54% for males and 44% for females; rates of childhood sexual abuse were 16% for males and 22% for females. The authors found that only about 9% of the abuse experiences recorded in the research interview had been entered into the clinical chart. The charts also contained several reports of sexual abuse that had been denied by the patient during the research interview. In these cases, the history in the chart had been provided by an informant, not the patient. The underreporting of assaults, both of childhood and the adult years, has been a familiar finding, and it is important to realize that this is not limited to borderline patients. It is likely that, compared to other studies, the somewhat lower prevalence reported here of childhood sexual abuse in female patients is a reflection of the more rigorous criteria for major abuse employed in this study.

Bryer et al. (1987) studied child abuse histories in women inpatients at a private hospital in Boston. Of 172 female admissions, 124 met study criteria, of whom 68 agreed to participate. Sixty-six usable data sets were collected. Patients were predominantly Caucasian, employed, unmarried, and Roman Catholic, with some postsecondary education; mean age was 31.8 + 11 years. Method of evaluation was the SCL90R (for severity of present symptoms), the Millon Clinical Multiaxial Inventory, and a self-report questionnaire inquiring in some detail about abuse experiences. Forty-eight (72%) of the 66 women reported a history of abuse at some time during their lives. A total of 39 women (59%) reported a history of abuse before age 16: physical abuse in 10 (15%), sexual abuse in 14 (21%), and both types of abuse in 15 (23%). There were 29 women (52%) who reported a history of sexual abuse experiences prior to age 16; of these 29 women, 12 (41%) were diagnosed as borderline personality disorder. Only two patients diagnosed as borderline did not have a childhood sexual abuse history. Patients with a history of either type of childhood abuse had higher mean SCL-90R (global severity index) scores than patients without an abuse history, and patients with both types of abuse had the highest scores of all. There was a threefold increase in the incidence of suicidal ideation, gestures and/or attempts in patients with an abuse history in childhood.

Chu and Dill (1990) also studied the rates of childhood abuse (before age 16) in women psychiatric inpatients in a Boston area private hospital. Ninety-eight patients (of 188 female admissions) met study criteria and completed usable data sets. By description, the patient population appears to be similar to that described in Bryer et al.'s (1987) study. In addition to the SCL-90R and the Life Experiences Questionnaire (Bryer et al., 1987), designed to investigate childhood trauma and home environment, the authors included the self-report Dissociative Experiences Scale (Bernstein & Putnam, 1986). Twenty-seven (28%) patients reported childhood physical abuse only, 12 (12%) sexual abuse only, and 23 (23%) both types of abuse. Thus, 35 patients (36%) reported childhood sexual abuse, either with or without accompanying physical abuse. If we add to this figure the 27 patients who reported physical abuse only, we reach a rate of 63% of the study population with histories of childhood abuse. Contrary to most other studies, Chu and Dill found greater severity of psychiatric symptoms in general in those patients with histories of physical as compared to sexual abuse.

The findings related to dissociative symptoms are interesting. Although the subjects in the study (abused and non-abused patients) had higher dissociative scores than the norms established for normal adults, few differences were found in clinical symptoms or psychiatric diagnoses between patients with high and those with low dissociative test scores. Patients with high dissociative scores were not clinically diagnosed more frequently with PTSD, multiple personality disorder, or dissociative disorder. Although the authors conclude from this that clinicians are overlooking dissociative symptoms when making diagnoses, other interpretations, such as that clinicians weight the reports of these symptoms less heavily or that answers on a self-report dissociative instrument do not translate into significant clinical symptoms, are possible. On the other hand, patients with high dissociative scores did show more auditory hallucinations and impulsive behaviors. In terms of dissociative scores and a history of childhood abuse, the only significant positive correlation was found in those patients with both physical and sexual abuse. The findings of this study underscore the difficulty both in collecting data and in knowing how to arrive at meaningful interpretations, especially with regard to dissociative symptoms. The case can always be made that when dissociative symptoms are not reported, or are inconsistently reported, it is because true dissociative experiences, by definition, are out of conscious awareness and easy recall much of the time. While this may be the case, one must be careful not to explain away any findings that are not in line with the sought-after thesis: in this case, that there is a close association between childhood abuse and adult dissociative symptoms and the derivative clinical diagnoses of PTSD and multiple personality disorder. This problem will be discussed again in the next chapter.

Margo and McLees (1991) evaluated 38 consecutively admitted female patients meeting study criteria (ages 18–45) on a 23-bed psychiatric ward of a university hospital in Syracuse, New York. Omitted from the study were those with less than an eleventh-grade education and those with current alcohol and drug abuse problems. Definitions and age limit (under 16) of abuse were adopted from Bryer et al. (1987). Of the 38 women included in the study, nine (23%) reported no abuse, seven (18%) reported physical abuse only, four (10%) sexual abuse only, and 18 (48%) both types of abuse. The prevalence for childhood sexual abuse (with or without physical abuse) was 58%. This figure demonstrates how selection of the study population affects the results. The decision to exclude women over age 45, many of whom would be expected to have straightforward depressive illnesses, probably leads to a somewhat higher abuse history rate in the study population, while, as the authors mention, the decision to exclude women with lower educational achievements (school dropouts), physical illness, and those with current alcohol and drug problems most likely eliminated from study several known and suspected risk factors linking early abuse to adolescent turmoil. In this study, 64% of abused women (versus 22% of non-abused women) had substance abuse histories. We cannot guess whether the two excluded populations balance each other out in terms of prevalence of childhood abuse in this inpatient study.

Forty-eight percent of abused patients (versus 11% of non-abused patients) had a personality disorder diagnosis, the majority receiving a diagnosis of borderline personality disorder (38% of the abused group). This also means that 62% of the abused group was not diagnosed as borderline. More specifically, nine of the 18 women (50%) with histories of physical and sexual abuse were given a borderline personality disorder diagnosis, compared to one of nine

(11%) with no abuse history, one of four (25%) with a sexual abuse only history, and one of seven (14%) with a physical abuse only history. While not supporting a simple linkage between childhood sexual abuse and adult borderline outcome, the data do suggest a relationship between severity of abuse and severity of symptoms, with those children experiencing combined (and therefore presumably worse) abuse being more likely to develop a borderline personality disorder.

It is possible that adult borderlines remember and present their past experiences more dramatically and more negatively than nonborderline patients, a factor that we shall have to reckon with in the next chapter. The women with abuse histories in Margo and McLees' study scored higher than those without abuse histories on the SCL-90R scales for anxiety, hostility, depression, and somatization, and the global severity index. There were no significant SCL-90R score differences between the three abuse groups (physical alone, sexual alone, both types of abuse), indicating, in this study, a lack of specificity between severity of adult psychiatric symptoms and childhood sexual abuse, as compared to any type of severe abuse in childhood. It is possible that the small number of patients in each abuse group precluded finding significant differences, but, as it is, the data point to childhood abuse of any type as a significant risk factor for severity of psychiatric symptoms once a psychiatric syndrome is present.

In a report from Leicestershire, England of 103 inpatient and outpatient women ages 16–49, Palmer, Chaloner and Oppenheimer (1992) found an overall rate of reported sexual abuse (before age 16) of 51%. Patients who were illiterate or actively psychotic, as well as those with eating disorders (reported in another study by the authors), were not included in the study. Thirty-seven women meeting study criteria refused to participate, most often before learning the nature of the research. The rates of abuse by ICD-9 diagnoses were 18 of 36 (50%) for manic-depressive illness; 18 of 36 (50%) for neurotic disorders; 2 of 5 (40%) for schizophrenia; and 15 of 26 (58%) for personality disorder. There was no association between diagnostic category and the overall rates of reports of childhood sexual abuse. The authors conservatively conclude that childhood sexual abuse experiences could have lasting effects of a kind which might increase vulnerability to adult psychiatric illness.

In the largest report to date investigating childhood abuse history and adult psychopathology, Brown and Anderson (1991) studied 1,019 consecutive admissions (947 patients) to an Air Force hospital in San Antonio, Texas. The population studied was 59% male (N = 601) and 41% female (N = 418). The average age was 30, with a range from 17–90; the sample included retired service as well as active duty personnel. Seventy-two percent were white, 14% were black, 8% were Hispanic, and 6% were Asian. Definition of sexual abuse was fairly broad — any sexual contact, including fondling — before age 18 by a nonfamily member more than five years senior or by a family member more than two years senior to the patient. Physical abuse followed a similar definition, except that fighting among peers was excluded.

Of the 947 patients interviewed, 166 (18%) reported a history of childhood or adolescent abuse. Eighty-six (9%) reported sexual abuse (with or without physical abuse); 94 (10%) reported physical abuse (with or without sexual abuse); 28 (3%) reported combined abuse, of whom 23 were female; 70 (7%) reported physical abuse alone, and 68 (7%) reported sexual abuse alone, of whom 20 were female. Seventy-one (17%) of the 418 women in the study reported childhood or adolescent sexual abuse. For both genders, the lifetime prevalence of illicit drug use was greater in those patients with a history of combined abuse. A diagnosis of borderline personality disorder was given to 3% of the non-abused patients, 13% of patients with either type of abuse, and 29% of those with combined abuse.

The most common admitting symptom for any of the abuse groups was suicidality. There was no significant association between homicidality and history of childhood abuse. The strengths of this study include the use of all admissions rather than establishing inclusion and exclusion criteria, and the inclusion of a large number of male patients in the study group. The major question about the study population concerns how fully one can generalize from a military population, which presumably has screened out some of the more disturbed segments of the general population, to a civilian population. On the other hand, all studies contain their own unique population characteristics, in terms of social class, race and ethnicity, and other factors relating to the catchment area and admission criteria to a particular psychiatric service.

A number of studies have investigated the incidence of abuse in outpatient and emergency room psychiatric populations. Briere and

Zaidi (1989) found that, when asked routinely about such experiences, 35 of 50 (70%) nonpsychotic women reported histories of childhood sexual abuse before age 17, compared to a report rate of 6% (3 of 50 patients) when the emergency room evaluator did not inquire directly about childhood abuse. Patients who had been childhood abuse victims reported more drug use, self-injurious and parasuicidal behaviors, and sexual and legal problems than patients without such a history. Thirteen of the 35 (37%) abused patients had received borderline personality diagnoses. All told, 22 of the 35 (63%) abused patients had been given one or several personality disorder diagnoses. As the authors point out, these were clinical diagnoses not derived from rigorous diagnostic interviews. The major finding of the study, underscored by the authors, is that a high proportion of nonpsychotic women seeking or referred to psychiatric services in an emergency room have histories of childhood sexual abuse, and that this important part of their life experience is likely to be overlooked by health care professionals unless inquired about directly.

Jacobson (1989), as a complement to her study (Jacobson et al., 1987) of psychiatric inpatients, investigated physical and sexual assault histories of 31 outpatients (of an eligible pool of 123) requesting psychotherapy at a university-affiliated clinic. The mean age of the 31 patients was 31; 26 (84%) were female; 23 (74%) were white and 8 (26%) were black. Eleven of the 26 women (42%) and one of the five men (20%) reported childhood (under age 16) sexual abuse experiences. Overall, 12 of 31 patients (39%) reported childhood sexual abuse and a total of 18 of the 31 patients (58%) reported childhood sexual and/or physical abuse experiences. Jacobson points out that a higher percentage of outpatients than inpatients (from the 1987 study) had histories of sexual assault as a child. While the relatively small percentage (25%) of eligible outpatients participating in this study and the likelihood of some self-selection bias make it hazardous to overextend the findings or explain discrepancies such as that mentioned above, Jacobson's data add to the growing consensus about the prevalence of childhood (and adulthood) sexual abuse in the lives of psychiatric patients.

In two related studies from a clinic in the greater Boston area, Surrey et al. (1990) reported on lifetime sexual and physical abuse histories in 140 women and Swett et al. (1990) on 125 men psychiatric outpatients. In both studies, the SCL-90R, Life Experiences Questionnaire, and DSM-III-R diagnoses were used. In the women's study, the 140 patients represented the usable responses from 146 women of a pool of 152 consecutive evaluations; in the men's study, the 125 patients represented the usable responses of 145 men of an eligible pool of 158 consecutive evaluations. Seventy-six of the 89 women who reported a history of abuse provided information about the age of first abuse. Of this 76, 56 reported abuse before the age of 18. Forty of this group of 56 were sexually abused, either as sexual abuse alone (N = 12) or in combination with physical abuse. Because of this incomplete reporting of age of first abuse, we can say that, at the least, 40 (31%) of the 127 women reported a history of sexual abuse prior to age 18. Later, in therapy, three women who at the time of the research interviews denied childhood sexual abuse experiences reported such a history, but these do not appear in the statistical analyses.

Of the 53 men for whom age of first abuse was known, 11 reported sexual abuse before age 18. Because of the incomplete data regarding age of first abuse for male patients, prevalence of childhood sexual abuse in the male patients cannot be ascertained definitively, but must be somewhere between 9% (11 of 125 patients) at a minimum and 13% (total of 16 of 125 patients reporting sexual abuse at any age) at a maximum. In both the male and female populations, severity of adult psychiatric symptoms was correlated with a positive history of childhood sexual and physical abuse, most particularly the depression, anxiety, and interpersonal sensitivity scales on the SCL-90R subscales and the Global Severity Scale.

CHILDHOOD ABUSE IN SPECIFIC
DIAGNOSTIC CATEGORIES

There have been several studies of the prevalence of childhood abuse in patients with particular psychiatric syndromes, most of which share several features in common with borderlines. Morrison (1989) interviewed 60 women with somatization disorder and 31 women with primary affective disorder matched for demographic characteristics from a large group psychiatric practice in San Diego. Thirty-three of the 60 women (55%) with somatization disorder, compared to five of the 33 women (16%) with primary affective disorder, reported a history of childhood sexual abuse (before age 18). This finding is consistent with other studies (Bryer et al., 1987; Surrey et al., 1990; Swett et al., 1990) in which high somatization scores on the SCL-90R were reported.

Of course, observations about the correlation of somatic symptoms and possible childhood abuse date back to the early Freud papers on hysteria and the more recent controversy engendered by Masson's (1984) accusations that Freud backed away from believing his patients' reports of childhood abuse by attributing such memories to the heightened imagination of neurotic women. Without delving into Freud's unconscious (or conscious) motivations, blind spots, and the cultural biases at the turn of the old century, it does appear that the pendulum of evidence and belief has swung into the opposite quadrant as we approach the turn into a new century. Students of cultural swings take notice, of course, that the pendulum does not stay stationary for very long, if at all.

Most recent studies (Sansone & Fine, 1992) have found a clear association between bulimia and borderline symptoms, i.e., many borderlines include bulimia among their self-destructive acts and many bulimics have significant borderline traits, although this association is disputed by Pope et al. (1987; see also Pope & Hudson, 1992). In a study (Waller, 1991) from Manchester, England, of 67 consecutive women with eating disorders treated on an outpatient basis with cognitive-behavioral therapy, 27 (40%) reported a history of sexual abuse before age 16. There was a gradation in incidence of reports of sexual abuse ranging from a low in restrictive anorectics (1 in 15), moderate levels in bulimic anorectics (7 in 13) and bulimics with anorexia (9 in 19), and high levels in bulimics without anorexia (15 of 20). The total number of abused patients in these last figures (N = 31) include five patients who were first sexually abused after age 16.

Waller discusses the problems in deriving conclusions about etiology from such studies. He points out, first of all, that the prevalence of childhood sexual abuse is not much higher than that reported in nonclinical populations and, secondly, the lack of timely disclosure of the childhood sexual abuse points to the presence of overall difficulties in family interaction, such that it is not possible to single out sexual abuse as the critical factor in development of an eating disorder. Waller suggests that while unwanted sexual experiences per se may not predispose to eating disorders, a history of sexual abuse would determine the nature of the eating disorder that develops due to other factors. The author backs off this general point, however, in view of the impressive correlation between bulimia and childhood sexual abuse and wonders whether such abuse has a direct causal role in bulimia without anorexia. Waller's discussion nicely conveys the problems in attributing unequivocal causality to complex attitudes and behaviors.

CHILDHOOD ABUSE IN BORDERLINE PERSONALITY DISORDER

With the background of reports of childhood abuse in non-borderline psychiatric disorders in mind, we can now review studies that focus specifically on persons with borderline personality disorder (see Table 2). Herman, Perry, and van der Kolk (1989) studied a group of 55 outpatients recruited from mental health centers and advertisements for symptomatic volunteers in the Boston area. There were 29 women and 26 men. Seventeen of the women and four of the men met DSM-III criteria for BPD. Of the 21 persons with BPD, 14 (67%) had been sexually and 15 (71%) physically abused before age 18; in all, 17 (81%) had been either physically or sexually abused or both. Of the 23 persons without BPD or borderline traits, nine (39%) reported physical abuse and six (26%) reported sexual abuse before age 18. Persons with severe trauma histories (more trauma, earlier onset, longer duration) fell almost exclusively into the BPD group.

Once again, the data fall short of permitting a facile etiological connection between childhood abuse and borderline personality, especially since the borderline subjects did not report current symptoms of post-traumatic stress disorder as measured by the Impact of Events Scale (Horowitz, Wilner, & Alvarez, 1979). The authors speculate that memories of the abuse had become integrated into the total personality organization and had essentially become ego-syntonic. This heuristic formulation permits the authors to conceptualize BPD as a complicated post-traumatic syndrome.

While such an hypothesis has important treatment implications, it falls very short as an etiological hypothesis. It is likely, however, that the outpatients and symptomatic volunteers participating in this study were much less symptomatic than patients recruited from an

TABLE 2

History of childhood and adolescent sexual abuse
in borderline and control populations

AUTHOR	POPULATION	BPD		CONTROL	
		N	ABUSED	N	ABUSED
Herman et al. (1986)	Female outpatients	12	8 (67%)		—
Bryer et al. (1987)	Female inpatients	14	12 (86%)	52	17 (33%)
Ogata et al. (1990)	Female inpatients	19	16 (84%)	13	4 (22%)
	Male inpatients	5	1 (20%)	5	0 (0%)
Zanarini et al. (1989)	outpatients	50	13 (26%)	55	3 (5%)
Herman et al. (1989)	outpatients	21	14 (67%)	23	6 (26%)
Shearer et al. (1989)	Female inpatients	40	16 (40%)	—	
Westen et al. (1990)	Adolescent female inpatients	27	14 (52%)	23	4 (17%)
Margo & McLees (1991)	Female inpatients	12	10 (83%)	26	12 (46%)

inpatient population. In addition, it is likely that persons who volunteer for a study or treatment program in response to a newspaper advertisement are not representative of the larger group of abused persons.

In a somewhat similar study of outpatients composed of 50 BPD, 29 antisocial personality, and 26 dysthymic/other personality disorder patients, Zanarini et al. (1989) investigated the prevalence of childhood abuse (verbal, physical, and sexual), neglect (especially emotional withdrawal by the caretakers), and early separation experiences. Overall, 75% of borderlines reported a history of some sort of abuse by their full-time caretakers; more specifically, 58% of borderlines reported a history of physical or sexual abuse, or both. In addition, although the levels were fairly high in the antisocial personality and dysthymic/other personality disorder groups, 90% of borderlines reported a history of disturbed caretaker behavior. There were no significant differences in separation experiences, and the role of neglect was unclear because it was less discriminating between the different disorders. The authors conclude that, although the results of their study underscore the importance of abuse in the etiology of borderlines, there does not seem to be any one type of negative childhood experience that in itself is sufficient for the development of all the clinical features of BPD. Furthermore, I would add, this study encounters the additional methodological risk of not only inquiring into specific abuse experiences, which are ordinarily of a discrete and objectively recognizable nature, but also of inquiring into subtle factors such as the perception of neglect and emotional withdrawal. We cannot be sure of the quality of information obtained in asking a troubled adult about the emotional nuances of parent-child interactions 20 to 30 years ago, especially if there is also a history of actual physical or sexual abuse.

In contrast, Ogata et al. (1990) studied the histories of 24 DIB-diagnosed (Gunderson, Kolb, & Austin, 1981) borderline patients and 18 depressed control subjects without borderline disorder hospitalized at the University of Michigan Medical Center. Seventeen of the 24 (71%) borderlines reported a history of childhood sexual abuse, compared to four of 18 (22%) of depressive patients. Five of the borderlines were male, of whom one was sexually abused in childhood. This means that 16 of 19 female borderlines in the study reported histories of childhood sexual abuse, the majority with multiple abuses. There was no depressed subject with a history of multiple abuses. Significantly more sexually abused patients than non-abused patients reported derealization, depersonalization, promiscuity, unstable one-to-one relationships, and chronic dysphoria (emptiness, loneliness, or boredom). In this particular population, there was a high prevalence of sexual abuse by relatives other than parents (grandfather, uncle, cousins), and nonfamily members. The authors comment on the relationship between sexual abuse and dissociative phenomena, particularly derealization, and are concerned that, in the presence of derealization experiences, the identity diffusion of borderline patients may be confused with multiple personality disorder. As they state, "informing a suggestible borderline patient that she may have multiple personality disorder may offer a new pathological identity and lead to inappropriate treatment strategies" (p. 1012).

In a second investigation from the University of Michigan, this time of adolescent girls (ages 14–18) hospitalized on the adolescent ward, Westen et al. (1990) studied 27 patients with BPD and 23 non-borderline controls. Fourteen (52%) of the 27 borderline patients and four (17%) of the 23 controls reported histories of sexual abuse. The sexual abuse was typically compound abuse, with the same youngster experiencing several forms of it, often in conjunction with physical abuse. In fact, 80% of the sexually abused adolescents also reported physical abuse. Some interesting correlations between particular symptoms as reported on the DIB and a history of sexual abuse showed up in the study: girls with abuse histories scored higher on impulse/action categories (self-injurious behaviors, drug use, promiscuity, assaults, manipulative suicide attempts) than girls without abuse histories; suicide attempts were correlated with a history of physical abuse, but not sexual abuse, and the girls without an abuse history scored higher on the derealization scale than girls with an abuse history. This last finding was unexpected and is in direct opposition to the finding of Ogata et al. (1990) from the same hospital, as well as to the findings of other studies. A second provocative finding was that girls with an abuse history scored a full 10 points lower on IQ testing, almost all of it accounted for by lower verbal scores. The authors speculate about the possible effect of severe traumatic experiences in the latency years on basic psychological processes and structures such as self-esteem, sense of identity, capacity to regulate affects, reality-testing, and cognitive processing. It is also possible that causality moves in the opposite direction, so that girls with lesser verbal skills are more vulnerable to predatory adults. In essence, however, the authors raise the question of the impact of chronic abuse on the child's evolving character structure. In their thoughtful discussion, they ask, while acknowledging that a definitive answer is not possible, if there is a difference between a "true" borderline and a person who meets borderline criteria (whether DSM-III or DIB) with symptoms and character style that appear to be related to a history of sexual abuse.

Shearer et al. (1990), in a study of 40 female inpatients with borderline personality disorder, found that 16 (40%) reported a history of sexual abuse occurring before age 15. Of the 16, 11 were incest victims. The authors found that history of sexual abuse was associated with a greater incidence of eating disorders, drug abuse history, and suspected temporal lobe epilepsy. There was no non-borderline control group in the study.

PATIENTS WITH HISTORIES OF CHILDHOOD ABUSE

The reciprocal approach to starting with patients with various psychiatric diagnoses and then investigating rates of childhood abuse in these groups is to start with groups of patients who have been abused in childhood and then see what the adult picture looks like. The major methodological risk in this procedure is to make the assumption that whatever troubles such adults have is directly attributable to the childhood abuse, as if no other experiences and factors were influential in the development of these individuals.

Herman, Russell, and Trocki (1986) studied two groups of adult women with histories of incest, a nonclinical sample (N = 152) of women identified as incest victims through a community survey of 930 women in the San Francisco area (Russell, 1986) and a group of 53 women outpatients who had participated in short-term therapy groups for incest victims at a clinic in the Boston area (Herman & Schatzow, 1987). Half of the community sample reported long-lasting and substantial deleterious effects of the childhood incest, while the other half considered themselves to have recovered fairly well. The community sample's perceptions of lasting harm were associated with the severity of the abuse experiences in terms of degree of violence applied, duration of abuse, and greater age difference between victim and perpetrator. The patient sample in general reported much more traumatic incest experiences, a higher proportion of father or stepfather incest (75% for the patient sample as compared to 28% for the community sample), and a considerably earlier age of onset of sexual abuse (8.2 versus 11.2 years of age). It should be noted that the patient sample had screened out persons with active alcohol or drug use, those who were actively suicidal and those without social supports; therefore, the Boston outpatient sample represents the less severely disturbed end of the spectrum of psychiatric patients with childhood incest experiences. The authors conclude that the "likelihood of a good recovery appeared to be highly related to the nature of the abuse experience. . . . With the more severe degrees of sexual abuse, however, few women were able to escape without long-term sequelae. . . . These results suggest that violent, prolonged, or intrusive abuse or abuse by a primary caretaker represents stressors that are beyond the adaptive capacities of all but the most exceptional children and that will regularly produce a long-lasting traumatic syndrome" (p. 1296).

Goodwin, Cheeves, and Connell (1990) reported data drawn from the first 20 participants in a 12-week group in the Milwaukee area for incest victims who had at least one psychiatric hospitalization. The group appears to have been a fairly dysfunctional one: all 20 women had had at least three prior psychiatric or substance abuse hospitalizations, 19 were on some form of disability, 19 had been given a borderline diagnosis and 18 a mood disorder diagnosis, and 15 had an eating disorder. There was a high incidence of flashbacks; dissociative symptoms; revictimization experiences both in childhood and adulthood, sometimes perpetrated by health care providers; multiple suicide attempts; and a diagnosis of somatization disorder. All had been sexually abused prior to age eight, and most had experienced multiple abuse. Most of the women had been involved with the legal system, although none met full criteria for antisocial personality disorder. Of the nine women who had borne children, only one retained continuous custody of the child. It is clear that the sample included in this report occupies the more severe end of the child incest spectrum, in comparison with the Boston area outpatient sample (Herman & Schatzow, 1987) discussed just previously. The differences in the two populations point out the necessity of defining one's study sample when drawing conclusions about the effects in adulthood of childhood sexual abuse.

Pribor and Dinwiddle (1992) reported a study of 52 women incest victims in the St. Louis area drawn from outpatient programs for sexually abused women. All women who took part in the programs surveyed were contacted; 64% agreed to participate in the research study. Comparison subjects (N = 23) were age- and race-matched women with no history of incest and were drawn from the same sources. The results of the study show that persons with an incest history have a higher prevalence of all psychiatric disorders measured than do those in the control (non-incest) group. This includes anxiety disorders, major depression, and alcohol dependence. More severe incest abuse was correlated with a higher risk for development of a psychiatric disorder. Half of the incest group had never seen a psychiatrist. Of those who had, almost none felt they derived benefit. Many never told their psychiatrist about the incest, nor were they asked. Since the investigation followed Washington of St. Louis diagnostic biases, there was no direct inquiry made into the presence of borderline personality disorder. This is an interesting example of how one's frame of reference precludes the acquisition of seemingly important information. What this study does show is that childhood incest is a nonspecific risk factor for development of one or several psychiatric disorders.

SUMMARY

All studies agree in broad outline in confirming what common sense and clinical experience tell. Sexual and physical abuse of children and adolescents are detrimental to their well-being and development. What the studies have told us additionally are that the prevalence of such abuse is much greater than we had appreciated, and that the deleterious effects persist into adulthood across a very wide range of personal and social functioning. Once we move beyond these broad and intuitively correct conclusions, we enter into realm of normal science, as Kuhn terms it, in which we have to do the hard work of carrying out the detailed studies and cautiously examining the relationships between the many variables. The hard work involves collecting and teasing apart the many factors designated as "causes" and the many features designated as "outcomes," in order to determine which correlations and relationships hold up under careful scrutiny. The danger that bias and predetermined ideas will color one's findings exists at all levels of investigation, from development of research instruments to selection of sample population to collection of data and, finally, to analysis of evidence. The problem of investigator bias is especially relevant to the topics we are studying here, for who does not feel strongly about child abuse? The next chapter will examine the evidence with a critical eye to methodology and conclusions, in order to obtain a clear idea of just what it is that we know and we do not know, and what limitations we should impose upon our hedgehog-like generalizations. This is especially important because the conclusions that we draw have major impact upon how we develop broad social policy to victims of sexual abuse (and their perpetrators) and specific treatment approaches.

3

Post-Traumatic Stress Disorder and Borderline Personality Disorder: Are They the Same?

It is difficult to stay neutral or unimpassioned about sexual abuse of children, nor is it clear that it is desirable to remain so. The offense is massive; the impact profoundly disturbing; the social response to date appears puny and ineffectual. There is risk that one can appear to be indifferent to the crime and its victims by standing off to the side as an observer.

Yet we are aware that the consequences of unrestrained enthusiasm for a cause can affect one's judgment, such as in assuming causal connections when there may be none or in attributing blame to innocent parties or events. This occurs not just in regard to lynch mobs and kangeroo courts, but also with social issues in which passion replaces reason and information, such as occurs, for example, in the public debates about the safety of fluoridation of drinking water. My analogous concern in this chapter is that our revulsion toward the crime of child abuse and our sympathy for the victims may interfere with an evenhanded evaluation of the relationship between childhood trauma and its presumed consequences in specific adult psychiatric problems.

One morning, on entering the clinic where I work, I notice a flyer on the bulletin board. It is written by a group called ARIA, which stands for Adults Recovering from Incest Anonymous. ARIA sponsors self-help groups based on an 12-step model for women who have experienced incestuous sexual abuse. Its message seems sound and responsible. The major problem I have with the flyer, and the only reason the issue is raised here, relates to a section entitled, "How do I know if I am an incest survivor?" There follows a four-column list of 34 items that are classified as "common indicators of sexual abuse." Some of the items are the symptoms traditionally associated with borderline personality disorder and, more recently, with sexual abuse: cutting or burning yourself; overeating or vomiting; tendency to sexualize relationships; splitting, psychic numbing; alienation from and hating your body; not remembering blocks of childhood; pattern of being a victim, especially sexually.

There are, in addition, numerous items on the list that are so nonspecific for sexual abuse as to encompass the majority of the population. Examples include: depression, abusing alcohol or drugs; needing to be perfect; not sure when or how to be assertive; tightly controlling emotional expression; behaviors you feel you can't control. These are basic human problems, or rather, basic human responses to problems, and while it is possible that incest victims too suffer from them, there is absolutely no evidence to think that any of these traits or symptoms have any specificity to sexual abuse. To relate all of them to incest only serves to obscure whatever important associations exist between abuse and its consequences. In addition, such suggestions that feelings of depression or anxiety should make one suspect childhood sexual abuse contribute to the present public presumption that practically anyone with any emotional problems was probably abused, one way or another, as a child.

The issue is not whether child abuse is horrendous or can have devastating consequences, but how to evaluate in a fair manner the evidence that links childhood abuse to specific types of adult problems, and how to consider contradictory evidence and alternative hypotheses so that we might gain a deeper appreciation of the complexity of the influence of such adverse events on human development. The state of the question is:

Is the experience of childhood and adolescent sexual and physical abuse the major cause of the maladaptive psychological and behavioral patterns seen in persons who are diagnosed with BPD and BPD-related syndromes? If so, then a corollary question is: Should the use of the borderline diagnostic category for these persons be replaced by a PTSD diagnosis?

The thesis to be examined in this chapter is well articulated in two complementary statements by Judith Herman (1992a) regarding BPD-spectrum disorders. The first statement relates to the overall hypothesis; the second to the magnitude of abuse as a causal factor relative to other factors:

1. "The common denominator of these three disorders [borderline personality disorder; multiple personality disorder; somatization disorder] is their origin in a history of childhood trauma. The evidence for this link ranges from definitive to suggestive." (p. 125)
2. "The most powerful determinant of psychological harm is the character of the traumatic event itself. Individual personality characteristics count for little in the face of overwhelming events." (p. 57)

The basic dilemma is that common to all large generalizations—that there are so many qualifications and exceptions to the major thesis as to render it unsatisfactory as an encompassing theory. The value of a unifying hypothesis (childhood sexual abuse causes BPD) in cutting through the tangle of confusing and conflicting evidence and providing us with a clear direction for practical action is compromised by the loss of appreciation of other important factors in the development of a complex human response.

In the previous chapter, I touched upon various problems in assessing the relationship between childhood abuse and borderline personality disorder. I will review them here in an orderly fashion, presenting arguments for and against the credibility of each side of the debate. The two basic issues to keep in mind are (1) whether the traumas in childhood cause the BPD picture, and (2) whether the brute facts of the abuse outweigh all other influences in determining who develops BPD.

PROBLEMS OF RETROSPECTIVE STUDIES

The first set of problems in evaluating the childhood sexual abuse-BPD connection relates to the inherent weaknesses of all retrospective studies that rely on personal memories rather than documents, charters, school and health records, or even corroborating testimony from other persons' memories. Problems of accuracy and authenticity of childhood memories are further compounded by the traumatic nature of the childhood events that the adults are remembering, or are asked to remember, although I must point out that there is no scientific evidence that traumatic memories of childhood are distorted more than non-traumatic, or ordinary, memories of childhood events. Much of the literature concerning child abuse and adult symptomatology stresses the "fact" that the traumatic experiences have caused distortions and repressions of memories of those events, but then proceeds to accept unquestioningly the memories that are uncovered or more fully recovered in therapy. We cannot have it both ways – at least not fully. Either traumatic childhood events give rise to distortions of the memories of them or they do not.

The problem is that we do not know which memories have been distorted minimally, which extensively, and in which directions. There is no resolution to these questions, but we need to continue, at every point along our investigation, to keep them before us as important and relevant to our initial inquiry: What is the relationship of childhood sexual abuse to borderline personality disorder? Our confidence in the answer depends to a large extent on our confidence in the evidence.

A second problematic question is whether childhood memories of borderlines are inherently less trustworthy than childhood memories of adults who are not borderline. Again, there are no answers; certainly, the trustworthiness of these memories has not been put to the test. It is possible, as mentioned above, that there is something about the abuse experiences in childhood that specifically causes distortions of the memories of the abuse events themselves and of childhood life in general for those individuals. An alternative hypothesis relates to the putative penchant of borderlines for dramatic and exaggerated presentations. It is possible that borderlines, by virtue of the nature of their disorder, remember and present their past experiences more dramatically and negatively than other patients do. This line of reasoning gets us into just one of the many circular arguments about borderlines: Is the theatrical style of the borderline the developmental result of childhood sexual abuse, or is it a core feature of a particular type of personality that then exaggerates all kinds of emotional reactions, and especially tends to sexualize the perception of events?

The third problem in evaluating the retrospective reports of childhood abuse also touches on some presumed attributes of borderlines. If borderlines are prone to idealization/devaluation as cognitive processes for perceiving and evaluating others, how can we accept without serious reservations their adult reports of their childhood environments? This problem relates more to the credibility of reports about the quality of the parent-child relationship (e.g., bonding and attachment behaviors, emotional neglect, enmeshment, affectless overcontrol, parent-child role reversals) than to issues of accuracy of memory, but the potentially distorting effects of idealization/devaluation must take their place in the list of cautions as we sift through the evidence.

The fourth problem regarding memory distortions of childhood events relates to the possibility that suggestible patients are being coached by their therapists as to the types of memories of abuse that they are supposed to remember that they do not yet remember. As with every issue discussed so far, this charge is hotly debated, with ad hominem and ad feminem attacks flying in both directions. There is no avoiding the issue, and it will surface time and again in different contexts within this book. I think that the major suspicions regarding the authenticity of childhood abuse memories center around two basic types of recollections: those in which the person has no recall of childhood abuse until a therapist strongly suggests that the person was abused in childhood, and those in which the recollections of abuse either begin to extend back in time before age three or begin to include fantastic stories of satanic ritualistic abuse. It is not that memories before age three do not exist, or that ritualistic abuse is nonexistent, but that the spread of these types of embellished stories has too much the flavor of stereotyped hysteria. I count myself among the skeptics.

In the past month, I have seen three patients whose memories of abuse first emerged under the persistent suggestions of their psychotherapists. One of these patients, a 30-year-old woman, was referred by her new therapist for a medication evaluation. In the course of the interview, I asked if there had been any abuse in her childhood, either emotional, physical, or sexual. She replied that she thought she had been sexually abused by her father when she was four years old. Yet she could not remember the occurrence of abuse. I inquired about the basis of her belief that she had been abused. She said that she had been in a family systems counseling group for five years and that the therapists had told her that she had the dynamics of an abuse victim and therefore had probably been abused. In fact, she telephoned her father, who lives in the South, and informed him of her suspicions. He denied it and appeared to be very offended at her suggestion. The patient still holds to the belief that she was probably abused. Near the end of the interview, I asked if there were anything else that might be important for me to know in my evaluation of her. Well, yes, she had been in a sexual addiction group until recently. "Are you sexually addicted?" I inquired, not being quite sure what a sexual addiction was. "Well, yes," she replied, "When I become involved with a man, sex becomes very important."

Argument by anecdote is dangerous, because we select our anecdotes to support our case. Demonstration of the existence of false memories based upon suggestions does not invalidate the presence of true memories of sexual abuse, but it does raise questions about our readiness to accept more and more bizarre and unlikely stories because we do not wish to risk offending our patients or causing further damage by disbelieving them. Nevertheless, the fact remains that the studies that causally relate child abuse events to borderline personality disorder rest upon the reported memories of highly emotional and traumatic events from childhood. These reports are subject to distortions of memory, deliberate falsification, and priming by professionals. While we accept, as a matter of common sense, the apparent finding that traumatic events in childhood may be partially or fully repressed (i.e., forgotten), we seem to avoid the complementary conclusions to be drawn from this observation, namely, that the "memories," when recovered, and especially when recovered with the helpful participation of a therapist, are subject to the same psychological processes of distortion that brought about the amnesia in the first place.

FALSIFICATION OF LIFE STORY

The issue of deliberate falsification is such a loaded topic as practically to defy objective evaluation. We know that some people lie about their life experiences and their illnesses. The reasons for this may be as varied as the individuals. Once we question the veracity of any narrative, how shall we know when to believe and when to question? To the person, including myself, who works with abused children or adults, the pragmatic answer is relatively straightforward: Believe what the person tells you. The few cases in which the narrative is fabricated or exaggerated will reveal themselves in due course and, if not, the overall odds and therapeutic benefit still favor believing the story. This solution, however pragmatic and ethical within the context of psychotherapy, is not acceptable in two particular types of situations: psychiatric research and accusations of criminal misconduct. In these areas, data must be sharply questioned.

In each of the clinical research articles reviewed in Chapter 2, the authors themselves raise, but never resolve, the issue of credibility. The paper of Herman and Schatzow (1987) is often the lone paper cited in defense of the truthfulness of the accounts of abuse. In this study, there was corroborating evidence of childhood abuse in 75% of 53 women outpatients in an incest survivors group. In the other direction, there are also a few cautionary articles in the literature that provide examples of fraudulent claims of abuse. Matas and Marriott (1987) present a case of a woman who claimed to be an adopted child who became an incest victim when she was age 16 for a six-month period. She described in much detail how she was tied down and repeatedly sexually assaulted by her adoptive father. After considerable psychotherapy and several psychiatric hospitalizations, a family meeting, long-postponed, was held and the patient tearfully acknowledged that she was neither an adopted child nor sexually abused by her father. But does lying about the adoption automatically invalidate the veracity of the abuse charge? Or can we use the pattern of dramatic prevarications as evidence suggesting that she was, in fact, a sexually abused person? Billig (1991) provides a discussion of the problems that arise in general with regard to deception in psychotherapy.

On the closely related topic of credibility of PTSD symptoms, Perconte and Goreczny (1990) compared the MMPI test results of a clinical population of Vietnam veterans with PTSD and veterans with non-PTSD psychiatric disorders and fabricated PTSD symptoms. The authors found that "scores on the MMPI F scale and PTSD subscale proved to be of no value in discriminating real from fabricated PTSD." Other workers have also commented on the difficulty of developing a discriminating PTSD profile on the MMPI (Koretzky & Peck, 1990; Wilson & Walker, 1990).

In June of 1992, the Minneapolis newspaper carried a horrifying story of three women bursting into the rural home of a 19-year-old mother and stealing her 19-month-old son. "Is nothing safe?" I wondered. Two days later, the boy was found safe, although hungry and mosquito-bitten, in a ditch two miles from home. The following day, the young mother confessed to abandoning the baby in the ditch and concocting the story. One explanation, offered by a relative, was that the young woman was upset that her new boyfriend was not paying enough attention to her.

Horror stories such as this one surface from time to time. Yet the fact that some people lie, for whatever reasons, does not invalidate the overwhelming evidence regarding child sexual abuse. But as the stories mount regarding ritualistic abuse and satanic cults such that every small town in America must be the scene of at least one coven dedicated to devil worship, somewhere along the line, the influence of mass media and human suggestibility must be factored into the assessment of the child abuse data. As Rich (1990) pointed out, the accuracy of the reports that go into most child abuse studies are usually uncorroborated and unconfirmed.

Suggestible persons are being instructed in detail about the types of events that occur in satanic rituals, a social phenomenon (the suggestibility, not the rituals) that probably accounts for the remarkable stereotypy found in the descriptions of these ceremonies. A similar observation has been made, although on the side of the angels, in the remarkable similarity in descriptions of near-death experiences. We all know what to expect: soft light at the end of the tunnel, a sense of peacefulness, a feeling of warmth. It is not surprising that those who have near-death experiences use the same imagery and metaphors. I am aware that there is an alternative to suggestibility as an explanation for the similarity of descriptions of these transcendental (or satanic) experiences, namely, that the similarity of the experience explains the similarity of description, just as a kick in the crotch would probably be described by most men in a pretty similar way. No advance suggestibility telling the man what it will feel like is necessary. People describe stereotyped satanic rituals and near-death experiences the way they do because that is how the events really happen. If only the devil were so unimaginative.

FALSE MEMORY SYNDROMES?

The brings us to the last issue to be raised in this discussion of the credibility of the data, namely the priming of symptoms by professionals and mass media. Those who are skeptical about the very existence of multiple personality disorder point to the enormous number of cases coming from a very small group of workers who appear to have a vested interest in multiplying the multiples. Merskey (1992) asserts that iatrogenesis seems to be the major etiological factor in the development of MPD. Up until the last two decades, the number of MPD cases seen across the country and the number reported in the literature were miniscule. Following the publication and movie of *The Three Faces of Eve* and, later, of *Sybil*, MPDs began turning up everywhere. The MPD lobby states that the multiples were always there, just as childhood abuse was always there, only that the psychiatric profession did not care to ask the right questions or know the truth. It is stated that, on average, the patient with MPD has had six years of contact with psychiatrists and psychologists before the existence of multiples is suspected and revealed. The alternative explanation is that it took the therapists, especially the last one who, by definition, is the "discoverer" of the underlying nature of the problem, six and a half years on average to instruct the borderline patient how to become a multiple personality. Yet Tolstoy could hardly come up with one hundred interesting characters in one novel. How could persons of lesser imagination approach or excel this? I do not wish to belabor the MPD controversy here, other than to state what is fairly obvious. There are fashions and trends in psychiatric presentations, and cultural trends which appear to shape the types of symptoms that patients develop and report, as well as the types of stories in which psychiatrists and psychologists become interested. The mental health professions must bear some responsibility for this.

There is an extensive psychological literature on memory research that has direct relevance to our considerations. It is well documented that false memories can be suggested to persons who then incorporate these suggestions into their memory and recall them with great confidence (Weekes et al., 1992). The events suggested may be trivial (e.g., a noise occurred the other night when you were asleep in bed) or significant (e.g., when you were five years old, you were lost at a shopping mall and found by a bearded stranger). What is more, some persons may then proceed to elaborate the pseudomemory in much greater detail than was included in the original suggestion. Second, contrary to traditional beliefs, eyewitness recall is not negatively affected by the emotional stress accompanying the event

(Christianson, 1992), but is subject to distortion and false elaboration based upon the suggestions of others. Barnier and McConkey (1992) reported the results of a study in which 30 high- and 30 low-hypnotizable subjects saw slides of a purse snatching, and then imagined seeing the slides while in hypnosis or waking conditions. The experimenter suggested the offender had a mustache (true), wore a scarf (false), and picked up flowers (false). Hypnotizability, but not hypnosis, was associated with false memory reports: more high- than low-hypnotizable subjects reported false memories. Context also influenced true and false memory reports: the formal rather than an informal test situation produced more false memory reports.

These research findings emphasize two critical factors that have relevance to our concerns about recovery of childhood memories: the suggestibility of the witness and the context in which recall occurs. High-hypnotizable subjects are more likely to recall and elaborate suggested memories than are low-hypnotizable subjects. Which psychiatric diagnostic groups score highest on hypnotizability scales? Patients with dissociative disorders (primarily MPD and PTSD) score highest on all measures of hypnotizability (Frischholz et al., 1992), compared to patients with schizophrenia, mood disorders, and anxiety disorders, as well as college student controls. This suggests that patients with dissociative disorders are most susceptible to the development of pseudomemories, given proper suggestions and conditions. What sorts of suggestions and contexts are we referring to?

It is precisely the strong and repeated suggestions by an authority figure and the peer pressure in a group therapy situation that set the context in which the suggestible, hypnotizable dissociative-prone patient begins to recall and elaborate abusive childhood events for which there was no prior memory. The demand characteristics of the situation, which include motivation to please the therapist and other group members, combine with the suggestible nature of some patients to produce pseudomemories that become more elaborated and are believed with more confidence as time and reinforcement move on.

The specific role of hypnosis in the recovery of childhood memories requires a further comment, since this procedure is often used to assist abuse victims in recalling their repressed memories. The community-university clinic where I work is receiving an increasing number of telephone inquiries about the availability of hypnosis for this purpose. The reply is best summarized in a report by the Council on Scientific Affairs of the American Medical Association (1985):

> The Panel has agreed that there is no evidence of increased recollection by means of hypnosis for recall memory of meaningless material or of recognition memory for any types of material. When hypnosis is used for recall of meaningful past events, there is often new information reported. This may include accurate information as well as confabulations and pseudomemories. These pseudomemories may be the result of hypnosis transforming the subjects' prior beliefs into thoughts or fantasies that they come to accept as memories. Furthermore, since hypnotized subjects tend to be more suggestible, subjects become more vulnerable to incorporating any cues given during hypnosis into their recollections.

An interesting development recently, clearly in response to the increase in the number of allegations and litigation secondary to the recovery of childhood abuse memories under the influence of an enthusiastic therapist, has been the formation of the False Memory Syndrome Foundation, with administrative offices in Philadelphia. This organization disseminates newspaper reports and scientific publications, and serves as a forum for exchanges between people who state that they have been falsely accused, often by their own children, of perpetrating sexual abuse.

There is need to place this entire discussion into a balanced perspective. I have reviewed studies that support the notion that it is relatively easy to create pseudomemories in suggestible persons, especially in a context supportive of this procedure. I must emphasize here that these studies do not necessarily undermine the credibility of what our patients report to us under ordinary circumstances. We need to keep separate a patient's spontaneous reports and memories, even in reply to direct inquiry, and those memories that finally emerge following the repeated suggestions by a therapist that the patient must have been abused in childhood. From a scientific and legal perspective, these latter reports are definitely suspect. Notwithstanding this, some of these reports are most likely true. The problem is that we do not know which ones are and which are not. The fact that so many of these memories arise in the context of what can only appear to be the marketing of dissociative disorders treatment programs gives us further pause for concern. Ultimately, each of us will have to make our judgments in a case-by-case fashion, but I would suggest that a fair degree of cautiousness is in order.

METHODOLOGICAL PROBLEMS

To move to a more technical problem in evaluating the child abuse literature, factors that must be considered include the nature of questionnaires used and sampling errors stemming from the use of non-representative populations. Questionnaires may not be sensitive enough or may be too sensitive for the information sought. Some questionnaires may be too general and thereby miss important information or somehow convey the impression that everyone may have a certain experience. Some questionnaires, such as the Beck Depression Scale, are obvious in what a positive response to each question reveals about the person, thereby allowing those who wish to appear more depressed to answer in kind. In a similar manner, the most commonly used dissociation scale (Bernstein & Putnam, 1986) asks very straightforward and suggestive questions (e.g., Some people are told that they sometimes do not recognize friends or family members; Some people have the experience of finding themselves dressed in clothes that they don't remember putting on. Mark the line to show what percentage of time this happens to you.). Most "multiple personality" patients appear to have a vested interest in being multiple and will argue with anyone who suggests that they are not. The problem with Bernstein and Putnam's Dissociative Experiences Scale (DES) is that for those who wish to appear as multiple, or as having dissociative episodes, it indicates how to answer the questions and may even suggest a few new experiences to report. The usefulness of these questionnaires depends upon the subject telling it like it is. We know that, for a variety of reasons, borderlines at times may chose to tell it other than how it is.

It can be argued that the same is true for most self-report questionnaires designed to elicit subjective symptoms. This is certainly true, and the more standardized instruments, such as the MMPI and the Millon Clinical Multiaxial Inventory, attempt to counter this problem by building in validity scales. The dissociation instruments, however, are composed of very simple statements that permit the subject to perceive the intent of the question and then decide how to answer it.

SELECTION CRITERIA

In deciding which group of persons to study, exclusion of certain types of behaviors and symptoms, such as, for example, omitting persons with alcohol and drug problems, may skew the data in ways we cannot guess. We may end up with a less disturbed population, or with a population that preferentially utilizes dissociative symptoms rather than chemically-induced avoidance techniques, or away from a population that may have genetic loading toward affective disorder and/or alcoholism. The results we obtain will be fashioned by how we define our study population. Similarly, the incidence of sexual abuse in our study population will vary depending upon how broadly or narrowly child abuse is defined and what cut-off age is selected to determine whether the abuse shall be counted in as childhood/ adolescence abuse. Therefore, the statistics about rates of abuse that emerge from any study must be evaluated in light of how the researchers selected their sample and defined its variables.

It is not that researchers ought not to select inclusion and exclusion criteria; every study has to define the domain of persons it shall consider, and the criteria are usually clearly described in the "methods" section of the report. The problem comes in primarily when the authors or others wish to generalize from the particular abused population as defined in the study to other abused populations. Often the review literature, or the secondary literature, tends to pick up the major findings in a few sentences and ignores the nuances and limitations of the study, such as the number of persons included, control groups, age range, gender, socioeconomic status, race, religion, and ethnicity. We do not know which of these factors matter, or in what ways, but we cannot assume automatically that we can generalize from one sample to another, or to the population of abused persons in general, or indeed, if any meaningful generalization can be made to such a heterogeneous group.

ARE PTSD AND BPD THE SAME?

This is a much less interesting and important question than it appears to be. The really important questions center around the second of the two assumptions stated at the beginning of this chapter, namely, that the experience of childhood sexual abuse overshadows all other factors in producing the BPD picture.

On the other hand, the issue of what to name the PTSD/border-line syndrome is, if not theoretically interesting, at least of political and social importance, because the terminology employed by psychiatry influences public awareness of the deleterious long-term effects of childhood abuse, and this in turn influences how people respond to PTSD/borderline persons. Furthermore, the issue of what diagnosis to tell to the PTSD/borderline patient personally and to place on insurance forms is therapeutically and pragmatically important for many reasons, which I will discuss later in the chapter. But scientifically and philosophically, the question of whether PTSD and borderline are the same thing is the wrong question to ask, because it buys into a sloppiness of language and concepts that dooms any attempt at a meaningful answer.

In a nutshell, the present concepts of PTSD and borderline are each so vague and encompass so many heterogeneous conditions that it is impossible to know what each one is, let alone whether they are the same thing. We do not know yet how to relate the many different causes and presentations of PTSD to each other, and do not know how it comes about that borderlines who have and have not been abused resemble each other. We do not know what the woman who has been viciously raped and the man who has been caught in a flood or earthquake have in common, nor what the Cambodian survivor of three murderous years of Pol Pot genocide and the Vietnam veteran have in common, in terms of a PTSD syndrome. Nor do we know what each of these different PTSD pictures has in common with the adult who was repeatedly sexually abused in childhood. Yet they all get lumped together under the broad heading of PTSD. The conceptual problem with PTSD reflects the age-old controversy between sharpeners and levelers, between those who stress differences and those who stress similarities. Terr (1991) has suggested a preliminary classification based upon whether the trauma was a single incident, which she designates Type I, or multiple, longstanding traumas, designated as Type II. Although there are obvious problems with a bipartite classification, since there are the inevitable crossover and mixed cases, this represents a good beginning from which to research the problem of the relationship of the varieties of trauma to the varieties of PTSD.

The second reason why asking if PTSD and borderlines are the same is the wrong question is that the rhetoric of advocacy uses so much hyperbolic language that all differences in depth and intensity of traumatic experience are obscured. Everyone nowadays is a survivor, everyone is courageously struggling and fighting against illness or an inhospitable environment, or against the system, or against a bleak childhood. It is not that life is sweet and generous to most; it can be and is grim to many. But the use of headlines and heroic language to describe the daily conditions of life place big and little hurts on the same plane. PTSD, if it is to be a useful construct, will have to distinguish between the normal human tendency to relive in the mind all unpleasant experiences and the variety of enduring patterns of severe psychological and physiological responses to overwhelmingly traumatic conditions.

INDIVIDUAL FACTORS IN THE PTSD RESPONSE

This brings us back to what I am proposing is the more interesting question, for we immediately recognize that different individuals respond differently to the same or similar stressor experiences. How can it be, as Herman (1992a) states, that the traumatic events themselves are the most important factor in determining the PTSD picture if, at the same time, we know that each individual responds to stress in his/her own characteristic way? In the face of this dilemma, which confronts all child development studies, the important ethical and empirical question is how to begin to tease apart those factors, apart from the brute fact of the "objective" trauma, that influence the response of the individual. The second question, one that is a little easier methodologically to approach, is how to break down the brute fact of the trauma into a more detailed analysis of the variables that go into the childhood assaults.

The problem all along in raising this complex set of questions is that it begins to sound like the victim is going to get blamed. Any suggestion that the environmental events are not totally responsible for the specific PTSD responses of each individual is taken as an exoneration of the perpetrator and an affront to all victims. Since much of the work done in the psychotherapy of PTSD/borderline is conceptualized as convincing the patient, one way or another, that she is not to blame for what happened to her as a child, then any thought that the child's traits and temperament contributed something to the abuse situation or to the specific shape of the PTSD response just sounds intolerable. What needs to be battled out with patients in this regard is their harsh moral condemnation of themselves more than their perception, distorted as it must be, of the events surrounding the abuse.

Green, Lindy, and Grace (1985) have outlined the major possibilities with regard to the relationship between character and PTSD. The first possibility is that character pathology and PTSD are relatively independent. People with and without character pathology have an equal chance of developing PTSD. The implication of this model, in terms of our present discussion, is either that the nature and intensity of the traumatic stress are the key factors in determining the development and severity of PTSD in each individual, or that there are important variables of which we are presently ignorant. The second possibility is that character pathology predisposes individuals to develop PTSD and to maintain symptoms over time. For example, Zweig-Frank and Paris (1991) have suggested that children who are needy and clinging may be more susceptible to sexual abuse by virtue of their neediness, or may be perceived as more vulnerable by predatory adults, thereby making them more likely targets for abuse.

The third possibility is that character pathology may function as a selector of those who will find themselves in a high-risk, potentially traumatic situation (Jenny, 1988). This would apply to some who volunteer for combat and others who seek out violent domestic partners. The problem with this formulation is that it ignores what has happened in each person's life that predisposes this person to select high-risk situations. The causal chain is seized in the middle, with the person as he appears in young adulthood, and does not address how that individual came to have the high risk-taking propensity in the first place. It is often assumed that, in fact, traumatic earlier life experiences are the determinants of such high-risk preferences, but to accept this hypothesis would be to assume the answer to the very question we have just said we need to investigate. Genetic influences may be fairly important here.

The fourth possibility is that character pathology may develop from the trauma, especially from the experience of repeated trauma. This would conform to Terr's (1991) Type II trauma, which she associates with denial and numbing, self-hypnosis and dissociation, and rage. Preexisting personality traits may harden into a disorder proper, or a personality disorder may develop de novo. This is the model that undergirds Herman's (1992a) statement that "Individual personality characteristics count for little in the face of overwhelming events" (p. 57). This model appears to be most relevant to the PTSD/borderline relationship and therefore requires further examination at this time.

In essence, Herman's statement by itself is untenable, whatever its advocacy appeal may be. For on the very next page, Herman acknowledges that "individual differences play an important part in determining the form that the disorder will take." The question of the relationship of personality to stress response is a much broader one than applies only to the child abuse-borderline personality disorder interaction. Most recent studies of PTSD associated with responses to natural disasters, such as floods and earthquakes, have found that the correlation between the amount of stress in a traumatic event and the resulting psychological problems is fairly low (Gibbs, 1989). This means that factors other than the stressful experience itself, such as gender, social networking, and personality traits, play an important role in determining type and magnitude of response.

There are many problems to stress research, including questions about how to try to quantify totally different types of events into "stress units," how to measure stress reactions in persons with different styles of displaying emotions (for example, is the person who cries or the person who is mute after a disaster more upset?), and how to decide that what is being measured in an individual, such as anxiety level, is a result of recent stress rather than a manifestation of prior maladjustment.

The technical problems in doing stress research and in attributing symptomatic responses and personality maladjustments to the traumatic experiences take on special meaning in relation to child abuse, precisely because the victim is still a child, and therefore more malleable in personality than is an older individual. In fact, we can say that problems in PTSD research are pale reflections of the problems in the development of the abused child, namely, the issue is not that specific symptoms arise, but rather that the ongoing experience of abuse shapes the developing personality. Basic components of personality, including identity formation, ways of relating to self and others, ways of feeling and showing emotions, ways of integrating unpleasant and discrepant events, approaches to problem-solving, defensive schemata, patterns of passivity and assertiveness, are distorted by the repeated traumatic experiences and the larger context of fear and helplessness in which the child is raised and must adapt.

All of this is common sense and everyday observation, supported by child development studies about the effects of destructive environments on the growing child. The problem, nevertheless, is to reconcile common sense psychology with the very strong research data that tell us that the home environment has less influence on the personality traits of the child than we ordinarily believe (Bouchard et al., 1990). How can we reconcile these contradictory hypotheses, one based on everyday observation that the home environment shapes the child and the other, clearly counterintuitive, but based upon solid research findings in behavioral genetics, that the home environment accounts for a small percentage of individual variability in personality and temperament?

This dilemma is well articulated in the play *Equus*, by Peter Shaffer, in which the adolescent Alan is sent to a mental hospital for evaluation and treatment after he blinds six horses with a hoof pick. Alan's mother, after a confrontation in the hospital during which she slaps her son, protests to the psychiatrist:

> Let me tell you something. We're not criminals. We've done nothing wrong. We loved Alan. We gave him the best love we could. All right, we quarrel sometimes — all parents quarrel — we always make it up. My husband is a good man. He's an upright man, religion or no religion. He cares for his home, for the world, and for his boy. Alan had love and care and treats, and as much fun as any boy in the world. . . . No, doctor. Whatever's happened has happened because of Alan. Alan is himself. Every soul is itself. If you added up everything we ever did to him, from his first day on earth to this, you wouldn't find why he did this terrible thing — because that's him; not just all our things added up. Do you understand what I'm saying? (p. 78)

This is a clear statement of the dilemma. Alan's mother protests that to blame the parents for everything the child does is to negate the very essence of the boy himself. Alan is his own person, more than the sum total of how he was raised. But the mother's plaint here is based upon her assertion that Alan's upbringing fell within the range of a normal home environment with normal, fallible parents. This distinction is the critical point when we evaluate the nature-nurture debate regarding childhood sexual abuse and development of the PTSD/borderline picture.

Sandra Scarr (1992), in an excellent review of recent developmental theories, summarizes the research findings as indicating that the environments most parents provide for their children have few differential effects on the offspring. The essential assumption here, according to Scarr, is that "most families provide sufficiently supportive environments that children's individual genetic differences develop" (p. 3). The very foundation of what we understand as normal child development is predicated upon the child being raised in the "average expectable environment." I would take this even further and state that even our "normal" diagnostic system for mental illness is predicated upon the child being raised in the "average expectable environment." The human species, in its long evolution, has developed a remarkable capability to adapt to a wide range of rearing environments and still thrive healthily. However, once the childhood environment departs substantially from this broadly defined norm, in terms of neglect, abuse, violence, and unpredictability, than all assumptions about the orderly process of child development go out the window. To quote Scarr, "Environments that fall outside of the species-normal range will not promote normal developmental patterns" (p. 5).

The child's specific environment becomes more critical in determining the personality of the growing child precisely as it deviates from the range of normal environments (Burgess, Hartman, & McCormack, 1987; Dodge, Bates, & Pettit, 1990; Kashani et al., 1992). When this happens, personality and psychopathology are skewed in a variety of ways that represent the strong effects of the deviant environment on the child's constitutional endowment. In this sense, Herman (1992a) and others are correct in asserting that childhood trauma is the cause of the PTSD/borderline picture. My reservation, as a skeptical fox, about this unifying explanation is that the generalization can be sustained only by ignoring many other factors, besides the abuse, that also influence the development of the abused child.

VULNERABILITY AND RESILIENCE

There is an ongoing body of clinical research in children, predating this particular BPD issue, that has explored concepts of vulnerability and resilience to stress. It is clear that a simple linear model in which response is directly proportional to stress does not accurately describe what happens to children. As Luthar and Zigler (1991), in their review of research on childhood resilience conclude, vulnerability and protective factors both interact with the risk variables (stress or trauma) to produce the level of adjustment reached by the child. The research literature also makes it clear that the earlier optimism regarding invulnerable children, based upon measurements of external behavioral adjustment (e.g., doing well at school), was naive. More recent studies that investigated internal factors of emotional health (e.g., symptoms of depression and anxiety) have shown that these "invulnerable" children have been more affected in their personal development than was apparent from behavioral measurements. It is likely that as the studies move beyond even the discernible psychiatric symptoms such as depression and anxiety to the more subtle personality changes that follow growing up in harsh environments, additional adverse consequences will be uncovered, despite the protective mechanisms available to these "invulnerable" children.

What are the protective mechanisms that the child potentially brings to the abuse situation? The list is long (Widom, 1991), representing overlapping concepts of dispositional attributes most probably based upon genetic and constitutional factors, but possibly also reflecting the interaction of such basic infant development concepts as secure attachment to a caregiver (Sroufe & Fleeson, 1986). The reader will perceive that even here, one backs into the nature/nurture controversy regarding how basic traits are developed in the young. By whatever means the child obtained his/her protective mechanisms, and of course, it is likely that the same parents who abused or tolerated abuse of the child may not have been adequate caregivers even at the infant stage, the following are some of the attributes which, if present, are thought to provide some degree of buffering to childhood stress: ability to be comforted, sleep-wakefulness states, physiological thresholds of arousal, intelligence, humor, attractiveness, interpersonal awareness and skills, and internal locus of control.

There are also familial and environmental factors that are important in providing protective mechanisms. A good relationship with at least one parental figure appears to be very important. So many of the cases that we see in our work with adults who were abused in childhood come from very disturbed homes that we tend to forget that sometimes the abuse occurred out of the home by neighbors or distant relatives, and that the home environment itself may not have been a destructive one. There are always rejoinders to this argument, suggesting that if the home were truly secure, then the child would have been able to reveal the abuse to the parent. This appears to be a post hoc judgment that, like other speculations, we have no basis to assume without specific knowledge. It is also a speculation that ignores the child's ability to think and imagine independently, to be its own soul, as Shaffer phrased it.

Finally, the basic point of all child development studies needs to be stated: the impact of the various protective and risk factors differs at different life stages. Thus, any measure of adult personality traits or styles of coping is affected by the effects of the abuse as it occurred in the context of a particular life phase within a particular environment.

CONCLUSIONS

To summarize, the import of the many studies of stress in childhood in general, and of the childhood environments of adult borderline in specific, do not permit us to take the position that there is a one-to-one relationship between severity of abuse and severity of symptoms. Yet those who assert such a linear connection are saying something very important which should not be lost just because they have overstated it. Other things being equal (which they never are), we can assume two things: (1) that there is a threshold of trauma beyond which abuse, if imposed upon any child, will produce an unequivocal PTSD syndrome, and (2) that there is a rough correlation among some composite measure of childhood sexual abuse variables (age of onset, duration and frequency of abuse, degree of intimidation and violence, relationship to perpetrator), personal and environmental ameliorative factors, and the immediate and long-term harmful consequences to that child's personality development, approach to life, and resiliency to future stress. To give a specific example of a long-term developmental effect of childhood sexual abuse that seems particularly to apply to the PTSD/borderline syndrome, the abused child's need to keep thoughts and images of the traumatic events out of consciousness, along with the conflicting need to rework the trauma, establishes a lifelong tension in that individual between denial and flooding.

Two issues need to be clarified in order for us to have temporary closure of these complex issues. To give an oversimplified answer to the oversimplified question of whether PTSD and BPD are the same thing, the answer is "No." Beside the general observation that most abused children do not develop a borderline picture and that not every borderline has been abused in childhood, we also note that cutting of oneself and patterns of victimization are not integral features of most PTSD syndromes. For example, I have interviewed more than 600 Southeast Asian refugees in the past eight years; many of them have PTSD and many want to die, but they do not engage in self-mutilative activities (Kroll et al., 1989). Their PTSD manifests itself in other ways. What this suggests is that there is something specific about childhood sexual abuse in our culture that skews personality development in certain individuals toward a pattern which we have up until now called "borderline" and are beginning to recognize as a PTSD syndrome. It also points out that the PTSD syndromes seen in Southeast Asian refugees, who have not all had identical traumatic experiences either, is very different from the PTSD picture that develops in response to childhood sexual abuse.

This brings us, a little indirectly, to the last consideration of this chapter, namely, what diagnosis to give to borderlines who have had significant abuse experiences in their childhood and whose personality style, psychiatric symptoms, and sense of self appear closely connected to the abuse experiences. I think the major struggle that we have about the issue of terminology here is that the term "borderline" is a terrible term and should be dropped from use. It does not convey anything helpful; it is a remnant of incorrect theoretical concepts of another era. It is of historical interest, as is neurasthenia and pseudoneurotic schizophrenia in psychiatry, stranguary in medicine, and phlogiston and ether in physics.

The great value of the PTSD diagnosis for adults who have experienced childhood sexual abuse is that it is one of the few diagnoses in DSM-III-R that meaningfully links a particular syndrome with a particular cause. It is very helpful to borderline/PTSD patients to frame up their present problems in terms of understandable, but now maladaptive, responses to past traumatic experiences. It outlines a direction for treatment. The therapeutic danger is, as expressed previously, that the therapist and patient also need to look at other issues besides the abuse, including those personal factors that makes each person's PTSD configuration unique. Otherwise the patient is at risk of losing an identity that goes beyond victimhood.

4

Self-Injurious Behavior: Cross-Cultural and Historical Aspects

In modern psychiatric practice and research we encounter a number of patients who engage in physically self-injurious behavior (SIB). Some of these patients suffer from a variety of psychoses, while others can be shown to have mental retardation and/or brain damage (Schroeder et al., 1978; Shore, Anderson, & Cutler, 1978). There is, however, a substantial population of self-injurious persons who, being neither psychotic nor brain-damaged, are usually placed within an Axis II (personality disorder) category (Conn & Lion, 1983; Winchel & Stanley, 1991).

Automatic assignment of nonpsychotic, non-brain-damaged individuals who injure themselves into the character disorder class is a psychiatric procedure with very limited explanatory or practical utility, since it is probable that at least some SIB, such as is conducted as part of a religious ritual, does not constitute psychopathology. Such a consideration suggests that SIBs can be arrayed along a dimension of health/illness, rather than only in terms of various illness categories (Favazza, 1987; Paris, 1991).

We can postulate heuristically that all SIBs involve some common grounding in neurochemical substrates and physiological pathways leading into the self-injurious behavior. In addition, it is likely that common neurochemical and neurophysiological sequelae result from the SIB, although we are not yet able to establish laboratory or PET scan norms that will distinguish between SIB reflective of psychopathology and SIB that forms part of socially or religiously supported activities. Indeed, we cannot assume a priori that such distinctions will be forthcoming, i.e., that there are neurobiological differences underlying differently motivated SIB. Nevertheless, the possibility, even the likelihood, that such neurobiological differences between "healthy" and pathological SIB will be found calls for the development of social, behavioral, and phenomenological classificatory approaches parallel to the biological studies, in order to delineate the variables that determine where on a health/illness dimension any particular SIB should be located.

At a psychological level, such variables include constructs relating to motivation, purpose, intention, and life experiences preceding the SIB, the meaning of the SIB to the self-injurious person, and the nature of cultural attitudes of support or constraint toward SIB. Clinical experience and research have elucidated the mind-set of persons who utilize SIBs in order to alter a noxious cognitive and affective mental state. Yet our understanding of the interface between those individuals who employ SIBs to relieve their suffering and society's role in sanctioning or condemning SIBs remains rudimentary. We need a clearer phenomenological description of the changes in mental state occurring in the context of self-injurious behavior, much as the model Horowitz (1987) has developed in his configurational analyses of psychological life. At the same time, we need to relate this structural analysis of human inner life to a classification of SIB in terms of cultural values and customs.

We start with the observation that, although psychiatry has tended to consider all self-injurious behaviors in psychopathological terms, some of these behaviors are sanctioned by most societies. One way to refine our understanding of the SIB population is to identify which self-injurious behaviors find social support and which draw social disapproval. We suggest that within the group of self-injurious persons who are neither psychotic nor mentally retarded, the SIB almost always includes a component of anticipated social response that relies upon a relatively predictable cultural context to provide meaning and coherence to the actions.

The initial identification of a public versus private dimension to self-injurious behaviors calls for the recognition of at least four basic configurations of social attitudes to SIB. First, there are self-injurious behaviors that express positive social values; the self-injurious person accordingly is held in high esteem. Second, there are self-injurious behaviors that appear to have no social value; the self-injurious person meets with social disapproval and is considered to have some sort of mental disturbance. Third, there is an ambiguous range of self-injurious actions that are considered pathways to socially valued performances, but, nevertheless, public disclosure of such behaviors meets with disapproval. Finally, there are individual life-styles that are associated with greater than ordinary risk of illness or accidental harm, but here there is much debate about whether even to place "high risk" life-styles on a self-injurious dimension.

PUBLICLY SANCTIONED SIB

First and foremost, public self-injurious behavior is a protest of the weak against the powerful, as well as a means by which the weak attempt to appease and honor the powerful. Within this broad construct, the configuration of public self-injurious behaviors forms a matrix of ritualized activities that are culturally institutionalized and controlled and that serve sanctioned and important social functions. From a religious perspective, self-injurious behavior has traditionally represented a sacrifice or a propitiation to the powerful gods, in order to gain benefits or avoid harm. Thus, one may make a sacrifice to avoid or cure an illness, to obtain a richer crop, to give thanks for such benefits already bestowed, and to mourn the dead and ease their travails in the afterworld. Alternatively, if one has behaved improperly or sinfully, a sacrifice through self-injury is made with the hope of avoiding the gods' anger and thus forestalling a worse punishment.

Examples of religiously sanctioned SIB include the ritualistic gashing of oneself with swords and lances referred to in the Old Testament (Lev. 19:28; Deut. 14:1; I Kings 18:28; Hos. 7:14; Jer. 16:6, 41:5, 47:5), the Sun Dance of the Plains Indians, in which warriors hang suspended from a sacred pole by thongs piercing their chest muscles (Brown, 1971; Powers, 1977); Hindu festivals in which devotees, while in a trance, pierce their cheeks with rods (Bowker, 1970); and the self-flagellations of wandering groups of Christian penitents in the Middle Ages (Henderson, 1978). Persons designated or accepted by a society to perform ceremonial self-mutilative religious rituals are usually not considered mentally ill; rather, they are given public respect and high status because they have the inner strengths to express deep values of the society in an manner that most members are unable or unwilling to do.

Sanctioned self-injurious behavior performed in a secular rather than religious context is similarly understood by that society as an attempt by the weak to embarrass the powerful and thus to alter the balance of power. The SIB is, in fact, one of the most powerful sanctioned protests of the powerless and disenfrancised. There are many modern examples, such as Ghandi's hunger strikes, the Irish Catholic hunger strikers, and the self-immolations more common to Asian cultures than our own.

The protest can only be successful when the self-injurious behavior draws upon some underlying values of the society that recognize the moral force behind the protest of the self-injurious person, such that public pressure and censure can be counted upon to bring about a settlement of the grievance. In the case of the student setting himself aflame in Tienanmen Square, this may have been consistent with his group's value system and was symbolically useful to the democratic protest movement, but it was totally ineffective for the moment because the repressive regime would not be embarrassed by traditional methods of protest into making concessions. Similar to SIB within a religious context, the person employing self-injurious methods for the purpose of social protest is usually not judged as mentally ill, but, on the contrary, often is given special status that accrues to the hero/martyr.

Finally, socially understood although not condoned, public exhibition of self-injurious behaviors can serve to demonstrate sincerity and intensity, as occasionally happens with love-struck youth or, more dramatically, with Vincent Van Gogh and his famous ear. Self-injurious behavior can also express group cohesion and identity. Examples include circumcision (rarely self-inflicted nowadays, but with several biblical references), tatooing, and scarification. A trivial example would be punching holes for the multiple earrings and nose-rings used to identify some adolescent subcultures.

PUBLICLY CONDEMNED SIB

The second configuration of self-injurious behaviors consists of those private, seemingly culturally devalued acts which serve to dramatize and perhaps resolve some personal conflicts of the individual. These behaviors are not seen as having socially redeeming merit. Examples are the wrist-cutting and arm-burning actions of individuals who thereby find themselves diagnosed as borderline, a term with clearly understood pejorative connotations (Gardner & Cowdry,

1985). Persons in our society who injure themselves under these intensely personal motivations and circumstances are usually considered mentally ill or emotionally disturbed and suffer decreased social respect and status. The same holds true for those persons who, obsessed by concerns about body size and shape, starve themselves or engage in bingeing and purging behaviors (Levin & Hyler, 1986).

In marked contrast to the social approval enjoyed by political hunger strikers, persons with "eating disorders" are considered mentally ill and in need of some sort of medical/psychological, and possibly legal, interventions. The social devaluation of self-starvation motivated by personal concerns about body weight and shape occurs despite the fact that our society has increasingly encouraged young women to become slimmer and slimmer. This paradox of social disapproval of behaviors whose goals appear to be socially approved has its echoes in the social attitudes toward self-starvation of the medieval ascetics.

SIB AMBIVALENTLY TOLERATED

This third category of self-injurious actions occupies an ambivalent middle ground between socially supported and socially devalued behaviors. In these cases, the laudatory nature of the goal seems to determine the social response, despite recognition that the behaviors may lead to long-term deleterious consequences, ranging from relatively trivial to very serious. Examples include self-starvation in ballerinas and steroid use in competitive athletes (AMA Council, 1990; Wilson, 1988)—in essence, those individuals in special categories of the entertainment and sports businesses. Outstanding performance in these activities is so valued by our society that the consequences of the means to excellence are usually ignored. Consideration of these examples points out that SIB itself is hard to define, especially as one moves away from the unambiguous cases of direct and immediate assault upon one's own body.

LIFE-STYLE CHOICES AND A TAXONOMY OF SIB

The range of what can be considered self-destructive behaviors is virtually limitless, dependent only upon the rigor and time-frame one employs in establishing definitional criteria. Furthermore, judgments of whether any particular activity is self-injurious or not are subject to a changing climate of social values and public opinion. Cigarette smoking and alcohol ingestion, social activities that once conveyed manliness and maturity, have only recently come to be viewed by some determined segments of our society as self-injurious behaviors, even when not done in excess (CDC, 1991; Rigotti & Pashos, 1991). Controversy exists about whether driving a car without a seat belt or riding a motorcycle without a crash helmet also should be considered self-injurious behaviors. Evidence of how quixotic and subject to public whim such judgments can be is provided by the example of the Minnesota legislature, which passed a law mandating that motorcyclists must wear crash helmets, only to repeal this law several years later in a capitulation to lobbying pressures (*Minnesota Statute Annotated*, 1992).

At issue are the rules by which particular examples of risk-taking behaviors, whether or not defined by law as illegal, come to be considered evidence of psychopathology (Apter, 1992). The more pointed question for the psychiatric profession is how far it wishes to go in defining socially undesirable, including indirectly self-destructive, behaviors as medical disorders. Thomas Szasz and others have, of course, attacked the psychiatric profession precisely on this tendency to expand continuously but inconsistently the domain of behaviors considered as symptoms of mental illness (Scull, 1992; Szasz, 1974).

A consideration of life-style choices highlights the difficulty that accompanies any attempt to develop principles by which to classify SIB. Life-styles involving unhealthy diets, insufficient exercise, use of legal mood-altering and consciousness-altering substances (alcohol, tobacco, coffee, tea, caffeinated soft drinks), strenuous athletic training regimens, and a host of sexually-related social behaviors that put one at risk of disease or assault can all be placed under the category of self-injurious behaviors.

Each proposed classification of SIB has its own limitations and exceptional cases, with examples that cross orderly boundaries. It may be that, when the goal sought is perceived to encompass lofty aspirations external to an individual life, such as union with God in the medieval ascetic examples and perfection in artistic expression in the modern ballerinas, then social disapproval of the means to the end is either slower to come or softened by a judgment that the individual sacrifices were justified. In such cases, the person's individuality is merged with the socially approved goals and therefore criticism is tempered with admiration.

PUBLIC AND PRIVATE SELF-INJURIOUS BEHAVIORS

Self-injurious behaviors may be enacted either in a public or private context or, of course, in a simultaneous or sequential combination of the two. In general, there is a public component to most self-injurious behaviors. This is certainly the case in those religious rituals mentioned above, in which prescribed and limited self-mutilative actions are an important aspect of a public ceremony. But even in our contemporary Western society, which, unlike most societies, appears manifestly to disapprove of all self-injurious behaviors and has no generally accepted religious rituals that legitimize self-injurious behaviors as an important component, most of those individuals who privately hurt themselves make their wounds public by bringing them to the attention of others.

There are exceptions. There are some individuals whose self-injurious behaviors are so private that discovery of them is usually inadvertent. Appreciation of these instances makes us realize that there must be some self-injurious persons (including those who never had contact with the mental health profession) whom we never discover. Such undetected cases in therapy patients usually involve ritualistic reenactments of childhood sexual abuse, such as tying oneself to bedposts, tightening ropes and belts about one's neck, pinching one's breast and genitals to the point of tissue injury, and lacerating one's genitals. Patients usually consider these acts extremely shameful and speak of such matters with great reluctance, if at all.

Indeed, if we examine those cases that do come readily to our attention, and there are many, we see that an important component to the self-injurious behaviors consists of publicly demonstrating one's wounds with the expectation of eliciting a response, usually supportive, from others. The self-injurious behavior in these cases is the individual's method of making a public statement. Often, in fact, the self-injurious activity is simplistically equated, by family members or those in the health field, solely with the public aspect of the behavior, and whatever relevant private meaning there may be in the motivation for self-destruction is overlooked, as in the familiar remark, "Oh, he is only doing it for attention." If we examine the responses of most mental health workers to self-injurious behaviors, we often notice a clear division in attitudes, with individual psychotherapists focusing on the private and ignoring the public statement, while inpatient and halfway house staffs and crisis teams usually respond to the public statement and ignore the private anguish. This has a clear analogy to the Middle Ages; the hagiographer and a few close associates of the ascetic claimed to understand the inner struggle underlying the self-injurious behaviors, while church authorities and family tended to judge these same behaviors as evidence of mental disturbance or chicanery.

In most societies, the essential feature of public self-injurious behaviors that form a recognized part of a religious or social system is that the cultural context renders the behaviors meaningful and understandable. The culture provides the text for decoding the symbolism expressed in the self-injurious behaviors. The social or religious milieu establishes a framework to make sense of otherwise highly aberrant actions. Specified self-injurious actions are defined as constructive behaviors only within the indigenous culture; the very act of defining a behavior as falling within positive social norms makes it understandable to members of that culture. Reciprocally, if the behaviors are not part of a normative behavioral code, then they are given negative social value. The actions and the actor are viewed as deviant, and most likely as mentally ill, for that is how one views idiosyncratic and seemingly capricious self-destructive behaviors that have no rational institutionalized meaning within a culture's social norms.

This last point leads us directly to a paradox, for the public display of self-injurious behavior by psychiatric patients appears to violate the social norms of our society, but nevertheless, we suggest, these behaviors have recently been characterized to represent, similarly to religiously and politically sanctioned self-injurious behaviors, a protest of the weak against the powerful. Mental health professionals have defined self-injurious behaviors in specific groups of individuals as the logical and comprehensible consequences of certain unfortunate events of childhood and adolescence (Herman, 1992b). This has the interesting effect, perhaps unintended, of establishing and shaping the social norms of how individuals who have been abused are expected to behave.

SELF-INJURIOUS BEHAVIOR AND CHILDHOOD ABUSE

As we have seen in Chapters 2 and 3, it has been well documented that over half the self-injurious, nonpsychotic patients in psychiatric inpatient and outpatient settings have been sexually or physically abused in their childhood or adolescence (Ogata et al., 1990; van der Kolk et al., 1991). In essence, we are speaking here of those persons with borderline personality disorders who more properly could be considered as suffering from chronic PTSD resulting from damaging childhood experiences (Herman, Russell, & Trocki, 1986). Cutting of the skin informs the public about what has happened to her in the only way she can figure out to communicate the information.

Acceptance of the significance of this public component of self-injurious behavior has shifted dramatically in the past few decades as new social norms have been created. When there was minimal recognition of the prevalence of childhood abuse and its possible role in the etiology of self-injurious behaviors, persons engaging in these activities were considered very deviant; their actions were incomprehensible, as the public ordinarily comprehends behavior, and therefore were viewed as evidence of severe psychopathology. Only recently, the public, in accepting the linkage between early abuse and adolescent and adult self-injurious behavior, has become more understanding, accepting, and supportive of the self-injurious person. With understanding comes a softening of judgment. Furthermore, it is not just that one has empathy with the victim and therefore criticism is tempered, but that, with acceptance of the causal connection between self-injurious behaviors and the larger environmental matrix encompassing childhood abuse, a social norm has been developed in which those who were abused in childhood are expected to injure themselves. We have institutionalized self-injurious behavior as the socially meaningful and legitimate way to express distress about incestuous abuse.

LINKAGE OF PRIVATE EXPERIENCE AND PUBLIC CONDUCT OF SIB

Before proceeding with an examination of self-injurious behaviors in medieval society, we wish to offer a hypothesis about the linkage between the public character of SIB and the psychological experience of self-injurious behaviors. Cutting of one's own skin is one way in which the PTSD/borderline works out at multiple levels the impact of the sexual abuse upon her. Recognition of this, nevertheless, should not let us lose sight of questioning just why cutting of the skin should be a way of responding to one's childhood traumas. The answers must be given both in social and private terms; however, if we look at the biological effects of self-injurious behaviors, it is clear that such behaviors alter one's state of consciousness. It also does many other things, such as reduce tension and agitation, punish oneself, and appease one's guilt, but, primarily as well as concomitantly, it changes one's state of consciousness (Hill, 1989; Ornstein, 1986). There are other ways of doing this, of course, and some of these ways are employed in other cultures and for other purposes. One can use alcohol or drugs or food; one can meditate, one can induce a trance state by staring at an object or listening to a repetitive sound; one can move rhythmically (Furst, 1977).

But for some in our culture, cutting or burning has become the most effective and reliable way to alter one's state of consciousness, at times when other methods fail and at other times as a preferred choice. The private aspect of self-injurious behavior as primarily a way of altering one's state of consciousness serves to bridge the gap between the biological and sociocultural components of SIB. If cutting of oneself alters one's state of consciousness, it must simultaneously alter one's neurophysiological state. In essence, cutting oneself is a way of manipulating one's brain chemistry (Hill, 1989). Without getting caught up for the moment in the direction of causality between mental and physical acts, we can trace through a chain of events that proceeds as follows: Distressed state of consciousness or dysphoric mood leads certain people to cut their skin, which leads to altered brain chemistry and physiology, which is perceived by the person as an altered state of consciousness, which is manifested by changed cognitive processing, changed imagery and associations, and changed mood. All of these events and actions are in addition to whatever the public significance and response (approval versus rejection) to the SIB might be, and in addition to whatever the psychodynamics (expiation of guilt, identification with the aggressor) of the SIB are. It is likely that, as we examine SIB in medieval ascetics, we will find that what the medieval ascetics and modern PTSD/borderlines have in common are not the psychodynamics, but the more basic biological pattern of altering one's state of consciousness in response to the experience of suffering, and the more public pattern of having the greater society provide meaning and interpretation to the SIB actions.

SELF-INJURIOUS BEHAVIORS IN MEDIEVAL ASCETICS

The examination of self-injurious behaviors in medieval Europe provides a perspective and understanding of the interaction of the cultural contribution to the biological events, private meaning, and social function of these behaviors. The group of persons in medieval Europe who come closest behaviorally to contemporary self-injurers were the religious ascetics (Kieckhefer, 1984; Weinstein & Bell, 1982). We are not suggesting at the outset that there exists an identity or close similarity of personality or purpose between medieval ascetics and contemporary self-abusers. The intention and social context in which a behavior is performed are essential ingredients to understanding that behavior. We should not too readily assume the opposite, however — that behaviors similar in appearance but from different cultures must automatically have little in common beyond their surface appearances. We need to assess the universals of human nature based on evolutionary biology and the particularities of diverse cultures. It may be that society's ambivalence toward many, but not all, types of self-injurious behaviors betrays a basic recognition of certain commonalities of suffering and idealistic aspirations in the persons who self-injure.

It is often protested when a comparison is made between medieval ascetics and modern PTSD/borderlines (or, in the older psychiatric literature, hysterics) that the medieval ascetics were operating out of a religious tradition that understood, supported, and encouraged their ascetic behaviors, whereas today's PTSD/borderlines are considered mentally ill and are discouraged from hurting themselves. But a close examination of the medieval records casts doubt upon both traditional assumptions. Medieval ascetics were not uniformly encouraged in their asceticism, nor are modern self-injurious persons uniformly discouraged. There was considerable criticism and opposition to the extreme behaviors of the medieval ascetics; conversely, there is more social support for today's self-injurers than we have tended to recognize.

Persons in the Middle Ages who engaged in religiously motivated self-injurious behaviors were called ascetics and were thought to self-injure as a way, among other things, of controlling the bodily, including sexual, demands and passions; imitating Christ's sufferings; becoming holy; and striving for union with God. Conditions in late medieval urban centers in western Europe were such that certain types of religious expression were permitted and encouraged which had not been possible or barely thought of, at least not in any major way, since the 4th or 5th centuries and then more in the Near East (e.g., the Desert Fathers) rather than the Latin west (Lawrence, 1984; *Lives*, 1980). The expressions of religiosity we are referring to are the dramatic excesses of physical asceticism and the states of ecstasy occurring in the context of meditation, prayer, and receiving of the sacrament of Holy Communion.

In the 12th through 14th centuries, certain religious segments of the population, such as the Flagellants and beguines, were breaking the conventional and proscribed boundaries of organized religious ritual and experience, and were exploring the farther boundaries of mystical experience and expression, with a new emphasis upon each individual's personal experience with God (De Ganck, 1991; McDonnell, 1954). One such pathway to God was through extreme asceticism, a pattern of behavior that seemed to have a particular appeal for adolescents and young adults (Kroll & De Ganck, 1986). There was, and still is, considerable admiration and fascination given to those who can endure suffering and deprivation beyond that which most of us can tolerate. In many cases, the saint's biographer was susceptible to this adulation, too, and often could not resist boasting about the ascetic feats of his particular holy woman. Despite official rulings and prohibitions against heroic self-injury, persons who engaged in extreme asceticism were often held up as models of virtue and attracted crowds of imitators, petitioners hoping for miraculous cures, and curiosity seekers.

The zealousness of youth, however, is rarely appreciated by the older generation. The medieval authorities, including parents, were no more pleased with the ascetic excesses of their youth than are today's authorities pleased with the self-injurious behaviors of PTSD/borderlines, even as we understand and sympathize with their reasons for hurting themselves.

OPPOSITION TO MEDIEVAL ASCETICISM

In the Middle Ages, the official position of the church, as expressed in papal and episcopal statements, surviving written sermons, and monastic regulations, was that a person should not practice heroic, or extreme, asceticism. Furthermore, the extreme ascetics were often considered mentally ill by their own families, the provincial church and secular authorities, and the local townspeople. Many times the shift of public opinion concerning the extreme ascetic from mad person to holy person occurred after the death of the ascetic, rather than during his/her lifetime. Since we know primarily of those holy persons whose reputations survived and benefited from positive public relations during the past 800 years or so, we no longer perceive the strong social disapproval that frequently occurred during their lifetimes. When we do know about it, as, for example, in the case of Francis of Assisi, the benefit of hindsight tells us that Francis was a true visionary and not a religious lunatic (Cousins, 1983). But that was not the opinion of his family or most of his contemporaries (*Bonaventure*, 1978; Green, 1985).

The church fathers and those who wrote monastic rules, such as St. Benedict, always stressed the need for moderation in asceticism, pointing out that excessive fasting and punishment of the body rendered the person incapable of discharging her duties and too weak to focus on God (Benedict, 1975). The church authorities, and others, were also aware that competitive asceticism led to vainglory in regard to man and God: toward man because such persons sought greater esteem and reputation; toward God, because the ascetics expected God to be influenced by their extreme behaviors, as they demanded grace, miracles, and visions from God, or merely insisted that God keep them alive on no material food. There were formal ecclesiastical and monastic rulings against excessive behaviors in connection with the Eucharist, such as the Cistercian ruling in 1261 that nuns who faint or go into a trance state following taking of the sacrament shall not be given the Host (McDonnell, 1954).

In many instances, families were strongly opposed to the religious preoccupations of their adolescent daughters and took measures to try to prevent further involvement in a religious life. Both Ida of Louvain (*Vita of Ida*, 1986) and Christina of St. Trond were pursued by their families, caught, and chained up in the family home. Christina, often referred to by her contemporaries as Christina Mirabilis, was so elusive that the man hired by the family to retrieve her, when he finally caught up with her, allegedly broke her leg with a cudgel. Later, after she escaped and was caught again, she was placed in a heavy yoke so she could not get away (de Cantimpre, 1986). The basis for the diagnosis of "insanity" by the family appears to be a cluster of outrageous adolescent behaviors that brought embarrassment to the wealthy merchant families. While one might argue that the families were opposed to their daughters' religious commitments for economic reasons, i.e., in order to force their errant daughters into obedience toward arranged and advantageous marriages, this assertion, while correct in part, ignores the fact that the attribution of craziness was not the only method of parental persuasion and coercion and, if anything, might harm the marital prospects of other children in a family. The label of craziness clearly was designed to discredit and disqualify the religious goals of the young woman. Such labeling and violent responses point to a strong social perception that young adults who behave in certain outrageous ways are indeed mentally deranged.

Another form of attack upon the young medieval ascetics was the censure by their colleagues or religious sisters. For example, the biographer of Lutgard of Aywieres (de Cantimpre, 1987) criticizes those who slandered Lutgard by their references to the "fantastic visions of insignificant women." When the Abbess forbade Lutgard to take the sacrament every Sunday because of the sobbing and fainting that would ensue, the other nuns supported the abbess. The nuns of Mont Cornillon became annoyed at Juliana for her excessive fasts, which made her too weak to do her share of work, and for pressing to receive a daily sacrament, although no one else was (*Life of Juliana*, 1990). When Juliana angered a visiting ecclesiastical dignitary by insisting that she was guilty of many sins which all knew she could not possibly have committed, the sisters let Juliana know that they were scandalized by her behavior. Juliana's biographer informs the reader that the devil inspired such malicious criticism of his holy woman.

Beatrice of Nazareth was frequently criticized by her sister nuns for the excesses of her fasting, flagellations, and ecstatic states (*Beatrice*, 1991). When she was ill as a teenager and in the infirmary, according to her biographer, she was not brought food, which was very unusual treatment for a sick member of the monastic community, an act that suggests that the sisters were expressing their disapproval of Beatrice's excessive asceticism which rendered her incapable of maintaining bodily strength and vigor, and perhaps their skepticism that Beatrice was really as incapacitated as she appeared. The sisters were applying a form of behavior modification very much in keeping with the approach of benign neglect sometimes advocated as a response to some of the infirmities and provocative behaviors of modern borderlines. But since it was highly unusual for the nuns in a medieval monastery to withhold caretaking of an ill person in the infirmary, this must be seen as rendering a judgment about their perceptions of the authenticity, or cause, of Beatrice's illness.

It may not have been merely jealousy that motivated criticism of the excesses in behavior of these women, but a realization by their peers that competition was going on to see who could be the most heroically ascetic or go into the most intense or most frequent ecstatic trances, and that many of the holy women seemed to enjoy their reputation for excessive zealousness, an enjoyment which rendered suspect the very motivational foundation of asceticism. Such concern for fame and glory was basically inconsistent with the professed purposes (humility, obedience, imitation of Christ) of their religious life. Finally, there was much concern, even if petty at times, that those women who were given to debilitating ascetic practices and prolonged trance states were not doing their fair share of the manual labor and that the burden of labor falling upon all the others was proportionately greater.

It is clear that, even within the religious community, heroic asceticism was not the norm and was often viewed as highly suspect and abnormal behavior. We tend to exaggerate the tolerance of medieval people for extreme religious expressions. In fact, it is precisely because these adolescents were so unusual, and continued their aberrant behavior into their adulthood, that they were talked about and became the subjects of biographies.

Nor should we think that self-injurious behavior was the only pathway to sanctity in the Middle Ages, such that the religiously intense young woman had no alternative but to pursue the extremes of asceticism. Although the Western medieval church had not yet developed a rich meditative tradition for altering one's state of consciousness similar to that of Eastern religions, there were, nevertheless, several examples of contemplative holy women, such as Julian of Norwich (1978; Bradley, 1984) and Hildegard of Bingen (1986; Flanagan, 1988) who were well-known and respected, and who did not pursue the path of heroic asceticism. Therefore, while we do not want to disregard the important influence of the intense spiritual revival of the 12th through 14th centuries upon the dramatic choices of religious expression of the young ascetics, neither should we exaggerate the acceptance of excessive behaviors that occurred in that medieval society.

The essential point here is that we are now, in the 20th century, taking notice of a handful of young women of the 12–14th centuries who pushed the newly emerging social and religious values well past the point of accepted societal norms and who may have used the cultural patterns prevalent in their society to express their own adolescent turmoil and conflicts in ways that were considered highly abnormal by their contemporaries. Asceticism was not simply the way one was normally expected to go about pursuing a religious vocation. Few people engaged in extreme asceticism; those who did did so with some encouragement, but almost always in the face of strong opposition and ridicule. If this formulation is accurate, especially in regard to the judgment of their contemporaries, then we need seriously to consider the points of correspondence between medieval ascetics and modern PTSD/borderlines in terms of neurophysiological factors, individual psychodynamics, and cultural reinforcers and deterrents. Earlier psychiatric attempts to equate medieval ascetics or visionaries with 19th-century hysterics have simply obscured rather than clarified deeper similarities and differences between the two SIB groups.

SOCIAL ATTITUDES TOWARD
SELF-INJURING BORDERLINES

In the late 20th century, the psychiatric and societal position toward PTSD/borderlines is an ambivalent one. At first glance, self-injurious behavior is considered a sign of mental illness. But despite the fact that self-injurious behaviors are formally discouraged, persons who injure themselves are given special status and recognition. They are provided with individual, group, and family therapy so that they can talk about themselves. They are placed in hospitals, often in very comfortable surroundings, with other similarly inclined adolescents and young adults, so that they can be cared for. They are strongly encouraged to talk about themselves and their experiences. If they continue to cut themselves, they are placed on one-to-one nursing observation in the hospital and, if an outpatient, may be given a "personal care attendant" to sit up with them, or watch them sleep, through the nighttime. Somewhat paradoxically, they are expected to give up their self-injurious behaviors under such encouraging and reinforcing conditions. All of this has been noted frequently in the psychiatric literature (Dawson, 1988).

In addition, mental health professionals explain to them and for them why they cannot stop injuring themselves, as if self-injury under altered states of consciousness, such as trance or dissociative states, is the logical, understandable, and inevitable response to present-day distress and emotional overarousal over past events, especially childhood sexual abuse.

All this suggests that, similarly to the Middle Ages, self-injurious behavior is a culturally-sanctioned and culturally-reinforced behavior. SIB is defined by the community as a relevant and meaningful, even sensible and understandable expression and response to certain emotional problems of adolescence and young adulthood.

COMPARISONS

Our final task is to examine the points of convergence and divergence between medieval and modern SIB. The points of similarity are as follows:

1. SIB is done predominantly by adolescent and young adult women.
2. SIB is done in a state of heightened emotional arousal.
3. The goal is to achieve an altered state of consciousness or an altered mood state.
4. There is an important public component to SIB. The self-injuring person displays the wounds publicly and, in turn, society responds, simultaneously caring for and protecting and criticizing and denigrating the SIB person.

5. Often the person is considered not fully responsible for the SIB, by virtue of acknowledging that the person is either in an ecstatic state (medieval times) or dissociative state (now).
6. Society provides symbolic meaning to the SIB by defining it in terms of cultural values foundational to that society: otherworldliness in medieval times; the sanctity of safe passage through childhood in modern times.

The points of difference between SIB then and now are more ones of content than of form:

1. The medieval self-injurious person was shaped by an image of a crucified Christ, while the modern person is haunted by an image of a violated child.
2. The goal of medieval asceticism was to remove the mental clutter and strivings of the flesh that interfere with union with God, while the modern goal of self-injury is to remove the intolerable imagery and visceral memories that equally interfere with attainment of a peaceful state.

SUMMARY

Some SIB occurs in nonpsychotic, non-brain-damaged individuals in all societies. Our modern society is exceptional in not designating an important cultural role for certain types of ritualized SIB. Nevertheless, ritualized SIB, performed in our society by PTSD/borderlines, is interpreted as a meaningful symbolic act and is simultaneously reinforced and discouraged. An examination of SIB by medieval ascetics suggests that, in medieval society, too, there was public ambivalence. The medieval populace was as suspicious yet intrigued by excessive SIB as we are. Yet, in each society, the prevailing value system gave the self-injurious persons the vocabulary and the conceptual tools to develop asceticism or symptoms as a meaningful behavior.

In both societies, caring professionals (religious in medieval times, secular in modern times) are caught in the paradox that their very understanding and sympathy for the suffering and aspirations of the young persons who engage in SIB have the effect of supporting and reinforcing the SIB. At the same time that sympathy is offered, there is also recognition in both societies of an unhealthy narcissism to heroic SIB that feeds on the intense self-centeredness accompanying SIB and on the public fascination drawn to such persons.

The paradox for the observer/therapist is that if one perceives only pathological narcissism, one does an injustice to the intense human protest and striving that underlies this type of SIB; alternatively, if one perceives only the damaged victim or the God-seeking ecstatic, one is unable to help modify the SIB in a way that permits the self-injurious person to move beyond the SIB. Ultimately, in the medieval and the modern cases, unrelenting SIB interferes with deeper resolution of the horrendous life experiences in the victims of childhood abuse, and with the achievement of a deeper mystical state in the medieval holy persons (Kroll & De Ganck, 1990).

In both instances, SIB is used to alter a troubling state of mind. The infliction of pain serves as an interruptive mechanism, which helps the person achieve a more conflict-free mental state. Mental clutter, flashbacks, disruptive imagery, and dysphoric mood states are temporarily suppressed through the act of SIB, enabling the person to reach a more pacific cognitive and affective state that, in addition, brings to some SIB persons a culturally heroic affirmation.

SECTION II

Psychotherapy Goals and the Therapeutic Alliance

INTRODUCTION

The substantive question is whether a person can do what at the time he thinks bad without acting under some kind of compulsion.

William Charlton, *Weakness of Will*

Getting into therapy with a trained professional in order to talk about one's troubles and problems is an activity that is accepted and even strongly encouraged in our society. The professions offering psychotherapy are respected and have relatively high status. Governmental agencies, insurance companies, and health maintenance organizations endorse psychotherapy and are willing, to a limited extent, to underwrite its costs. The judicial system relies upon therapy at times as an alternative to incarceration. A dentist who recently pleaded guilty to sexual relations with his patients was ordered into "boundary therapy" by the judge as part of the plea-bargaining arrangement. The judge and other parties involved (prosecution and defense attorneys; the local dental association; the state professional licensing board) must assume that the dentist's behavior can be meaningfully framed as stemming from "boundary problems" and that psychotherapy, rather than a jail sentence and loss of license, is the appropriate and effective legal response to this type of unprofessional behavior. Religious institutions establish counseling centers and refer their parishioners to therapists. Persons who are troubled are expected to and usually are motivated to "get themselves into therapy" with a trained, competent professional psychotherapist. Clearly, society believes, or acts as if it believes, that psychotherapy is relevant and efficacious for a broad range of personal and interpersonal problems and, furthermore, views the person who gets into therapy as taking a positive step to help himself or herself.

Granted that our society encourages persons with troubles to go into therapy and designates the therapist as the proper person to talk to when having problems of a certain type, it still is important to ask what it is that individuals expect when they go into therapy. The answer must be more complex than just "to get better." Patients bring themselves into therapy for a variety of reasons, some of which are constructive and some destructive. The latter reasons may also be referred to by the older term "neurotic," meaning that the behavioral patterns are unconsciously driven and motivated to maintain maladaptive defenses at a cost of personal growth, maturation, and flexibility. We recognize that the notions of healthy and maladaptive styles involve basic value judgments which are themselves embedded within our culture. Valued traits such as autonomy, self-sufficiency, and openness are only virtues in a society that defines them as such; perhaps obedience, interdependence, and silence are equally or even more virtuous. In my work with Southeast Asian refugee families, for example, it is likely that the thrust toward autonomy in the younger generation is perceived as selfishness by the older generation, raised with more traditional values based upon the centrality of kin relationships.

The problem of value judgments regarding reasons for entering into psychotherapy becomes prominent in the therapy of PTSD/borderline persons, as therapist and patient struggle to tease apart acceptable and unacceptable behaviors and to reach a consensus about goals. In life, not just in therapy, persons with PTSD/borderline disorders are caught up in repeating old issues, old scenarios, old injuries. The essential problem of these individuals is that, having been unable, often for obvious reasons, to resolve their core issues constructively, they remain locked into a repetition of using old patterns that once may have been necessary and adaptive, but are now maladaptive by most reasonable standards. Each seemingly new encounter leads through old hurts to a new, yet familiar failure, thereby confirming and reinforcing the characteristic distortions of perception and behavior that were created by, or arose out of, the earlier injuries and hurtful experiences in the first place.

The PTSD/borderline patient is ceaselessly enveloped and tormented by an ongoing, intrusive stream of consciousness consisting of memories, flashbacks, and internalized voices of condemnation that blend with self-critical denunciations, even as he/she tries to go about the daily business of life's routines. The concomitant feeling states of rage, helplessness, disgust, and inchoate emotional arousal that combine with visceral sensations of pelvic and abdominal pain, shortness of breath, and headaches become so pervasive that they cannot be driven from prominence. One's total consciousness is ever at risk of being flooded over or split apart into dissociated and seemingly unrelated pieces of the past, at times with photographic-like accuracy and at times with haphazard distortion.

Yet, almost paradoxically, the person with PTSD/borderline disorder is not only a passive victim to a stream of consciousness gone beserk, but also an active agent, intentionally evoking painful memories, reviewing old fragments of childhood abuse, seeking repetitions in the present of past patterns of predatory relationships and high-risk situations, and setting up with a sense of increasing tension a chain of associations that will culminate in self-injurious behaviors followed by a rapid collapse of tension and perhaps a few moments of quiet before the entire process begins anew.

The contrary or, indeed, contradictory perspectives by which the core issue of PTSD/borderline persons can be described and understood is a fundamental philosophical dilemma in all of psychiatry and psychology. The PTSD/borderline person suffers from a disorder of the stream of consciousness. The philosophical dilemma relates to the problem of how best to conceptualize such a disorder, of whether to use the language of volition or the language of compulsion.

Seen from the outside, the PTSD/borderline can be described as (1) engaging in repetitive maladaptive behavior, (2) appreciating somewhat what he/she is doing, and (3) being responsible for his/her willful behavior. Seen from the inside, the person whom we describe as PTSD/borderline (1) is the passive viewer-participant of a stream of consciousness that he/she does not control, (2) has a narrow perspective in which the present experience is powerfully driven by the scripts of the past, and (3) lives his/her own life in a subjective sense of compulsivity and desperation.

There is no philosophical resolution to this dilemma; it is the free will/determinism problem become real in the realm of psychotherapy of persons who have been damaged in childhood by abusive caretakers and other representatives of the adult world. The resolution of this issue for the patient and therapist must be a pragmatic one; which convention of language—that of volition or that of compulsion—will be most helpful in the joint enterprise of psychotherapy? Which language will give the PTSD/borderline person the best chance of changing the runaway, tormenting stream of consciousness and the pattern of self-destructive behaviors and problematic relationships?

The implications of the different approaches are clear in conception, even if muddled in execution. The language of volition is also the language of blame; it holds the patient responsible and interprets failures to change behaviors in terms of weakness of will. The language of compulsion absolves the patient of responsibility and reframes the notion of failure into irresistible impulses determined by readily understandable mechanisms involving cause-effect relationships. Just how it comes about that a society decides what actions are understandable from what antecedents is an interesting topic, but it is clear that, in our modern technological culture, self-injurious behaviors are accepted and pardoned as a logically and psychologically understandable response to childhood abuse.

One's premises are both revealed and betrayed by the language one employs. Perhaps we can compromise between the polar opposites of volition and compulsion: One does not have volition over one's thoughts, but one does over one's actions. But surely this will not do in either direction. We seem neither totally powerless to shift our attention or focus of consciousness nor totally in control of our actions, especially under conditions of sufficient duress. Any psychology that acknowledges the existence of mental states and an inner life will take cognizance of mental activity that occurs outside of one's conscious awareness and of actions that subjectively appear to be driven or compulsive.

In Section II of this book, I will try to work from a different compromise. In general I will use the language of volition, but I will disengage it from the language of blame. I will speak of what it is that the patient wants in therapy and from therapy, as if the volitional component held dominance over the compulsive in the hierarchy of motivational factors. The patient's reality, of course, is not so simple; habits, drives, vulnerabilities, patterns and perceptions shaped by past experiences, basic temperament, genetic endowment, psychological defenses, existential despair—all of these and more enter into the complex and possibly indeterminate series of actions that the therapist confronts in therapy and that get sifted through and responded to by the therapist's own perceptions and habits developed by his/her own life experiences.

In view of this complexity, which prevents adherence to any simplistic volitional theory of human nature, I will take the liberty of requesting that the reader attribute to my language of volition a relativistic or "as-if" quality. The discussions analyzing PTSD/borderline patients' goals in therapy are intended to be understood as if volition were limited, partial, and at times practically nonexistent, rather than that the patient is merely being willful in pursuing his/her goals and in resisting the therapist's stated or unstated goals. Reciprocally, it is to be understood that the patient is not merely displaying weakness of will when he/she continues to engage in destructive patterns within and without the therapy hour. Of course, the same considerations apply to the actions of the therapist, as we shall have cause to examine later.

The patient comes to the therapist wanting help, but what does "help" mean? First and foremost, it would seem, the patient wants relief from his/her intolerable situation. Accompanying the quest for relief, however, is the entire history of how the intolerable situation came to be and of previous attempts and strategies to find relief. If endeavors to find relief up to the present time have involved what could only be judged as maladaptive and self-destructive behaviors, one would certainly anticipate that some of these same maladaptive patterns will be tried out in therapy.

In therapy, as also in life, the PTSD/borderline patient is caught up in repeating old issues. One can say that he/she suffers from an error of viewpoint, a faulty world-view, in which his/her way of looking at life leads him/her repetitively to perceive all situations the same way. Unable to strive for constructive changes, the patient is in the grip of old mythologies and scenarios. Among the many consequences of being stuck in this repetition of painful memories and exploitative expectations from others, two particular patterns of driven behavior have special relevance for the therapeutic problems under discussion here. These are that the patient appears to wish for two things from the therapist and nothing from the therapy.

The patient wishes, first of all, to have his/her needs gratified by the therapist. Second, the patient wishes to have one more arena and opportunity with which to replay old issues. These are not the goals that the therapist has for the patient. The therapist wishes to have the process of therapy, rather than what he/she gives directly to the patient in therapy, magically heal the patient. The therapist wants the patient to give up the old maladaptive patterns of behavior, but hopes for this to occur not from what he/she is pressured into personally giving to the patient in therapy, but from what the patient gets out of the process of therapy, such as insight or a corrective emotional experience. Thus we have an inherent conflict in the very structure of therapy: Two parties participating in a "single" enterprise, but each with motivations and goals different from the other; each committed to the therapy process differently.

Therapy, according to this model, is a series of frustrations, accommodations, and betrayals. The patient slowly has to relinquish his/her more neurotic goals in order to capture and keep some degree of love and respect from the therapist. The therapist slowly comes to realize that the therapeutic procedures that he/she thinks ought to have the most value for the patient, such as rational understanding and mutual cooperation, are not what the patient is working for, and that he/she (the therapist) is being asked by the patient to give much more than logic and interpretations. The patient is demanding engagement, not analysis. Out of this struggle of conflicting goals and methods comes a compromise in which both parties must give and give up more than they initially bargained for.

Ultimately, for therapy to be successful—that is, for the patient to change along constructive lines—the patient must give up more than the therapist gives up. Therapy fails under two general conditions. The first is when the patient is unwilling (in the language of volition), or unable (in the language of compulsion), to give up his/her demands for direct gratification from the therapist and the continuation of the pattern of reworking old issues in the same old, maladaptive ways. The second is when the therapist agrees, tacitly or openly, to provide the direct gratifications which the patient seeks or even encourages the patient to seek these, or when the therapist is unwilling or technically unable to discern the patient's old maladaptive patterns in order to work constructively with the patient via confrontation and interpretation rather than by participating in (and thereby reinforcing) the patient's acting out.

The notion of the "therapeutic alliance" has been introduced by therapists (never by patients) to signify the means by which therapist and patient work together toward the same ends. Its absence is seen as the failure of the patient (never the therapist) to engage in a collaboration when therapy happens to go awry. But giving credit to the therapeutic alliance for the successes of therapy is like crediting the scoreboard for the home run that produced the score. The therapeutic alliance represents the result or end point of successful therapy; it is the evidence of effective therapy, not the mechanism by which therapy works. Friedman (1988) has an extensive and thoughtful discussion of this very point. The therapist cannot wait for the therapeutic alliance to develop in order for therapy to proceed. The therapist need not, indeed cannot, effectively do anything special to help it develop, since such attempts usually fall into the category of nontherapeutic gratification done in order to pacify the patient, purchase affection, and keep the patient in therapy, and therefore are likely to complicate and interfere with therapeutic progress.

The therapist's tasks are relatively simple to state and exceedingly difficult to accomplish. The therapist has to:

1. Discern the old patterns.
2. Point out — confront — help the patient become aware of how these old patterns and intrusive streams of consciousness operate in his/her life and their consequences.
3. Possibly trace the old patterns back to the childhood injuries, experiences, and responses. I say "possibly" because it is not clear how fully this procedure of reconstructing the past can ever be done or how necessary it is in order for the patient to give up the old patterns, or when it is even harmful to dwell excessively on old traumas.
4. Struggle with the patient in therapy and resist the patient's attempts to make the therapist a source of unreasonable gratifications and a participant in playing out old issues.
5. Provide affirmation of the patient's intrinsic value and permission for healthy growth. This involves the therapist's maintaining a real presence in therapy without the excesses of regressive gratification or seductive exploitation that undermine the work of therapy.

The reason these tasks are difficult to accomplish is that it is impossible in human interactions, of which psychotherapy is but one example, to avoid all gratifications between the actors; I am not even suggesting that such an austere goal would be desirable. There is gratification in the basic sociality between two humans, in their coming together, in their acceptance of one another, in their meeting one another with respect and dignity. To these basic ingredients, the therapy situation adds both the benefits and the burdens inherent in an unequal relationship: The patient obtains a listening person who theoretically will be affirmative and nonjudgmental, and who will not get caught up in the patient's old maladaptive patterns; the cost is that the listening person gets paid to be a listener, does not share reciprocally in personal disclosures about him/herself, is less emotionally vulnerable, sets most of the rules, and maintains boundaries that sharply and artificially limit the degree to which the relationship may evolve.

Chapter 5 will discuss the therapeutic issues centering around the matrix of the PTSD/borderline patient's search for gratification from the therapist and the therapist's ambivalent responses. Chapter 6 will discuss the related issue of replaying old maladaptive patterns in the context of therapy. The discussions will develop out of the concepts that are represented schematically in Figure 1. Although Chapter 5 relates primarily to the two left-hand boxes and Chapter

FIGURE 1

Therapy Issues

	GRATIFICATION OF NEEDS	REPLAY OLD ISSUES
POSITIVE	Validation: Affirmation and permission Nurturance Having someone care Grieving Refocus of anger Role modeling	Verbalization and catharsis Testing trust issues Cognitive repackaging Establish proper boundaries Internal locus of control
NEGATIVE	Dependency Rescue Sexualization Entitlement	Acting-out Victimization Identification with aggressor Avoidance of old tapes External locus of control

6 to the two right-hand boxes, it is clear that there is considerable overlap in how patients work both of these issues within the context of therapy. Figure 1 is a schematic model and as such leaves out, either intentionally or inadvertently, many other perspectives of therapy. It will be helpful to the extent that its own perspective touches upon some very important issues that are a key to understanding in detail the ways in which the psychotherapy of PTSD/borderline patients gets sidetracked.

5

Gratification of Needs

It is remarkable that such a unlikely enterprise as psychotherapy should work at all. The fact that it does at times is a testimony to the strength of cultural values in establishing and encouraging special healing rituals in which members of a society can participate. It is also testimony to the rewards inherent in certain types of human relationships, even when formal rules establish limits and boundaries to the relationship. Essentially, despite the many defects, there are sufficient satisfactions and anticipated benefits accruing to patients in psychotherapy to keep them, in most cases, hooked into the therapy process. These constitute both the normal and legitimate gratifications that occur within the sociality of two humans and the fantasied as well as real gratifications that inevitably occur to a greater or lesser extent in all therapy situations. Such gratifications are not necessarily related to getting better, for unsuccessful as well as successful therapies appear to endure and provide a sense of satisfaction. What seems to keep the patient in therapy are the satisfactions of the transference.

What sorts of gratifications accrue to the therapist? At a positive level, the therapist enjoys the human interaction within the therapy, just as the patient does. Therapists obtain the satisfaction, in addition to the material rewards, of undertaking a theoretically helping activity that is consistent with their own sense of ethical and valued behavior. Therapists may also enjoy engaging the patient at both an intellectual and emotional level in the service of untangling puzzling behavior patterns. All of these socially meritorious and moral motives, however, can shade into their more self-serving and egoistic counterparts. Along with the public recognition and respectability that society bestows upon the various sorts of therapy practitioners, there are also personal and baser motives and rewards that derive directly from the types of one-to-one interactions that are unique to the therapy situation. These more personal motives, which cannot

110

be entirely absent even in the best of therapists, might ordinarily be of no great consequence in a casual relationship, but take on great importance as they begin to dovetail with the patient's own neurotic vulnerabilities and permit exploitation of the power imbalance inherent in the therapy relationship.

For patients whose life experiences have taught them that their only worth is as a source of gratification to others, such as to gratify father's sexual desires or mother's needs to be taken care of, the problem of vulnerability to exploitation will be intensified and reinforced in interactions with therapists who use the therapy situation to enhance their own needs for power, flattery, and emotional dominance, or who merely enjoy being experts who can tell someone else what is best for them and what is not. The patient quickly learns which particular responses will elicit warmth and approval — or anger and rejection if these are the meaningful reactions — from the therapist. In such situations, the therapist participates in playing out the patient's old self-destructive issues and thereby contributes, usually unwittingly, to the worsening of the patient's problems.

VALIDATION AS A NECESSARY GRATIFICATION

Although the notion of gratification in the context of therapy usually has a pejorative connotation, there are, in fact, several areas in therapy in which gratification derives naturally from the very process of therapy and is healthy and therapeutic. The sense of warmth and acceptance that occurs when two people talk with one another in a positive manner is the first example that comes to mind. For many patients whose early years were filled with conflict or deprivation and whose present lives are relatively unfulfilled, such positive interactions in therapy can be very meaningful. Furthermore, the positive social interaction between patient and therapist establishes a foundation for the more specific therapeutic work relating to a sense of validation of the self.

The notion of validation is of central importance in the treatment of PTSD/borderline individuals because so many of their childhood experiences have both directly and subtly invalidated their right to exist, to maintain privacy and boundaries, to develop their own individuality, and to have quiet confidence in the accuracy of their own perceptions and judgments. Correspondingly, adults raised under conditions that invalidated their existence have learned to question their own integrity, perceptions, and reasoning abilities. These doubts are pervasive; they exist in the very marrow of the PTSD/borderline person.

There are two aspects of validation which need to be considered here: affirmation and permission. Affirmation is a relatively straightforward concept; it speaks to developing a sense of essential worth as a person. There is risk that, in practice, the artificial pursuit of affirmation can shade imperceptibly into seductive and facile expressions of approval, e.g., "I'm okay, you're okay." Affirmation in therapy relates to working out with patients some awareness of the sources of their very negative attitudes about themselves and beginning to change these attitudes in a positive direction. It is a lifelong task.

Permission in therapy is more loaded than affirmation, for it borders on attitudes of condescension and superior judgment on the part of the therapist. Yet, as we shall see, permission to express grief, anger, even selfishness and entitlement often has to come from the therapist, for patients have long ago incorporated notions that they possess no right to have such "self-centered" feelings. Persons, even as adults, who have been raised to believe that they are worthless except insofar as they are the targets of frustration or desire of others, do not believe that they have any legitimacy to resent their maltreatment or to place their own dawning awareness that something is terribly wrong over the judgments of the adult world. To complicate matters, however, patients often oscillate between a sense of worthlessness and the apparently opposite notion of entitlement. Worthlessness and entitlement, each stemming from the same damaging childhood experiences, represent formidable cores of psychopathology and treatment resistance.

The present discussion will focus on affirmation in therapy. Issues of permission will be raised later, although, realistically, affirmation and permission are two faces of the same coin.

AFFIRMATION

The patients about whom we are speaking have, in most cases, been raised with consistently negative judgments about their own worth, attractiveness, competency, intelligence, sexuality, and morality. They have little hope that they can effectively influence their future in any other than a progressively destructive way. For example, most PTSD/borderline women have been told by fathers or other male predators that they are whores, good only for sex, and that they are so unbalanced that no one would believe them if they were to reveal the story of their abuse. They have been told by mothers that they are incompetent and selfish and will never amount to anything. Because of their own predilection, as a way of reworking old injuries, to seek out predators and to sabotage potentially healthy relationships and enterprises, the adolescent and young adult experiences of these patients have only served further to confirm the dire predictions of others and their own sense of futility and essential depravity.

The therapist's tasks in the face of the patient's consistently negative and damaging self-image are relatively straightforward and clear in overall direction, but very complex in specific execution. Therapists must place themselves squarely on the side of affirmation, but cannot do so naively or simplistically. Merely telling patients that their perceptions are off and that they are not horrible persons will not do, although, at times, this message too needs to be communicated. There are associated messages that could also be directly transmitted, such as, "You have worth by virtue of your existence as a person, you have dignity, you did not ask for what happened to you."

But if life were so uncomplicated that simple, heartfelt rebuttal were sufficient to undo years of emotional and physical battering, we would be living in a utopia. Why should the patient believe the therapist, who can be perceived as merely being "therapeutic" in dispensing compliments and who therefore can be discounted? Affirmation of the patient has to permeate every interaction between patient and therapist, even when the therapist is giving the patient a hard time. Affirmation shows up in the respect the therapist has for the patient and for the painful enterprise that therapy represents for the patient. Affirmation does not consist of the male therapist telling the female patient that he loves her, or giving her a hug to comfort her and show her that she is not such a terrible person, that she is not an untouchable. Such actions lead to expectations that cannot or should not be fulfilled, and therefore are ultimately ineffective and deleterious.

ESTABLISHING HEALTHY BOUNDARIES
AS AN ASPECT OF AFFIRMATION

Finally, affirmation in therapy consists in the recognition conveyed to the patient of his/her need for clear and healthy boundaries. This is done not just intellectually, but by the therapist's respect for the patient's ideal boundary definitions, despite the patient's misinterpretations, as evidence of indifference or rejection, of the therapist's scrupulous regard for clear boundaries. Furthermore, since the patient's boundaries are often vague or defective, the therapist must at times take an active role in deciding where the patient's boundaries are best established, even when it entails not listening to the patient's requests for certain actions on the part of the therapist. This point is clear when the patient's request constitutes an obvious boundary violation, such as a request for sex, but not so obvious at other times, for example, when the patient requests that the therapist give information about the patient to other persons. Overriding a patient's wishes or apparently legitimate requests carries its own risks to the therapeutic relationship, such as the therapist falling into the attitude of omniscience. Nevertheless, the therapist must decide when the "reasonable" request or the apparently innocent involvement of others in the protected therapeutic relationship is a set-up that calls for interpretation rather than compliance. Too often, patients are able skillfully to get others to collude in violating their boundaries, which represents yet one more repetition of previous patterns of intrusive interactions with others. The following example illustrates the subtle and apparently unremarkable ways in which this may occur.

CASE 1

Mr. A, a single stockbroker age 32, has been chronically suicidal for many years. He has begun work with a new therapist, and appears to be committed to therapy with her. He has discussed with her aspects of childhood abuse that he had not revealed before. Suicide threats and attempts have been dealt with in the present therapy in a fairly low-key style, even when brief hospitalizations have been necessary and instituted. In essence, the risk of suicide has been accepted as part of the working background with this patient. Toward the end of the first year of therapy, the patient makes an appointment to see a lawyer, ostensibly to get his financial affairs in order. Enough hints are dropped at the meeting that the lawyer becomes suspicious, asks a series of personal questions, and deduces that Mr. A is planning suicide. The lawyer then writes a letter to the therapist, whose name he has extracted from Mr. A, asking that she call him "upon receipt of the letter" in order for the two of them (lawyer and therapist) to work out a treatment plan for Mr. A. The letter includes a signed release of information statement.

The therapist is faced with an interesting situation. Mr. A has succeeded in alarming the lawyer, who is unaware of the chronic nature of the problem and is unsophisticated in recognizing this type of acting-out. The lawyer, in addition to having genuine concern for Mr. A, is behaving like a lawyer in covering himself legally. From the viewpoint of the therapeutic process, however, Mr. A.'s decision, so to speak, to seek out a lawyer to make a will and then to intrude, seemingly innocently, his personal issues into the discussion with the lawyer such that the lawyer contacts the therapist, represents a piece of acting-out. Although the acting-out occurs on many levels, I have brought it up in the present discussion of boundary problems because Mr. A, first, was unable to maintain proper task-related boundaries with the lawyer, even though we can hypothesize that this was his intent all along, and second, has tried to get his therapist involved in talking to the lawyer about him and in either jointly setting up a rescue plan for him or getting into a fight with the lawyer over his care.

The therapist, in today's litigious climate, must decide whether it is safe to give the lawyer the cold shoulder by refusing to participate in the little game that Mr. A has set up and thereby risk future accusations and lawsuits should Mr. A suicide, or else to comply with the lawyer's request for a conference to discuss and make decisions about the patient, thereby collaborating in the patient's acting-out in a way that will certainly compromise the therapist's freedom of therapeutic action in the future and may set up a chain of events that are unforeseeable by all involved. It is impossible to predict where such an initial action may lead, once the patient succeeds in pulling others into what needs to be a private therapy relationship. I am not suggesting that the therapist should never involve family members or others when suicide is threatened. Many times this is the only ethical action to take, if the therapist is convinced that suicide is imminent. This is always a judgment call. However, if the therapist does have to involve others, then therapy moves to a different level, as the intrusion of the therapist into the real life of the patient and involvement with the patient's family or acquaintances are themselves topics that need to be worked through in therapy, once the risk of suicide subsides to base level.

In this present case, the therapist wrote a brief letter to the lawyer acknowledging receipt of his letter, stating her intention to discuss the matter with Mr. A, but refusing to discuss the matter further with the lawyer. She then raised the issue with Mr. A in therapy as an example of his problem in maintaining healthy boundaries for himself. The suicide component of this brief adventure was not ignored, but was not made the central focus; instead the focus was the patient's use of indirect threats of suicide in an attempt to induce the therapist into violating the integrity of the therapeutic relationship. Despite the seeming reasonableness of the lawyer's request, the therapist should no more give in to this type of pressure than she would hand the patient a razor blade in exchange for a patient's promise to substitute cutting himself for killing himself. In working with the patient over this incident, the therapist was careful to maintain a neutral stance regarding the lawyer; the essential piece of therapeutic work involved an examination of the patient's faulty boundaries and of his attempt, through acting-out, to force the therapist to become directly involved in taking care of him, as well as to collaborate in a conspiracy against him.

I have raised the problem of proper boundaries within the context of ways in which the therapist can legitimately affirm a patient's intrinsic values, even when the patient appears to be undermining such efforts. The patient continues to work on his/her agenda, which is often shaped by the desperate need for affirmation, set against his/her own deep beliefs that affirmation cannot be genuine or deserved. These negative beliefs about self-worth mitigate against the simple device of complimenting the patient or contradicting the patient's self-condemning statements. This is why, for example, it is usually more helpful initially to characterize patients' attempts to involve others in negative interactions as symptomatic of boundary problems than as manipulative acts, the latter representing an interpretation which the patient can only perceive as criticism from the therapist.

While all forms of criticism of the patient need to be avoided, its counterpart, praise, can be equally problematic. From a technical point of view, if the therapist gets caught up in the *content* of an "affirming" dialogue, while ignoring the *process* — what it means to give praise to patients, or what it means to side with them and criticize others who have condemned and damaged them in the past, or what it means to a patient to get hugs from the therapist — then therapy usually will not work because the patient will either distrust the intent of the therapist or begin to work the therapy to get more compliments and other gratifications rather than to gain perspective on the power of negative self-imagery throughout the years. In addition, joining with the patient in criticism of family members means criticizing those aspects of the patient herself that she has incorporated from family members; complimenting the patient may inadvertently repeat a pattern of flattery en route to sexual abuse by a family member. It is not that praise and encouragement have no place in a therapy that combines supportive and exploratory work. Rather, there are levels of significance for the patient regarding supportive statements from the therapists about which the therapist probably has no understanding or inkling, because the background of the patient's life has not been developed in detail in the therapy. I am not suggesting therapeutic paralysis; nevertheless, the therapist will have to give thought to the multiple layers of meaning of seemingly simple and straightforward support and affirmation.

The essence of therapy, ultimately, is not to gratify patients, but to work with them so that they can begin to find healthy gratifications outside of therapy. Within the therapeutic framework, however, it is important to convey to patients that they have intrinsic value. The therapist's task is to do this properly and pervasively and without perverting the therapy, without therapy deteriorating into a mere series of compliments and gratifications. The same is true for issues such as nurturance and caring. These are areas of conflict for patients; in the patient's life, episodes of simulated caring by others have often served as antecedents and entrapments for later abuse and rejection. Nurturance and caregiving by a therapist can never be enough to make up for what was not given earlier. The "corrective emotional experience" should not be understood literally as an indiscriminate panacea. But what therapists give of themselves is genuine, although primarily symbolic and very limited, and carries no price tag. It is legitimate for the patient to want more; the therapist has to accept and convey this legitimacy without being condescending or rejecting. But it is not legitimate for the therapist to give more, to attempt to satisfy these needs of the patient. It would no longer be therapy.

Validation as Permission

Conveying the legitimacy of a patient's own emotions, desires, and need for self-respect brings us to the notion of permission. There are times when patients know what to do in order to help themselves but do not think they have a right to do it, or else do not even think of a particular course of action because they have long ago abandoned (or never developed) consideration of ways to affirm themselves. For example, some patients who receive vicious and sexually intimidating telephone calls from the father or stepfather who abused them in childhood are unable to break off the telephone call. They do not feel they have a right to do this; they must hear out the verbal abuse, although it almost inevitably ends up with the patient hurting herself after the call. While, as I indicated above, there are many dynamic issues involved in why the patient cannot, or does not, hang up the telephone, it sometimes is sufficient for the therapist to tell the patient that it is all right to put the telephone receiver down on the cradle. It is legitimate for the patient to take this small physical step, although symbolically large, toward self-protection and self-affirmation. The deeper reasons for the patient's inability to protect herself will come up again and again on many kinds of issues; they need to be examined, but first, if possible, it is useful to help her begin to assert herself on some basic levels.

Validation of Grief and Anger

There are other important healthy needs of the patient that can be acknowledged and worked with in therapy. Helping patients grieve over what they have missed, over what might have been but was not, and over what happened that should not have, is crucial for the therapy to provide a structure within which grief over the past can be felt and expressed. How much self-pity is helpful in the grieving process is not calculable, but a therapist can agree with patients that they have had more than their share of misfortunes without encouraging them into martyrdom, excessive entitlement, or bathos. Some life stories are truly heartbreaking; the therapist is not called upon to intensify indulgence in misery, although the patient may wish this, nor to preach stoicism. Perhaps, prior to getting into the painful therapeutic work of helping patients place their harsh life experiences into perspective, bearing witness by hearing out the story is sufficient for the moment.

Alongside grief work is the patient's need to refocus anger. In most cases, patients have directed their anger against themselves with words and action. Patients castigate themselves with all the criticism that others have leveled at them, and carry out punishments and penances against themselves. I am not suggesting that this is all there is as explanation and cause of self-injurious behaviors, but certainly anger directed toward the self is at the center of much of the self-destructiveness seen in borderlines. It is not effective for the therapist simply to tell the patient that she should not be angry at herself, nor is it effective for the therapist to tell the patient that she should be angry instead at those who have hurt her. Such platitudinous dictums ignore the complexity of human dynamics and learning. In most instances, the patient has concluded long ago that she is to blame for her misfortunes, if not by her bad and provocative behavior, then simply by existing. The patient's ultimate remedy for the mistake of existing, of course, is suicide. Although arguing with the patient about the focus of her anger is usually ineffective, nevertheless, the patient has to begin to shift some of her anger to more appropriate targets, or at least to understand that anger at oneself is the result of hurtful experiences in the past. Much of this work in therapy falls under the heading of cognitive restructuring and will be discussed later.

In a broad sense, the patient needs suitable role models, and the therapist can help provide this. It is not that the therapist must be, or is, a paragon of virtue; just being a reasonable and thoughtful human being will do. But of course, many individual behaviors and values of the therapist get role-modeled. The therapist can be non-judgmental; the therapist can accept the patient; the therapist thinks before acting; the therapist does not respond punitively or with rejection; the therapist establishes clear and healthy boundaries; the therapist maintains emotions within a normal range of intensity; the therapist does not blame; the therapist is non-exploitative and does not get enmeshed, but nevertheless cares for the patient. I am not trying to define the ideal therapist. These behaviors and dispositions constitute part of the routine and expected conduct of the therapist in therapy. Departure from these norms constitutes departure from the broad range of good therapy.

This compendium of healthy gratifications of patient needs in therapy is not exhaustive, nor are the various categories mutually exclusive. The basic issue is that the patient has emotional needs that may legitimately be gratified in therapy and usually, in fact, are gratified automatically (although not without self-consciousness) by virtue of the structure and process of therapy itself. The therapist needs to give thought to these areas, but not worry about them. The degree to which certain needs of the patient are gratified, and the extent to which these ought to become focal points early in therapy, will vary greatly according to the clinical status of the patient, conditions of therapy, and personality and orientation of the therapist. Excesses of gratification, as well as failure to process the patient's wishes in this direction, will interfere with or even sabotage therapy. But a therapy that does not provide affirmation of the patient, either openly or at least by attitude, is not much of a therapy at all.

PROBLEMATIC GRATIFICATION OF NEEDS

There is risk in placing value judgments on the different ways people perceive and pursue their needs. The concept itself of "need" is complex and has entered into popular language as well as psychological jargon to the point where it can mean anything to anybody. As used here, need clearly refers to something other than the basic physical necessities of life: oxygen, light, warmth, clothing, shelter, and food. Our common evolutionary heritage has formed us into social creatures, and our specific hominid evolution has made us into self-conscious, symbol-using individuals. For all but a few very exceptional persons, humans require social communication and interpersonal connectedness to be emotionally and psychologically healthy. In Western culture, a positive sense of oneself as an individual, most likely derived from social connectedness, is also considered either necessary or evidence of psychological health.

Certain persons, whom we designate as borderline by virtue of how we define the disorder, are locked into relatively rigid patterns of defining and pursuing the details of their needs maladaptively and self-destructively. Yet this statement, without qualification and commentary, is too general; it is true of all patients with character disorders and traumatized pasts. What is it that PTSD/borderline individuals specifically are doing wrong? Wherein lies their problem, and how is this manifested in the therapy situation?

The problem in doing psychotherapy with PTSD/borderlines is twofold. First, in terms of goals, the patient's pursuit of gratification of needs takes priority over motivation to work in therapy toward constructive change. Second, in terms of behavioral style, the manner in which PTSD/borderlines relate to the therapist is patterned to obtain gratification of their needs rather than to facilitate the process of change. The problems are not insurmountable; rather, in a sense, the uncovering and resolution of the divergent goals of patient and therapist and the examination of how the borderline behavioral style is manifested in therapy become the very heart of the therapy. Divergent goals and maladaptive styles only become unmanageable problems when the therapist is either unaware of the patient's agenda or, worse, when the therapist actively colludes with the patient in the pursuit of his/her goals. This is not meant to imply that the PTSD/ borderline has no motivation to work in psychotherapy toward constructive change, or that therapeutic cooperation is impossible, or that the patient relentlessly and singlemindedly tries to subvert all forward progress to the gratification of needs. The therapist needs to capitalize on moments of positive motivation, but not be so enthusiastic about the potential for progress that he/she does not perceive those times when the patient's defenses reassert themselves.

Often the patient's negative goals are vague and desultory, reflecting the influence of the current situation upon a background of self-destructiveness and dismal life experiences. The specific goals come and go, at times with little intensity; it is the inexorable pattern, and the readiness to exploit an unreflective response from the therapist, that pose the therapeutic problem. Here is an example.

CASE 2

Ms. D is a 30-year-old single, college graduate, bisexual woman with a history going back to early childhood of brutal sexual and physical abuse by both parents. She has spent the last two years in and out of private and state hospitals for self-injurious and assaultive behaviors. She is doing fairly well as an outpatient, in that she has not cut for several weeks and has recently had a job offer that has bolstered her positive feeling for herself. After she tells her therapist about the job offer, she says:

Ms. D: I enjoy coming here to see you. Do you enjoy having me come here?

Therapist: Why do you ask?

Ms. D (*with a smile*): There you go again. Can't I ask a simple question? Does everything have to be examined?

Th: No, not everything does. But this one does.

Ms. D: I don't know why I ask. (*pause . . . then a big smile*) I can't believe that I would tell you this. . . . I had the thought of seducing you.

Th: No kidding? How long has that thought been there?

Ms. D: Oh, I don't know. Maybe for a few weeks. Oh, I'm so embarrassed. I used to be afraid of you. You remember that time we had to have a session in another office, and I almost freaked out? Now it seems like it would be fun to seduce you.

Th: Did it seem to you that you could succeed?

Ms. D: I don't know. You're pretty straight. But I usually am able to. I once seduced my dentist; it was a woman and we had an affair. I can be a very persuasive person.

Th: What would seducing me accomplish?

Ms. D: It would make me dominant. I would have power. That's what it would do.

Th: Dominance rather than love, like when you were older and would walk into the bathroom when your father was taking a bath, and you'd be looming over him?

Ms. D: That's right. Oh, I can't believe it. If I did it, I'd probably tell my friends, and they're such feminists, I'm sure they'd report you. So I guess I couldn't tell anybody.

Th: That would really give you power. I could lose everything. I would really be dependent upon you.

Ms. D: Yeah, even money. Naw, I couldn't do that to you. Say, how'd we get into this in the first place? Oh yeah, now I remember. Do you enjoy seeing me?

Although therapists are often lampooned for the "technique" of answering a question with a question, this brief example provides anecdotal justification for the practice. So, the first point to discuss is: Why not answer the question? The therapist could have answered positively, which would be truthful, and in this manner at least temporarily bolster Ms. D's self-esteem. It would be simple: "Yes, I do enjoy seeing you. What is more, I look forward to our sessions." Would the first sentence without the second be acceptable? After all, it does affirm her. Would adding the second sentence move to the edge or beyond of seductiveness? It is either an unnecessary embellishment or a bid for ingratiation or seduction. There are other areas in which the therapist compliments Ms. D, such as for doing well at college in the past (as they discuss her future) or for not cutting herself for a week. Ms. D's question was too disingenuous to give a direct reply, but not because the therapist really believed, even after her intent was revealed, that answering it positively would have encouraged seductiveness. In fact, the therapist suspected that seduction was not uppermost on Ms. D's agenda when she asked the question, but only came to mind after the therapist asked her why she asked.

The main reason for not answering directly in this relatively low-intensity interaction was precisely because it would have blocked the discussion that ensued. We cannot, however, be entirely sure about this. The therapist could have answered "Yes, I do," and then asked why she asked. But two problems would arise here. First of all, gratification of the wish might have substituted for verbalization of it (although, initially, the wish was for a statement of reassurance or affection, not for sexual interest), and secondly, the thought of seduction would then have been related to the therapist's positive response rather than having to stand as the psychological progression of her own thought processes. As an alternative to answering her question directly, the therapist could have chosen to investigate a more intrapsychic arena, instead of the interpersonal one that was examined. This would have involved focusing on her train of associations leading back to childhood abuse, rather than remaining in the present and future tense, looking at the impact of her impulse upon her relationship with the therapist. The therapist matter-of-factly told Ms. D that he thought that the power issue was linked to Ms. D's childhood and adolescent experiences with an abusive father but chose not to push for further memories, preferring to keep the discourse at the interpersonal level.

In fact, in the discussion that followed, the themes of power and dominance, leading back just briefly to some reflection about her father's influence on her later relationships with men (seduction of the man without real interest or investment) were more important than any transient though of seducing the therapist. With few exceptions, this particular patient had been extremely cautious about speaking of her early life experiences and the therapist did not wish to push her into this area every time the opportunity, via a casual remark, seemed to present itself. This was in keeping with his technical therapeutic plan to work the therapy primarily at an interpersonal rather than intrapsychic level of discourse. The reason for this decision, as well as the basis for referring to it as a "technical" one, was that the pragmatics of this patient's defenses and vulnerabilities at this particular point in therapy called for a focus in therapy upon the here and now, including a scrutiny of how she related to the therapist, rather than a push for her to recover memories of incest and violence, a tactic that in previous therapies had provoked psychotic thinking and explosive behaviors. The decision, again, is a technical one, in that it does not reflect a unifying treatment philosophy that the most critical and important work of therapy consists of examination of interpersonal relationships as opposed to intrapersonal dynamics. It is a technical decision in that it is judged to be the proper tactic to guide the therapy at that particular stage of their work together.

Let us return to the topic of gratification of needs as the goal for being in therapy: The patient was not asking for insight or perspective or change. She was signaling that something was troubling her that, from the therapist's viewpoint, needed clarification. The therapist was not sure yet what the issues were, but they appeared related to her feelings toward him at the moment and how she perceived he felt about her. It turns out that Ms. D was struggling with some dominance/passivity conflicts, and perhaps feeling unlovable or vulnerable or anxious about possible abandonment by her therapist, a theme that recapitulated childhood experiences with mother. In response to these anxieties, Ms. D resorted, either in reality or fantasy, to a familiar behavioral diversion from uncomfortableness stirred up by her relationship to a man; she would seduce him. She knew this would have disastrous results for each of them. Yet the thought was there, and it was only the somewhat casual refusal to answer a seemingly unimportant question that permitted the conflict and uneasiness to be even approached.

The "unimportant" question, however, was not ostensibly directed toward either a sexual or a dominance theme, but merely toward a fairly routine and common issue in the therapy of PTSD/borderlines: "Do you care about me?" As such, the interaction would appear to fall more into the realm of what I have designated as the pursuit of healthy needs. It is precisely in this area that therapists, either by virtue of their own therapeutically naive kindness or by misapplication of a theoretical stance about borderlines that states that a positive transference and a "holding environment" must be actively fostered, think to facilitate the progress of therapy by purposefully gratifying the patient's need for affirmation. The desire for affirmation and for having someone care are important and legitimate needs of the PTSD/borderline patient. The therapist is obligated to judge whether providing some gratifications of these needs beyond that which is ordinarily provided within the context of the therapeutic relationship is helpful or harmful to the progress of therapy and, ultimately, to the progress of the patient. In this particular example, a wealth of responses could have done the same thing, as long as the therapist were clear about where he was going and what needed to be done. The therapist tried to tailor his responses to Ms. D's question ("Do you enjoy having me come here?"), such as to provide affirmation without losing sight of the fact that important issues beyond the need for affirmation were involved.

As a last comment, this example also illustrates another very common, often problematic interaction in therapy, that of the therapist being caught off-guard during low-intensity exchanges. There are apparent, or real, arid periods in all therapy, and other times when not much else but small talk and evasion are the bill of fare. It is not the case that a patient's every comment is a pearl in disguise, ready to be recognized and held up to scrutiny. But sometimes, within the course of either low-intensity or even tedious monologues or exchanges, an off-hand comment is tossed out that has unsuspected importance because the patient has decided or recognizes, perhaps only after it is said, that much is riding on the response. The importance of the off-hand question is not related to the information-content of the answer, but to the process of interchange between patient and therapist and to what is signified by the therapist's willingness or refusal to answer the question, as well as what the underlying meaning of the therapist's answer might be.

GRATIFICATION OF DEPENDENCY NEEDS

The borderline concept arose, even before the term "borderline" was specifically applied, from the appreciation that some types of patients became worse when treated with intensive psychodynamic psychotherapy. This notion of regression in therapy still remains operative as an organizing principle for the recognition and treatment of PTSD/borderline patients. While the more dramatic examples of regression in therapy often center around acting-out behaviors such as cutting and other self-destructive actions, the persistent demands for attention, therapeutic time, advice, solace, sympathy, caretaking in general, and personal involvement of the therapist beyond the conventional parameters constitute major challenges to therapists working with PTSD/borderline patients. Unkind descriptions, such as "bottomless pit" and "insatiable," reflect the intense ambivalence with which therapists approach what they perceive as the unreasonable claims of the PTSD/borderline patient.

In a sense, then, there are two therapeutic issues. The first is how best to deal constructively with patients' covert and overt demands that the therapist meet their dependency needs. The manner of phrasing the problem this way does not imply that there is a single "best" way, or that a "good" way in one context is suitable for a changed context. The second therapeutic issue is how therapists can suitably insulate themselves from the recurrent struggle with the patient over gratification of needs without becoming harsh and mean-spirited or, alternatively, excessively protective of their own sensitivities and backing away from the patient. The depleted therapist is no longer able to work therapeutically with the patient.

CASE 3

Ms. E is a 37-year-old divorced woman, a paralegal by training, who has functioned poorly for the past eight years by virtue of emotional lability, self-injurious behavior, and an interpersonal style in which great emotional demands placed upon others lead, when unmet, to a pervasive sense of wounded entitlement and threats of suicide. She has had several years of weekly psychotherapy and now meets with her female therapist on a monthly basis.

Ms. E's usual style of interaction in therapy was to complain bitterly for the first half-hour of each session. Several times, when she had exceeded the informal allotment of time devoted to the therapist's uninterrupted listening, the therapist would gently suggest that they needed to move beyond the complaints to the patterns underlying them. Ms. E would reply with vehemence that she "wasn't done yet."

On one particular day, the catalog of complaints was endless. Her county social worker was unresponsive to her needs; the food stamp coordinator denied her application for food stamps; when she went downtown to argue her case (unsuccessfully), she emerged from the government center only to find a parking ticket on her car; when she argued with the nearest policeman, who happened to be directing traffic, he told her that he had not given her the ticket and would not write out a statement for her that she really was legally parked; she went to an auto junk yard to buy a tail light reflector because someone had backed into her car and she got into an argument with the junk yard dealer, who ejected her from his lot; a few days later, someone else backed into her car in a shopping center and drove away; her mother told her (once again) that she always was an ungrateful and difficult child. After reciting this list to her therapist, the patient con-cluded, from these and other events, that people were inherently selfish, that she did not deserve such unkindnesses and did not care to continue living in an uncaring world, and that the only remaining response was to kill herself.

The therapist had five minutes in which to muster a reply. She assumed that any inquiry or suggestion that, perhaps, Ms. E's behavior had some-thing to do with how others responded to her would be experienced as blame, as one final insult from the last person potentially available to provide support. It had been attempted before, under more propitious cir-cumstances, but Ms. E had not able to step back and evaluate her own contribution to interpersonal disasters. The therapist had discussed pre-viously Ms. E's demands that she (the therapist) tell her what to do or leave her with some message or suggestion that would give her hope and help her get through the week. The therapist had never done this directly, although she had at times discussed positive actions, such as finding a part-time job or volunteer work, that might begin to balance the consistently negative experiences in Ms. E's life.

This time, the therapist decided to shift from content (tell me what to do to feel better) to process by picking up on a theme that had been discussed before, namely, that the immediate leap from specific distress to threats of suicide precluded other problem-solving options, as well as the possibility of obtaining some perspectives upon herself as an actor in the drama of her own life. With anger and conveying a heavy sense of inevitability, Ms. E stalked out of the office.

For those who like to know the endings of stories, or at least of chapters, the therapist sat on her anxieties about Ms. E and, much to her surprise and relief, Ms. E showed up two weeks later at a local mental health workshop in which the therapist was participating. Ms. E was in a fairly good mood; however, she was angry that she had sent her registration form too late to the program committee and therefore was denied admission to the conference, and had to sit out in the hall during the first half of the program.

This vignette provides an example of unrequited dependency needs. What does the patient want? She is not asking how she can change herself, although at times she will voice discontent about herself. If we listen to her words through many sessions, she wants the therapist to agree with her that the world is unkind and unfair and that she does not deserve the treatment she gets. The therapist can certainly support the first and sympathize with the second. But Ms. E wants more. She wants the therapist to provide a counterbalance to what the world has done to her. She wants the therapist to say the soothing words that will take away the pain and make her feel accepted and loved. Further, she wants the therapist to provide her with some rationale for continuing to stay alive, some reason to hope that the world will treat her better than it has in the past. I do not think that the therapist can legitimately do this. Ms. E and her therapist have even discussed religious and spiritual issues at times in the context of the meaning of life, but Ms. E is angry at God because God asks too much and has not responded to her prayers for relief.

It is not that questions of the meaning of life cannot be discussed in therapy. The questions are legitimate; the answers are not particularly within the expertise of the therapist, although this is a much more complicated issue than can be delved into at this point. More to the point, to tell a patient what to think about the meaning of life or how the therapist resolves her questions about the meaning of life is to ignore the process of psychotherapy while being caught up in the content. It is also to reinforce the patient's dependency upon the therapist, who pretends to have discovered the answers to life's existential dilemmas.

The patient wishes that the therapist would gratify her dependency needs. The patient wishes to be taken care of and comforted. This is an issue for therapy; it needs to be worked on as does any other strong theme in the patient's life. The demand or request, whether conveyed directly or by way of either anger or helplessness, need not—indeed can not and ought not—be satisfied. Let us consider the problem as if it were stated in a paradigmatic form: "I cannot get better unless I know that you care for me!" This unverbalized statement is operative within all requests Ms. E makes. In addition to the content of a request (Can I change my appointment time? Will you give me an extra 10 or 15 minutes? May I telephone you? Where are you going on vacation?), the patient is going to interpret the therapist's response as an indication of whether the therapist cares. In most cases, therapists perceive the hidden agenda of "Do you care for me?" that is carried along with the request, and moderate their answers according to what they judge are the important therapeutic issues present at that particular time, taking into account the long-term goals of therapy.

The problem arises when therapists, even if aware that some testing is going on, nevertheless feel obliged or justified, whether from theoretical stance or personality, to convey to the patient, perhaps even to convince the patient, that they really do care. Theoretical justification for gratification of dependency needs is supported by the psychodynamic "deficit model" of borderline etiology, which assumes that the patient is unable to maintain an internal holding-soothing environment (Adler, 1985), or by a Rogerian notion of maintaining positive regard for the patient. But these considerations are misapplied to such situations with PTSD/borderlines. Of course the therapist should be a caring person—if we could agree on what a caring person is and how a caring person behaves. But that is not the issue. The issue is a technical therapeutic one that arises when therapists think that they need to provide a special assurance or demonstration to the patient that they care.

This is an example of a countertransference problem in which the therapist needs the presence of a patient to confirm that he/she (the therapist) is a caring person. A central feature of most therapists' self-concept includes the notion of oneself as a caring person. This respectable aspect of the therapist's personality usually is affirmed by the very fact of being a therapist. But the PTSD/borderline patient forces the issue by calling into question whether the therapist really cares and, in essence, whether the therapist is a caring person at all. In such a situation, there is a likelihood that therapists' responses will be determined as much by their needs to reaffirm to themselves that they are indeed caring persons as by what is therapeutically called for at the moment. Furthermore, future therapeutic disasters are set up when the therapist agrees with patients (by responding to their distress in a protective manner) that, in fact, they cannot get better unless they know that the therapist cares. Trying to prove to the patient that the therapist cares leads to many untherapeutic interventions as well as many missed opportunities to invite the patient to examine how his dependency needs affect his interactions with others and to question how he perceives himself.

CASE 4

Ms. F tells her therapist that he lied to her about the dates of his vacation. She had called the answering service asking for the therapist at a time when he had told her that he would still be away, and was told by the operator that he was back in town. The patient, in session, went on to tell the therapist that he was one of the very few persons in her life upon whom she could rely and that, if she could not trust him in terms of when he will and will not be available, she will have to discontinue her therapy with him. She was partially correct in her understanding about the therapist's vacation schedule, and he felt badly about this seeming deception. The therapist tried to clarify how they had managed to miscommunicate, but it was complicated and he did not wish to go into great detail. Even as he was explaining, he was uneasy about what he was doing, suspecting that his explanation was excessive and, therefore, technically in error. He had rushed in to reassure Ms. F of his essential trustworthiness, both at present and in the future.

The accusation and explanation of dependability did not become a major focus in the session and patient and therapist proceeded to other issues. But this is precisely the point I am trying to express. Even in relatively minor ways, it is a mistake to respond to the content rather than the process of the patient's grievances about whether the therapist cares. The opportunity to examine some of Ms. F's basic assumptions about herself, the therapist, and the therapeutic relationship was missed. The therapist had responded as if what Ms. F said were true, that her trust in his reliability (to be there when he says he will be here) and stability are two of the few things that sustain her through hard times. Perhaps this is even subjectively true for her. The important therapeutic question, then, at this point in therapy is why, if it is true, would she be willing to jettison this relationship so quickly, why she would be so unforgiving of the therapist. It is possible that it relates to a pattern in her life of idealization/devaluation; it is possible that her reaction is justified from her point of view by traumas and disappointments that have happened earlier in her life. The therapeutic issue is that, so long as the therapist rushes in to reassure Ms. F that he cares, they will never discover the significant themes which are camouflaged by her hurt and hurtful response to him. Examining the nature of her attachment to the therapist, and the tension that develops as the ambivalent nature of her bond to the therapist is put to this relatively minor test, should take priority over reinforcing the attachment or making the relationship more comfortable for the two of them.

Although all patients legitimately wish to have a therapist who is concerned about them and who is committed to providing conscientious and thoughtful care, it is a classical PTSD/borderline issue to get more caught up with whether the therapist cares in a very special way than whether the therapist is conscientious and effective. The PTSD/borderline patient wishes to have a relationship with the therapist that is intense and special and personal. For example, consider the use of medication with psychiatric patients. When medication is prescribed for a depressed patient, the medication either works or not. If not, the patient reports this fact to the therapist and the patient is given a trial of another medication. The patient and therapist do not get caught up in whether the therapist cares for the patient or not. This difference points to a core quality of the PTSD/borderline patient, of what it means to be a borderline, and in what ways borderline patients differ from depressed patients who are not borderline. The difference between the depressed and PTSD/borderline patient is that the issues that the borderline has about being lovable or not, cared for or not, rescued or abandoned, become primary and get played out in therapy. The depressed patient merely wants to get over the depression.

There are times when therapists' needs to demonstrate that they care lead into more obviously problematic and nontherapeutic maneuvers.

CASE 5

Ms. G is a 29-year-old single mother on public assistance who has been in psychotherapy for about one year. She is troubled by loneliness, low self-esteem, unclear memories of possible sexual abuse in her childhood, and troublesome relationships with men since adolescence. Often she is belittled and verbally abused in these relationships. She often feels that she has been sexually exploited, although she initiates much of the social contact that leads to sexual activity. At times she wishes just for the company of a date and resents that it becomes sexual; at other times she acts upon her own sexual fantasies. In therapy, she and the therapist have settled into a pattern in which she tells him how badly she feels, and he tells her that she really is a worthwhile person. The therapist often gives Ms. G a hug at the end of the session in order to show her that she is acceptable and lovable, and that she ought not to demean herself. Ms. G protests that she does not deserve hugs, but allows the therapist to prevail.

Ms. G is preoccupied intermittently with hurting herself and with thoughts of suicide. At times she calls the police to tell them she is suicidal, but when they arrive at her home she states that she is better and does not need to go to the emergency room. During one therapy session, she appears particularly distraught and mentions plans to kill herself during the weekend. The therapist, caught in a quandary about whether to insist upon hospitalization in the face of the Ms. G's refusal to enter the hospital voluntarily, proposes that, if she will call him on the telephone during the weekend, he will not insist upon hospitalization. Ms. G reminds the therapist that she lives out of town and cannot afford the telephone tolls. The therapist gives her his telephone credit card. Ms. G uses the card to call the therapist several times daily during the weekend, and then several times nightly during the next week. They often have long conversations in which he tries to talk her out of being so suicidal.

The number of evening and weekend phone calls increases until the therapist tells Ms. G that she is calling too frequently and that she will have to return the credit card. To her credit, Ms. G has not used the card to make other toll calls. Ms. G protests strongly that the therapist does not care about her, that all his fine words about never abandoning her were lies, that he, like everyone else, finds her loathsome and undeserving. Now she really might as well kill herself. The therapist remains firm about limiting the telephone calls to several short calls per week, but tries to make up for it with increased statements about how he really does cares for her and with increased frequency and closeness of hugs.

Ms. G states that she wishes to discontinue therapy. She expresses regret that she has allowed herself to become dependent upon the therapist; she should have known it would only result in another betrayal of her trust. She decides to contact a rehabilitation agency to look for work. The agency contacts the therapist, who states that he thinks the patient is too sick to withstand the pressures of work, and that she needs more therapy. He mentions that previous attempts at employment have led to suicidal behaviors. The agency refuses to work with Ms. G to find employment without the therapist's approval, and Ms. G, angry with her therapist yet pleased with what she perceives as his demonstration of attachment to her, agrees to continue therapy. The suicidal fervor diminishes somewhat, as therapy returns to a "Do you care for me?/Yes, I care for you" mode.

Several months later, there is another crisis when Ms. G confesses that she has many sexual fantasies about the therapist, and he states that these are unacceptable. He suggests that the frequency of therapy sessions be decreased to every other week. Ms. G becomes upset and threatens suicide.

When the therapist moves to give her a hug, she hits the therapist and knocks a lamp over. She runs out of the office, but calls later that day, only to hear her therapist tell her that he can no longer work with her in therapy. At the end of the next day, the therapist arrives home to find Ms. G, in her car, blocking his driveway. She wants to convince the therapist not to discontinue therapy with her; she cannot be persuaded to move her car. The therapist drives to his neighbor's house and calls the police. By the time they arrive, Ms. G has left. That evening, she telephones the therapist several times, asking him to reconsider his decision to terminate treatment with her. The therapist holds firm and states his intention to file charges against her. Ms. G overdoses, calls the police, and is hospitalized. Two months later, she initiates a lawsuit against the therapist, claiming sexual abuse, failure to treat properly, and abandonment.

What has happened here? The therapist is a well-intentioned and caring therapist; the patient has entered therapy asking for relief of her bad feelings about herself. Yet therapy ends up a disaster, hurtful to patient and therapist.

The therapist has incorrectly assumed that he and the patient had congruent goals. The therapist assumed that the patient was in therapy to gain understanding of herself so that she could begin to act differently in the outside world. The patient, however, was in therapy to get her needs met, and the therapist inadvertently gave her ample reason to believe that this would occur. He responded to her distress by thinking that he could provide sufficient nurturance for her so that she would feel better about herself and could then go out to face a hostile or indifferent universe. He also thought that the professional surroundings would provide the warranty of respectability such that he could exchange hugs with Ms. G in an unambiguous enough manner that she would not develop amorous expectations. He believed that she would understand that his interest in her was as a fellow human in pain, not as a sexual object for his gratification.

Ms. G interacted with the therapist as she had with other men in her life. She tried hard to please him and to be a good patient. She conveyed her great despair to him and, although always expecting rejection, was pleased and surprised to see that he responded to her with warmth and caring. She was not clear as to whether he had sexual intentions toward her, since this was how most other men related to her. She was willing to see it through, as long as the therapist was willing to continue to be caring and supportive. As the therapist began to back off, the patient became more and more hurt, angry, and desperate. She felt he was accusing her of feelings that he had encouraged her to have.

Two technical mistakes indicated that therapy was going awry and heralded the denouement. The first was the substitution of hugs in place of the hard work of therapy. It truly is sad that the patient feels the way she does about herself, and that these feelings and negative self-concept appear to be the result of years of adverse experiences and exploitation by others. The role of therapy is to have the patient examine how the past has made her what she is and how she herself has developed certain maladaptive patterns of thinking about herself and interacting with others, especially men, in response to problematic life experiences. In the course of therapy, the patient will, of course, repeat with the therapist some of these maladaptive patterns. It is the therapist's task to make the patient aware of the style in which she seeks help, not to participate in the maladaptive interactions or to think that his hugs and caring, however genuine, will undo all that has happened to her.

The telephone credit card bespeaks of the same difficulties. This is not something the therapist had ever done previously and, undoubtedly, if a colleague were to consult with him on a similar issue, he would advise against such an action. Nevertheless, his action indicates that he lost perspective. He thought that he was legitimately demonstrating care and helping the patient avoid hospitalization or a suicide attempt. While, to the patient's credit, she did not abuse the credit card by running up a large long-distance phone bill, she did escalate the time and emotional demands upon the therapist. Eventually, the therapist concluded that he had to try to set limits, and when he did, the patient reacted to the limits as abandonment.

The question of suicide threats has to be discussed briefly here; it will return when we discuss rescue attempts and reworking old issues. Therapists have taken on, in our society, the responsibility for predicting the future and, peculiarly and contradictorily enough, changing it. How therapists have allowed themselves to be delegated with this task or have, in fact, convinced society that they are the ones who could do it is an interesting piece of social history that deserves more attention than it has received. It is clear that therapists are not particularly good at predicting the future, but, having agreed that they could, they now find themselves in the strange position of taking responsibility (or being made responsible) for the actions of persons whom they only see for one hour a week. There are 168 hours in a week; how anyone who sees a person for one hour can predict what that person will do during the other 167 hours of the week has always been a mystery to me. Prediction is difficult enough when the person whose actions we are trying to predict is giving it to us straight, that is, telling us what he/she really thinks and feels. But in the case of patients with personality disorders who have been exploited in the past and who are in a tangled transference relationship with their therapist, the task of prediction is impossible. There are too many other reasons for telling a therapist (or the police or a minister) that one is suicidal that have very little to do with wanting to die. With PTSD/borderline patients, the list of "other reasons" is a long one, but essentially can be subsumed under the two categories that we are examining: gratification of needs and reworking old issues.

Many borderline patients have learned that talking about suicide has powerful effects. Therapists, not wanting their patient to die and fearful of malpractice litigation, have tended to respond dramatically and excessively to threats of suicide. I am not trying to be casual about the topic of a patient's suicide. Suicide is always a possibility in patients whose very entrance into therapy is characterized by self-destructive urges and actions. The problem is to differentiate, as best as possible, those situations in which a suicide attempt of high lethality is likely and those situations in which talk of suicide is used to accomplish other personal and interpersonal purposes. There are well-known risk factors that one can put into the prediction equation, but even the presence of these risk factors does not allow accurate prediction to the individual. For example, in a detailed study of 1,906 patients hospitalized with affective disorders, a statistical model based upon identified risk factors failed to identify any of the 46 patients who committed suicide (Goldstein et al., 1991). Most persons who meet the high-risk characteristics do not go on to suicide (Blumenthal & Kupfer, 1990; Roy, 1986). The recognition must always be present that, in events of low probability, prediction is hazardous or impossible. Even the supposedly strongest risk factor, a history of serious suicide attempts, is not helpful in prediction of the individual situation because more than half of the deaths by suicide occur in persons who never made previous attempts. As discussed in Chapter 1, borderline patients with histories of self-mutilation (without accompanying major depression or alcohol dependence) are at very low risk of suicide (Fyer et al., 1988; Kreitman & Dyer, 1980; Kullgren, 1988; Paris, Nowlis, & Brown, 1989; Shearer et al., 1988; Stone, 1990).

In the particular case under discussion, the patient had a long history of suicide threats, with no history of serious attempts. This is no guarantee, of course; suicide is always an option, and suicide "gestures" can be lethal due to misinformation about drug toxicity, failure of the rescue party to arrive on time, other miscalculations, as well as increased seriousness of intent compared to previous attempts. The therapist has to accept the reality that he/she is far from infallible. Nevertheless, to continue to respond to the borderline patient's suicide talk as if it constituted an imminent threat is to encourage such threats, as well as to undermine all therapeutic efforts.

Suicide talk in this case had become the medium of exchange whereby the patient could convey her emotional needs in a therapeutically standardized manner, rather than stating the unacceptable: that she wished to have prolonged and meaningful telephone conversations with her concerned therapist six times during one weekend. In essence, if it takes a suicide threat or attempt to get the therapist to show that he cares for her, then some PTSD/borderline patients are prepared to follow through with this action, or at least to drop many hints and make many threats that they will kill themselves. When therapists permit themselves to get caught up in the content of suicide and suicide prevention and rescue ventures, effective psychotherapy temporarily ceases.

In the case just described, Ms. G is an adult, living in the community, and taking care of herself and her child. When she expressed thoughts of suicide, the therapist responsibly asked her whether she thought she needed to be hospitalized briefly in order to protect herself from her own impulses. Since the patient declined, therapy should have proceeded with an examination of what was transpiring in the patient's life, and in the therapy situation, such that the therapist felt compelled to take upon himself responsibilities that belong to the patient, namely, the prevention of her own suicide.

There are many times when the issues are not clear, when the ambiguities and complexities of the situation make it impossible to know what the patient intends at the moment or will intend the next hour or day. These are not easy moments for a therapist, but the foundation of therapy is that the therapist agrees to work with patients to help them make changes in their lives, not to be the provider of their emotional needs or to act as rescuer or the guarantor of their safety. The therapist simply cannot play these roles, and to try to do so is to court therapeutic disaster.

CASE 6

Ms. L is a 48-year-old unmarried woman, unemployed and living alone, participating in volunteer office work for a few hours per week, who has been followed at a community clinic for the past eight years. During this entire time, she has been seen twice weekly for an hour and a half each session by the consulting psychologist. This is the only psychologist for an agency that serves a fairly large suburban community. For the past three years, she has also been seen weekly by a vocational rehabilitation counselor in order to talk about her volunteer work and prepare her for an expansion of work hours and responsibilities. She also meets with her county case manager once every two weeks. She spends about 10 to 15 hours during evenings and weekends on the telephone crisis and suicide line. The treatment philosophy of the suicide and crisis program has been that a crisis worker is not to terminate a telephone conversation with a suicidal patient until the patient is able to contract verbally or give some equivalent assurance that he/she is no longer imminently suicidal. In Ms. L's case, this usually takes about 45 minutes to an hour. If Ms. L calls on a night when a crisis counselor whom she does not like is on call, she will hang up and wait until the following day to call.

The psychologist is aware that not much therapeutic work is being done in therapy. He feels morally compelled to maintain three hours of "therapy" per week, however, because he is convinced that Ms. L will kill herself, as she has threatened to do, if he decreases her contact hours.

Despite all these threats, Ms. L has never made any suicide attempts beyond minimal aspirin overdoses. The suicide crisis team is at their wit's end, but cannot get administrative backing to start limiting Ms. L's crisis calls.

What has happened here is that everybody's therapeutic roles have become severely compromised. Instead of reevaluating an obviously wasteful and unproductive treatment approach, the team, split among themselves, has become locked into a rigid pattern of providing strong reinforcement to a patient's manipulative style of interacting with her caregivers. Whatever else the individual and organizational dynamics might have been that created and perpetuated this situation, there has clearly been an inability to discriminate between serious risk of suicide and the use of suicidal threats as a means of solving problems of loneliness and meaning in life.

The discussion of the therapist's responses to suicide talk points out the overlap between gratification of dependency needs and gratification of rescue fantasies. The two issues are related although not identical.

GRATIFICATION OF RESCUE FANTASIES

CASE 7

Ms. H, a 32-year-old divorced assistant librarian, arrived at her therapy session dressed in a floral sundress cut quite low, with a thin strip of black lace outlining the top of the dress. There were obvious scratch marks extending up from the cleavage of her bosom.

Although she initially appeared to be in a good mood, Ms. H proceeded to narrate a succession of frustrating episodes and interpersonal failures. She had been feeling increasingly isolated and desperate about her inability to convey this to others and receive some needed caring responses. For the past month she had been letting a young man live in her apartment. He slept in the living room, provided some companionship, but was often caught up in his own affairs. There was no sexual involvement between the two.

Ms. H was feeling particularly lonely one Saturday night and conveyed enough of this mood to her roommate so that he suggested that they drive to the park and take a walk around the lagoon. They returned to the apartment around 11 p.m. Ms. H was still feeling very upset and went into her bedroom with several kitchen knives. She tried to scratch her wrists and chest with a knife, but it was too dull. She went out to the kitchen and took an electric knife sharpener back into the bedroom with her. She did not plan to kill herself, but rather wished to interrupt the self-conscious stream of criticisms with which she was tormenting herself. Staring at her hand and wrist, she began to feel that she was going crazy. After cutting her wrist and chest superficially, she felt as if she could not voluntarily move her body. Her hands were trembling and her head was shaking, and as she watched blood drip down her arm, she could not speak or move. Her roommate, finally becoming aware that something was transpiring, opened her bedroom door and walked in. Ms. H was still frozen in her position, unable to respond to him. The roommate shook Ms. H, held her, tried to get her to respond, and finally asked if she wanted him to call an ambulance. With great effort, she shook her head "no" and with this was able to begin moving and speaking again.

After settling down somewhat, Ms. H, ignored again by her roommate, left the apartment and drove to the house of a young minister from a religious sect who had been trying to convert her. It was by now after midnight. He came out and spoke with her for a while. Her wrist and hand were still bloody, but it was dark and he did not notice, nor did she tell him, what she had done. She felt he would condemn her for doing such a thing. The conversation was unsatisfactory and she left, driving around for a while and deciding if she should park in an empty garage somewhere, leave the engine running, and thus kill herself. She finally decided to go home and went to sleep. The next day there was a church picnic which she had planned to attend. Instead, however, she stayed in bed all day, feeling hateful about herself and convinced that the picnic would only be one more social disaster in which she would be rejected by men and end up feeling even worse about herself.

The therapist's response to hearing this story was initially empathic and supportive of how desperate she seemed to feel about herself. He briefly commented that her sense of neediness was legitimate and not something for which she had to condemn herself. He inquired about her inability to convey her sense of emptiness more directly either to her roommate or to the sect minister, noting that she knew the minister could not see her bloody wrist in the dark, and commenting on her wish that he would nevertheless divine how desperate she felt.

The therapist also commented on her low-cut dress, wondering if she was checking out whether he would notice the scratches, just as she had tested the minister to see if he would notice her bloody wrist. Ms. H acknowledged that she was aware, in selecting this dress, that a discerning observer might notice the scratches, but also protested that, after all, it was almost 90 degrees outside. The therapist agreed with her weather report, but commented again on her indirect, or nonverbal, manner of conveying her distress to him. Why should she have to demonstrate the scratches, he inquired, since she had already told him in words that she had scratched her wrists and chest? But, of course, at the time she selected the dress to wear to the session, she was not sure she would tell her therapist about the chest scratches. The low-cut dress permitted her to demonstrate how badly she had felt at the time she cut herself, as well as to check out if the therapist noticed the scratches, had she instead chosen not to tell him about them.

The therapist did not comment on the possible provocativeness of the location of the scratches in terms of seeing if he would notice them. The theme of hurting herself in order to get others to take care of her seemed more important at the moment than whatever sexual significance there might also be to the sun dress. He accepted the likelihood that the scratches were made initially to convey something to her male roommate, and only secondarily, when the opportunity arose, were displayed to him. Her style had been to exhibit her wounds, whether emotional or physical, to see if the other person cared enough about her to notice and respond.

Ms. H then reflected on her shame at her self-mutilative behavior and her sense that the therapist would disapprove and give her a lecture, just as she feared the minister would do, rather than respond compassionately as she hoped. She let the therapist know that she was still thinking about suicide. The therapist did not inquire into whether she had a specific plan for suicide, but commented on how she was giving him the same opportunity to rescue her that she had given to the other two men who had been so involved in themselves that they had failed her miserably. She acknowledged that she wanted the therapist to say something that would make her feel better and that would give her a reason to go on living, but denied that she wanted to be rescued.

The therapist raised the issue, since the end of the session was nearing, of whether she had to wait until she felt better before she could be with people or whether being more sociable and productive was a way of getting to feel better about herself. He repeated an earlier statement that it is hard to feel good about oneself when one is isolated and unproductive, and that feeling better about herself would follow rather than precede a sense of achievement and worthwhileness. In making these comments, the therapist semi-acquiesced to her demands that he leave her with something positive at the end of the hour. It was, of course, not quite what she wanted. It did put back upon her the task of digging herself out of her morass and could even be taken by her as implicit criticism, in the sense that he was saying that she knew what she had to do to begin to feel better and that, if she did not do it, the burden fell upon her, not him. In his decision to make these brief comments, the therapist was shifting from commenting upon the process whereby she demanded that he recognize her distress and take responsibility for her emotional state of mind to commenting upon the content of her request. He was telling her how to feel better, namely, that if she did something she feels good about, she would begin to feel good about herself.

Should the therapist have stayed purely in process to the bitter end, by insisting that the issue, from a therapeutic point of view, in this session and all other sessions, was not to squeeze some hopeful words out of him, but to examine the pattern whereby such demands permeate and ruin many of her interactions? I am not sure. I suspect that his response about "good works" both expressed his annoyance at her recalcitrance and provided a token of what she wanted. The session ended as a stalemate. The therapist did not offer a rescue plan and Ms. H did not relinquish her discourse on suicide, but neither did she accelerate the threats.

In this particular case, rescue fantasies are operative in and outside of therapy. The patient spends a fair amount of time and energy in conveying, especially to men, through words and deeds, her great distress and her preoccupation with suicide. She meets with intermittent success, in that, occasionally, a man will drop whatever else he is doing and spend several hours talking with her. She is not interested in a sexual relationship at these times and will reject one if offered. In general, she has not been able to develop sufficient signals of charming female helplessness that rescuing types find irresistible. Perhaps the absence of sexual cues accounts for this. What happens, instead, is an upward spiral of conveyed desperation that only succeeds in pushing away the targeted rescuer. There are times when Ms. H is aware of this pattern and can monitor her behavior to refrain from telling a new acquaintance within 10 minutes that she is suicidal in a manner that practically demands expressions of support and concern, but she finds it difficult to sustain a neutral or positive dialogue more than briefly. Therapy often repeats such interactions, with a tug-of-war developing between Ms. H and her therapist. His insistence that they process those behaviors that are designed to elicit rescue attempts seems to prevent therapy from contributing to her problems and keeps the therapist from making the more obvious types of therapeutic blunders with ill-designed rescue responses, but it has not changed her style of interacting with men very much.

The next case is another example in which rescue themes play an important role in the patient's mental life, real-life behaviors, and therapeutic interactions. The behaviors involve greater risk-taking and vulnerability to the violence of others. Unlike Ms. H, this patient has been the victim of a more violent form of childhood abuse, which might account for the differences in fantasies and acting-out behaviors.

CASE 8

Ms. J is a 26-year-old single woman, part-time student, part-time health care worker, who has a history of horrendous physical and sexual abuse by her mother during the early to mid childhood years. One day, at the end of a women's group therapy session, Ms. J announces that she is going to walk the 12 blocks to the major crosstown avenue. It is late evening, dark, and the neighborhood that Ms. J must traverse is not a safe place for a woman to walk alone. Several members of the group offer her a ride, but she refuses. One of the two women group therapists, who is also Ms. J's individual therapist, gets a little angry and confronts Ms. J about her intentional risk-taking behavior. Ms. J remains implacable and insists upon walking. In fact, nothing happens on the walk and she arrives safely at her destination.

This interaction, occurring at the end of group, was processed with her therapist at their next individual therapy session. Ms. J acknowledged that she was, of course, very aware of the risks involved in walking at night through that particular neighborhood. In fact, she was driven, if one may call it that, by a fairly specific fantasy in which she would be assaulted and, most likely, raped during the walk. The police would be called and she would be taken to the emergency room of the county hospital. There, according to the imagery as it is played out in her mind, she would sit huddled in the corner of an examining room, knees up to her chest, face in her hands, mute. The only words she would give out would be the name of her therapist. The nurse would call the therapist, who would come down to the emergency room. The therapist would hold Ms. J and cradle her in her arms. Only then would Ms. J allow herself to cry and to speak; only then would she tell what had happened to her. She would be comforted by the therapist, as she had been by her mother after her mother sexually abused her. In the present fantasy, unlike the childhood reality, the persons of the abuser-rapist and comforter are split into two separate individuals.

Ms. J narrated this story with considerable embarrassment. What she acknowledged to her therapist was that she spent a great deal of time with her rescue fantasies and that at different times they were more or less operative in her real life. Sometimes they would just remain fantasies; at other times she would try to bring them about by placing herself in risky situations. She realized that this was "stupid," to use her own words; nevertheless, the preoccupation with themes of rescue by her therapist (or others at different times) following sexual violation was so powerful that it threatened to take over much of her waking thought. Ms. J also realized that she often played out the assault-rescue theme in minor ways within the therapy hour. She found herself speaking and acting in ways designed to get her therapist angry at her. Only when the therapist became angry at Ms. J for risk-taking behaviors or became involved in a rescue operation did Ms. J feel that the therapist really cared.

Ms. J was aware of the potential, if she pushed the therapist too far in therapy sessions, for the therapist's expressions of concern to turn into anger and back again into concern. In fact, this very ambiguity allowed for a tension of anticipation, since she was never sure that the therapist would respond in a caring rather than a destructive manner, despite all the evidence testifying to her therapist's warmth and positive regard for her. She always envisioned the next time, when her therapist might lose her composure and her "pretense" of caring, and repeat the nightmare of mother's assaults upon her in childhood.

Passive silence characterized many of Ms. J's therapy sessions. She related, with some chagrin, that sometimes she maintained silence to test the therapist's commitment to her. There were other reasons for Ms. J's passivity in therapy. Her childhood experience was one of never knowing when she would be assaulted by mother. If she walked through a room and spoke to mother, she would be beaten for interrupting mother. If she walked through a room quietly, she would be beaten for rudeness in ignoring mother. Often the beatings, justified according to mother by Ms. J's "bad" behavior, would evolve into brutal sexual attacks. If she screamed or even cried when she was beaten or sexually assaulted, she would get it worse. If she did not cry, the abuse might go on until she cried. She never knew which behavior would provoke which reaction. Ms. J thinks that one of the results of these experiences has been a retreat into paralysis. Since any actions or verbalizations might lead to assaults, the best course was inactivity and silence. These, too, could and did lead to beatings, but passivity seemed less dangerous.

At times, the beatings would be followed by special closeness and soothings. Such childhood experiences were played out in therapy as wishes for comfort freely given without being linked to sexual abuse, alternating with fantasies of the full spectrum of reenacted childhood violence in which the therapist must beat and sexually abuse Ms. J as the necessary prelude to comforting. Even if the rape were done by a person other than the therapist, it would be worth it if only the therapist would comfort Ms. J. The themes showed up over and over again, but appeared to be giving ground slowly as the therapist remained steadfast in her positive and warm concern for Ms. J, without losing perspective on the importance of maintaining clear boundaries.

For therapy to move beyond the benefit, considerable as it is, of the corrective emotional experience achieved by a relationship to a therapist who responds positively and without the expected anger or assault, however, the mode of therapy has to begin to shift from content to process. In this particular case, patient and therapist need to talk about the intrusion of the abuse-and-rescue fantasies into the ongoing interaction of therapy itself. As the patient develops the

capacity to replace acting out to achieve gratification from the therapist with discussion in therapy of her fantasies, in which the therapist
participates in the pattern of abuse and reparation, the power of the
fantasy is weakened. The patient can no longer present a semblance
of cooperation while secretly pursing other goals. To name the process is to weaken its power. This is not to suggest that the fantasy
(in this case, of being beaten and then rescued, or of just being
rescued) is so readily abandoned; rather, once named and exposed,
it cannot be translated into action in the therapy as easily, and it can
be scrutinized each time it appears in one of its many disguises.

Gratification of Sexual Desires (Fantasies)

Although I have presented the case of Ms. J under the heading of
gratification of rescue fantasies, it is apparent that rescue themes
overlap both with the pursuit of gratification of several other needs
and with the replaying in therapy of old issues, namely victimization,
passivity, and comforting. These categories are artificially dissected
here for the sake of orderly discussion; in reality, however, they are
intertwined. The drive for gratification of neurotic needs almost of
necessity involves repetition of some hurtful pattern from the patient's life. The following case continues the discussion of divergent
goals in therapy between patient and therapist. The patient's goal in
this particular situation was to have a sexual relationship with the
therapist. While the therapist was not entirely innocent of encouraging the patient's sexual fantasies, the events that occurred seemed to
be more the result of the therapist's naiveté and failure to process
the direction of events in therapy than any malevolent design.

CASE 9

Ms. K is a 33-year-old divorced woman who entered into therapy with a
woman therapist five years ago in order to get a grip on her chaotic life-
style. A previous course of therapy in her early twenties, with a male therapist, had ended in a sexual relationship with him. Although Ms. K had not
reported him, several other women had, resulting in prosecution of that
therapist, who subsequently left the area.

Upon entering this current course of therapy, Ms. K reported anxiety
symptoms, sleep problems, occasional alcohol abuse, moodiness, unsatisfactory relationships with men, and frequent self-mutilative behaviors (cut-

ting of arms and legs). Attempts to treat these problems with a variety of antidepressant and antianxiety medications had not been successful, possibly because of limited compliance on the part of Ms. K, who would periodically overdose with some of the medications and wind up in the emergency room.

Ms. K had been having an affair for several years with a married man who is alcoholic. This relationship was characterized by a fair amount of verbal abuse, occasional physical assaults when the man was intoxicated, and two incidents of forced sex. She spoke in therapy of breaking off the relationship, but had not. She continued to hurt herself, often in response to arguments or insults from her boyfriend or other men. She had dated several other men during the past few years, but these encounters, too, ended up in unsatisfactory sexual liaisons. She had answered ads in newspapers as a way of meeting men, and reported that she had gone to bed with three men in one day upon occasion.

After several years of therapy, a time during which there was little if any improvement, Ms. K suggested to her female therapist that perhaps she should switch to a male therapist, since her major difficulties seemed to be in her relationships with men. She suggested a particular male counselor at the agency, whom she had seen briefly for marital counseling ten years earlier, prior to her divorce. This proposal was discussed with the agency staff, including the prospective male therapist. All agreed, in light of the lack of progress of therapy to that point, that a transfer of therapists seemed reasonable. Ms. K began therapy on a weekly basis with her new counselor.

The new therapist soon noted that Ms. K had a very poor opinion of herself. She blamed herself for staying in a relationship with an alcoholic man who abused her and called her derogatory names. She felt unloved and unlovable. She described overwhelming urges to cut herself in response to these negative feelings about herself. She reported an incident of rape following a party when she was 16 years old. She blamed herself for this. She made vague reference to the possibility of sexual abuse as a child, but was unable to shed more light on this.

The therapist began to work on self-esteem issues, reassuring Ms. K that the rape occurring in her teen years was not her fault. Therapy focused on Ms. K's attempts to break off the relationship with her abusive and alcoholic boyfriend. The therapist encouraged her to do this, and became upset when Ms. K reported another incident of physical abuse, in which Ms. K could have called the police, since the boyfriend passed out, but chose not to do so. Ms. K wept in anger and humiliation and the therapist gave her a hug to console her. Ms. K felt better and was able to have a better weekend. Therapy went on, with brief periods of seeming progress, as judged by decreased self-injurious behaviors and improved moods, alternating with setbacks in which Ms. K cut herself and sought out her abusive boyfriend.

After three years of therapy with the present therapist, Ms. K is essentially unchanged in terms of self-injurious behaviors, emotional lability, involvement in a series of apparently unsatisfactory love affairs, and marginal employment. Somewhere along the course of therapy, Ms. K has become sexually attracted to her counselor or, rather, more attracted, since she later acknowledges that her sexual interest in the counselor motivated her to ask for a transfer to him as a therapist in the first place. She is preoccupied with thoughts of a sexual liaison with the therapist and, undetected by him, often smokes marijuana prior to her therapy sessions. She wonders whether he is attracted to her and is not sure if the hugs, now occurring at the end of most sessions, are innocent or evidence of his sexual interest in her.

Quite rapidly, Ms. K's life takes a turn for the worse. She is accused of seducing and having sexual relationships several times with a 16-year-old boy whom she met when she was working part-time as a library aide. The police, in the course of their investigation, obtain a search warrant for Ms. K's home and discover many pornographic magazines, a few pieces of sexual apparatus, and a diary in which she has written about a sexual affair with her counselor, describing how she would arrive at therapy without underclothes and the therapist would masturbate her with his hand while hugging her and she would do the same for him. The therapist is charged with these offenses and, despite his vehement denial, is fired by the agency.

Soon after the initial sexual allegations against the therapist are made, Ms. K withdraws them, stating that they refer to the therapist of 10 years earlier and have been made up in anger over the present therapist's refusal to become sexual with her. Two weeks later, she rescinds this statement, contending that the therapist had, in fact, committed the sexual acts as described initially. Criminal and civil trials ensue.

The therapist contends that, while, in retrospect, he may have been incorrect in giving hugs to Ms. K, absolutely nothing more ever occurred. He saw Ms. K in an office right off the lobby of the agency building; the office door did not have a lock and the shades were never drawn. He contends that Ms. K must be reporting the seduction that occurred with the therapist ten years ago, and is now using the accusation against him as a way of deflecting attention from her own wrongdoing with a juvenile.

The therapist acknowledges that Ms. K had made a few sexual overtures to him during the third year of therapy, but that he indicated to her that a sexual relationship was out of the question. He thought that Ms. K had been sufficiently convinced of this to give up further attempts and that he had dealt with the attempted seduction therapeutically by not reinforcing it. He did not chart these behaviors because the agency was in a small town and he did not think that confidentiality of sensitive chart material was possible. For the same reasons, he destroyed several letters that Ms. K had sent him proposing amorous ventures. In essence, he had acted to protect Ms. K in a manner similar to the way in which Ms. K and other abused patients characteristically act to protect the males who assault them, namely, by not documenting or reporting the incidents.

The possibility of false accusations of sexual misconduct with a patient is one that every therapist faces. We work with patients on a one-to-one basis behind closed doors. Sexual intimacies are often an important part of the content of discussion and can easily lead to emotional arousal on the part of the therapist and patient. Feelings of closeness and protectiveness can develop as the therapist hears of and relates to the traumas and harsh experiences of the patient's life. Even in those cases in which the therapist's conduct has been exemplary, there is still the possibility of false accusations. Such accusations are probably rare and, although one may always wonder if some subtle exchanges have gone on to encourage sexual fantasies in those cases when a false accusation is made, the fact remains that therapists, by the very nature of the work, are vulnerable to such charges even in the complete absence of provocations.

We ordinarily assume, correctly or incorrectly, that many, perhaps most, accusations of sexual exploitation of a patient by a therapist are accurate. Although, in general, credibility is usually given to the patient, this still leaves us with the problem of the occasional false accusation. In the face of a therapist's denial that sexual exploitation occurred, and in the absence of corroborating evidence from other patients or the judgment of peers, there is no absolute way to determine the truth of the matter.

In reality, whether a seduction happened or not is not the issue for the present discussion. At the moment of accusation, there can be no exoneration. The therapist cannot prove innocence; even winning his litigation can be taken to show only that the patient cannot prove guilt. The very fact that the patient was angry enough to want to retaliate and hurt the therapist is indicative of the therapist's failure to understand and track the therapeutic process as it was unraveling. We can only surmise what it was that might have occurred to lead to such a dramatic and damaging accusation and such a failed outcome to therapy. The therapist was caught up with some vague notion that, if only he provided enough affirmation and evidence of positive regard, Ms. K would be able to like herself and give up her self-destructive patterns. He misperceived the risks that expressions of affirmation and warm regard, extended by way of compliments and physical touching, would shade off in the patient's understanding into sexual invitation and seduction, setting up promises that can only lead to disaster whether fulfilled or denied. The patient was not provided with a framework within which to get her life under control or to make it sensible in terms of her previous life adversities.

What a nightmare for patient, therapist, and all others caught in the vortex of accusations and defenses. After ten years of therapy and three therapists, the patient is worse. There has been no progress either in therapy or in the patient's life toward stabilization or cessation of self-mutilative behavior. She has not gained any appreciable perspective on the nature of her pattern of unhealthy relationships with men. But if this were all that had happened with the last five years of therapy, we would acknowledge that therapy with Ms. K, as with many PTSD/borderline patients, was a failure. I do not say this indifferently or casually. Therapeutic failures are never a matter of indifference, but, nevertheless, they are not rare with PTSD/borderline patients. There are patients who do not get better in psychotherapy, and we have no reason to claim that, if only they had had different therapists, the outcome would have been more successful. But in this case, therapy was not just unsuccessful; it was damaging to all concerned.

Yet, in reviewing the events, other than the injudicious use of hugs presumably to solve therapeutic problems that would have been better off verbalized and ungratified, there were no gross mistakes, no single blunder that could be identified, no persistent insensitivity or exploitation of the emotions of the patient. The therapist was kind, warm, well-intentioned. He was respected by other patients and his peers; he appeared competent and serious in his work.

The failure in this case, for we must consider it as such, was in getting caught up in the content of the patient's problem, in what must have appeared to be an endless therapy. The patient would move from crisis to crisis, and the therapist would try to help the patient solve or manage her crises. Although Ms. K would often present herself as the victim of male predators, it was abundantly clear that she sought out these men, at least in part, as sexual partners. The therapeutic failure is that Ms. K remained, or was allowed to remain, in therapy at a clinic for eight years without ever acknowledging the extent of her own sexual preoccupations, including her ongoing fantasies of a sexual liaison with her second therapist.

The therapeutic problem, from this point of view, was not that Ms. K had problems with men; that was why, so the therapist thought, she sought out therapy. The problem was that Ms. K maintained a stance in therapy about herself and her goals in therapy that was patently untruthful. Her goal in therapy was not to change herself, but to maintain a myth about herself as victim by demonstrating that all men are exploiters, including the therapist, and also, by the way, enjoying the fantasy of a sexual liaison with him. This is fair. At some level, one cannot fault the patient for acting out her psychodynamics. That is why she is the patient.

I realize that it sounds as if I am either facetious or terribly cynical in stating, on the one hand, that it was fair for Ms. K to present herself dishonestly in therapy and, on the other hand, taking her to task for this and suggesting that there was no desire on her part to use therapy as a vehicle for change. A patient may want to get better, whatever this may mean to each person, in addition to staying in therapy to gratify her needs and replay old scenarios. We do not have to speak of patients' motives for being in therapy in terms of all or none. But, in this particular case, Ms. K's small degree of motivation to change was vastly overshadowed by her drive toward gratification of her sexual fantasies. She remained in therapy because of the amorous excitement that accompanied her actual and fantasied involvement with her therapist, plus whatever psychodynamic significance such involvement, and the intertwined theme of victimization, held. I say that this is "fair" of a patient to do because it is expected and understood that the very problems that bring a patient to therapy will show up in therapy, and must be worked on within therapy.

If a patient is dishonest to herself and others, she will be dishonest in therapy. The therapist knows this in a theoretical way; the therapeutic task is to apply it to the individual therapy in an ongoing manner. The therapist can usually count on at least some degree of cooperation and mutual agreement on methods and goals; in this case, on the other hand, there appears to have been little or none. The therapist's problem was that he did not appreciate the gravity of the situation. The solution would have been to challenge the patient again and again, in various ways, regarding her motivations and goals for herself in therapy.

Is it reasonable to expect a therapist to discern that he and the patient are working in different directions? Can we not all be fooled? The answers, of course, are "yes" to both questions. We ordinarily, somewhere along the course of therapy, ought to be able to discern that there are major problems in the course of therapy. Nevertheless, we can be fooled. Sometimes, the cost of being fooled is very costly to patient and therapist. While there is no single technique to prevent therapeutic disasters, paying more attention to process rather than content provides the best chances that therapy will include a series of righting responses when things go astray, somewhat similar to a gyroscope or the use of frequent compass readings when one is a little lost. In addition, peer or supervisory consultation when the course of therapy with long-term patients appears stuck or deteriorating is often helpful or even essential.

To cite just one particular problem in Ms. K's therapy, as often happens in therapy with PTSD/borderline patients, there is just no point in repeatedly telling a patient that she should terminate a hurtful relationship with a male predator or that she should call the police. There is not much gain in telling a patient (or anyone else) more than once or twice something she already knows. The important questions instead become: (1) What stops you from ending your relationship with this man and why do you not call the police? and (2) Why are you in therapy? The therapist may also ask himself at such a moment why he is persisting in telling the patient what to do when she obviously is not interested in doing it.

I am not necessarily against informing a patient about safe houses and women's shelters and 911 emergency telephone numbers; perhaps she does not know about these or does not recognize that her situation justifies their use, or perhaps she needs some encouragement. But after the matter is discussed, and information and encouragement are given once or twice and not acted upon, a different therapeutic issue emerges. The therapist need not give up on the patient, but the focus must change from content to process and, as part of this, the therapist must rethink just what it is that is happening in therapy. After the therapist rethinks this, he must present his thoughts to the patient as many times as it takes to get therapy back on track.

Gratification of Entitlement

· The topic of the sense of entitlement in a person's life is a particularly emotional one, for it touches upon several universal themes by which we judge the quality of our life in relation to others and to what we think we deserve. Entitlement is the feeling or appraisal that we deserve better than we are getting, that we are unappreciated and therefore cheated in what the world has given us, or that, conversely, we have not deserved the lumps and hard times that have come our way. A perverse variation of such themes, often referred to as a negative entitlement, also exists in the form of a person's secret belief that he is getting more good things than he really is entitled to, that he is evil and deserves punishment or, at least, exposure for the imposter that he in fact is. In both possibilities, which often coexist, there is an imbalance, a lack of harmony, between what a person gets and what he believes he deserves.

In therapy with PTSD/borderlines who have been sexually abused, both conditions of entitlement invariably exist in parallel, each presenting their own dynamics and therapeutic challenges. The contradictory themes of "I deserve better" and "I deserve worse" are obviously intertwined and inseparable human responses to adversity, since they derive as responses to the same core experiences. Nevertheless, each pose very different therapeutic problems. Furthermore, the theme of negative entitlement, "I have done evil and I deserve all the bad things I get and more," while itself very prevalent with PTSD/borderlines, presents not so much as a drive toward gratification of needs in therapy as the replaying of old issues.

Briefly, the theme of "I am a bad person and deserve bad things (punishments) in my life" is a somewhat easier issue to tackle in psychotherapy—easier, not because the patient gives up these beliefs more readily, but because the therapeutic approach, whatever combination of exploratory and cognitive restructuring interventions are used, is relatively uncomplicated in its main outline. Cognitively, the therapist challenges the negative and self-blaming percepts of the patient; psychogenetically, the therapist explores with the patient that which the patient already knows intellectually, but has not integrated into his self-image: that the patient is not a bad person and does not deserve the self-inflicted or acted-out punishments.

The major issue preventing a naive absolution of guilt is that the patient knows of secret fantasies and actions of complicity or masochistic surrender to provide the lie to the therapists's often bland reassurances to the patient that "you are not to blame." In such situations, the details of the reasons for guilt and "deserved" punishments may have to be explored and heard by the therapist. Otherwise, the therapist is in the same unhelpful situation, in saying to the patient, "You have done nothing wrong," as the therapist who continues to tell the battered borderline how to get to the women's shelter. The information may be essentially correct, but totally ignores the complexities of the patient's emotions and dynamics.

On the other hand, the initial problem in therapy with the person who says "I deserve better from life," is that he is correct. In a banal sense, who does not deserve better from life? But, more pointedly, the patients who come to therapy out of horrendous childhood abuse situations have in fact deserved better. They did not ask for or deserve what they got. They were not given "the average expectable environment" in our culture in which to grow up and develop their personalities. They truly are victims. The therapist does not deny this; the therapist can agree with the patient that the patient deserved better, that she was shortchanged by life, that she has been damaged by life's adversities. This is an important piece of therapy that often goes under the general heading of validation. There is no problem to this. The Book of Job has provided a framework for us to think about the seeming arbitrariness of evil in the world.

The therapeutic problems arise because the patient does not necessarily announce his issues with entitlement, but instead plays them out in the process of therapy. These issues show up as expectations and demands for extra sessions, telephone calls, reduced fees and special arrangements, expectations of gifts, and signs of being favored above all other patients. As such, these entitlement behaviors also fall into the general domain of seeking gratification of needs. The presence of entitlement does not replace or supersede the gratification issues but, where present, add an extra dimension that may complicate therapy if not acknowledged and addressed.

SUMMARY

All patients in therapy attempt to structure the therapy so as to obtain various gratifications from the therapist. This statement is itself a normative description of the nature of the therapeutic relationship, and is not specific to the therapy of PTSD/borderline patients. It also does not involve a value judgment, such as implying that patients ought not to do this. Seeking gratifications is integral to the therapy situation and constitutes much of the essential ground for therapeutic work. Problems arise in the therapy of PTSD/borderlines because of the particular type of intense transference responses that seem to develop as a legacy of the childhood abuse experiences.

The therapist, too, seeks and derives considerable gratification from his/her work with the patient, a topic discussed at length by Friedman (1988). When the gratifications sought by the therapist involve an emotional (or sexual) exploitation, then these occasions, too, take on special destructive force because of the nature of the patient's abusive childhood experiences.

The next chapter examines the second of the two general themes commonly found in the therapy of PTSD/borderline patients: reworking old patterns and traumas.

6

Replaying Old Patterns
and Traumas

Humans are constructed with a rich inner life that continually reexperiences the past and rehearses the future. This is not something that we have a choice about; it is as basic as breathing. We can hold our breath for a minute or two, or alter our respiratory rate, or breathe deeply or shallowly or spasmodically, but breathe we will. Similarly with our mental life, we can conjure up specific images willfully at times; we can interrupt unpleasant, or pleasant, reveries at times, only to have them return; we can focus our thinking or let it drift, but think we will.

Furthermore, life experiences that are accompanied by strong emotional arousal are replayed in our thoughts more extensively and intensively than experiences of lesser or neutral emotional tones. Contrary to traditional beliefs that emotional stress interferes with accuracy of recall of the stressful events, more recent research on real-life experiences and laboratory simulations have demonstrated that certain critical details and some circumstantial information of emotionally arousing events are less susceptible to forgetting, compared with detail information in neutral counterparts over time (Christianson, 1992).

Remarkably enough, we are also constructed with built-in mechanisms to dampen down emotional arousal and cognitive flooding when the intensity of stimulation becomes too much—becomes, by definition, overwhelming. A dramatic example of such an inborn mechanism is the gaze aversion that occurs in infants under stressful situations, which has the effect of lowering the pulse rate that had accelerated in response to the stress.

The mechanisms by which disturbing information and emotions are modulated can be described at basic neurophysiological levels (refractory periods following nerve excitation; inhibitory neurotransmittors and inhibitory neuronal synapses), at psychologically unconscious levels (defense mechanisms; personality style), and at the ordinary level of conscious psychological experiences (forgetting; distraction of attention; dissociation).

The particular mechanisms by which we think about or avoid thinking about past events are less at issue here than the basic observation that at an experiential level our mental life consists of an ongoing stream of consciousness. This is the fundamental given of human existence. Part of this ongoing stream of consciousness is an imaginative reprocessing of a variety of past experiences. We are not limited to a literal representation of what actually happened, just as we are not bound in our rehearsing and fantasizing about the future to only those events that we are certain will actually occur. The form and content of our mental reprocessing stretch from an admixture of relatively accurate memories, replays of events as they "really" happened, distortions based upon the real event, and dreams, nightmares and fantasies that take the real event as a starting point and proceed outward to the further reaches of one's creativity. This goes on in all of us, practically all the time.

When the mental processing becomes too intrusive and unpleasant, or when the damping down of the distressing stimuli (e.g., by dissociating) interferes with functioning in important life activities only marginally related to the original series of events, then the person begins to experience what is by consent called psychological symptoms. A certain number of these distressed or symptomatic persons will seek out counseling or psychotherapy. Reciprocally, psychotherapy promotes itself, and is perceived in our society, as the modality of interaction most suitable for helping persons who are stuck in a cycle of reexperiencing in thought, emotion, and action their unpleasant past events.

If it is so that persons come into psychotherapy because they continue painfully to experience their past in thought and action, it is no surprise that these disruptive patterns will also show up in the psychotherapy. In fact, the core of psychodynamic theory of psychotherapy is built around this organizing principle, and a variety of terms have been developed to describe different features of a broadly conceived repetition compulsion as it gets played out in therapy. The basic principle of psychodynamic psychotherapy is that the patient will repeat, knowingly or unknowingly, in interactions with the therapist those critical life experiences and relationships that continue to trouble the patient. Without getting into the issue at this time of whether the behavior is volitional, intentional, or driven, the fact remains that the patient will act as if motivated to replay old behaviors in relationship to the therapist and the therapy situation.

Just as seeking gratification of needs will occur in therapy in constructive and destructive ways, so too will the replaying of old issues show up in therapy in a blend of constructive and destructive ways. But whereas some of the healthy modes of gratification of needs, such as role modeling and some degree of nurturance, can theoretically begin to occur almost immediately in the therapy as an accompaniment of the interpersonal transactions, the case is different with regard to the possibility of replaying old issues in a constructive way early in therapy. By virtue of what it means to be locked into a maladaptive pattern of replaying old issues, the patient cannot readily begin to reframe new relationships and new interactions in anything but the old assumptions, interpretations, and responses. Since the very goal of therapy is to have the patient replace destructive patterns and perceptions with healthier ones, it is unreasonable to expect this to happen at the beginning of therapy.

But the simple contrast that I drew between the patient being able to accept constructively the gratifications that come from the relationship to the therapist while still persisting in a destructive replay of old issues is in reality more complex and requires a second turn of the analytic screw. There is no reason to think that the patient is able to derive healthy gratifications from the human sociality that occurs in the context of a therapeutic situation, since the patient's dominant life experiences up to that point have not prepared him for trust in any relationship. For example, the charade of caring about the patient may have occurred in the past primarily as the prelude to a seduction. Why should the patient expect otherwise from the therapist?

So it turns out that both gratification of needs and replaying of old issues will occur predominantly in therapy in disruptive patterns, and only slowly, as therapy begins to work, change in a healthy direction. At the same time, it is clear that the distinction that I have drawn between gratification of needs and replaying old patterns is an artificial one, derived from the necessity to lay out complex relationships schematically in order to examine them. In a basic sense, mobilizing one's efforts to bring about the desired gratification, for example, of a rescue attempt involves a replaying of old patterns of behaviors and a reexperiencing of old traumas, for the rescue attempt will most likely be unsatisfactory or worse.

As I carry out this dialogue within myself — reasoning out similarities and differences, developing a dialectic in which a statement is made, then qualified in order to develop a more nuanced statement that more closely approximates the complexity of what the patient is experiencing in therapy — I am aware of the tortuousness of the process. I realize that obscurity of the subject matter is a poor excuse for obscurity of the writing. Yet simplification of the topic will not do. All that is left is to keep approaching the topic again and again, from different and, at times, the same vantage point, until a clearer focus is obtained.

To go at it again: Whereas some gratification of needs even early in therapy may have a healthy component that is relatively free of the neurotic quality that drives the attempts to get one's needs met, this is not the case in reference to replaying old issues in therapy. In this latter case, replaying old issues is invariably an intrusive process that, in addition, functions as a form of treatment resistance. In view of this, it will be easiest to discuss the topic of replaying old issues in therapy in the reverse order from that presented in Figure 1. The shift from destructive to constructive patterns of replaying old issues represents both the actualization and the evidence that therapy is beginning to work. The shift is usually fairly undramatic, being seen more as the absence of destructive patterns. The gains, nevertheless, are significant when they occur: tolerating an unpleasant mental state rather than cutting oneself is dramatic, but in an understated way. In order to proceed to the healthy by way of the unhealthy patterns, I will first discuss the concepts that have been traditionally used to describe replaying old issues destructively in therapy.

ACTING-OUT AND TRANSFERENCE REACTIONS

Acting-out and transference reaction are the usual terms used to express the notion of replaying old patterns. The terms are intertwined, but not identical. Yet we cannot fully discuss one without either of the other two. Replaying old patterns, acting-out, and transference reactions are three ways of looking at the same behavior occurring in the context of therapy. When an old pattern of behavior interferes with the, so to speak, smooth flow of therapy, we describe it as a form of acting-out. "Acting-out" in therapy is itself a shorthand expression for "acting-out a transference reaction." In a sense, acting-out does not so much interfere with therapy as it becomes part of the working out of therapy.

In trying to tease apart the meanings of these three concepts, we bump into the richness and inherent ambiguities of language and the leakage of technical terms into ordinary speech. Acting-out is one of many psychoanalytic expressions that have entered into common parlance. The term has become so broadly used as to dilute all specificity of original meaning; acting-out is now the equivalent of acting-up, that is, a bit of misbehavior or some sort of recognizably problematic behavior. Its linkage to the psychoanalytic construct of "acting-out is contained in the notion that the behavior or misbehavior is somehow the expression of a network of feelings and thoughts that are not directly verbalized, but instead are put into action. The original psychoanalytic notion also contained the sense that the acting-out person was unaware of the particular underlying thoughts and feelings that were driving the acting-out behaviors. Replaying old issues is a form of acting-out when it is evoked in the context of therapy.

Let me pursue the similarities and differences just a little further. Acting-out is usually considered a form of treatment resistance. The patient, instead of perceiving, examining, and verbalizing an uncomfortable or conflictual mental state, resists acknowledgment of whatever is struggling to emerge into consciousness precisely by initiating an action that simultaneously expresses and shifts attention away from the mental content that is to be avoided. The range of acting-out behaviors is theoretically infinite, but in reality reflects each person's characteristic way of doing things. Acting-out need not be dramatic, such as cutting one's wrist or throwing a chair; for example, silence in therapy in response to perceived hurt or rejection is as much a matter of acting out as is dramatic action.

Although acting-out, by definition, is a form of treatment resistance, not all instances of replaying old issues are primarily treatment resistance. I make this statement with some hesitation and reservation, for the therapist must always consider whether treatment resistance is part of the patient's agenda when the patient is caught up in replaying an old issue in therapy. The immediate cause for my obsessional reservation is that it is possible, for example, that the patient may dissociate in therapy when remembering childhood sexual abuse incidents, and that such dissociation is a characteristic and, by this time, automatic response to intrusive abuse memories, but may not be treatment resistance. The therapist must also ask, however, whether this particular episode of dissociation represents the usual pattern of tuning out the painful imagery and emotions associated with the abuse scenario itself, on the one hand, or, on the other, an attempt by the patient (a collusion of unconscious and conscious motives) to avoid the work in therapy of examining the significance of a range of feelings and thoughts that are connected to the abuse, such as despair, self-blame, and anger at self or others. If the latter, the shift to a dissociated state may be an example of treatment resistance, because it is used effectively to prevent, for the moment, further psychological work on coming to terms with the abuse.

Recall for the moment the discussion in the introduction to Section II about the language of volition versus the language of compulsion. Although I write in terms of shifting into a dissociated state, I do not make a distinction, since I do not know whether the patient is doing this voluntarily or not. Although we ordinarily assume that the patient is the passive recipient of alterations in his state of consciousness, it is naive to ignore the fact that altered states of consciousness can be self-induced, and that even the term "dissociated state" is itself a very vague one that encompasses a range of types and intensity of altered states. If one views the shift into an altered state as something that the patient does, it is reasonable to ask the patient to try to resist going into a dissociated state, in order to continue the therapeutic direction of the moment. This is not the same as telling the patient with pneumonia not to cough. If the patient cannot do this (stop dissociating, not coughing), then the therapeutic work shifts (rather than ceases altogether) to the intrusion and, eventually, the meaning of the dissociated state. It is essential that the therapist maintain a double vision with regard to dissociative states as they occur within the therapy session, dealing with them not only as important and interesting statements about the mental life of the patient, but also as instances of treatment resistance, as a form, so to speak, of acting-out.

The right half of Figure 1 (p. 108) shows in schematic form some of the principal ways in which old issues get played out within the context of psychotherapy. The list is not intended to be comprehensive; one would have to be disrespectful of human ingenuity even to attempt a complete listing of categories of replaying old issues. Furthermore, there is a degree of arbitrariness in selecting just these factors, a fact made clear by the degree of obvious overlap of several of the categories. Despite the reductionism present in all schematic presentations, it is nevertheless helpful in focusing on and clarifying important aspects of a process. Much of the therapy of PTSD/borderline patients will invariably consist of recognizing and responding to the behaviors encompassed within Figure 1. Therapy will be effective or ineffective, or even hurtful, to the patient depending upon how these patterns are dealt with in therapy.

The gap between theory (or schemata) and the real therapy session is enormous. As Friedman (1988) has pointed out, theory does not even come close to conveying the intensity of the struggle between patient and therapist and the pain felt by each. I mention this because I do not want to give the impression that one merely has to point out various patterns to the patient and the course of therapy will take care of itself. The patient brings to the two issues of gratification of needs and replaying old issues the full intensity of emotions and maladaptive perceptions that have marked her life course up to this point. These are urgent matters, and the patient's desperation to interrupt old destructive patterns is matched by a drivenness to prove the accuracy of a distorted world-view and rework old painful experiences.

Finally, although the destructive element to reworking old issues is usually most apparent, especially in undermining therapy, there is often a constructive, even if overshadowed, component to the repetition. There is a sense in which one strives for mastery of the actual situation, or of one's emotions in a situation, in reworking the issue again and again. The patient who continues to test the therapist for evidence of betrayal can still be pleased that betrayal has not occurred, even if not convinced about security in the future. Practicing establishing better boundaries by fighting with the therapist is a step toward health for the patient, even though the immediate effect is that of treatment resistance. Both pieces, the constructive and destructive, are present in the same interaction; the therapist will have to struggle to maintain a fair view of what the patient is doing.

IDENTIFICATION WITH THE AGGRESSOR

The patient who has been the target of childhood abuse demonstrates a variety of distortions in everyday interpersonal relationships. One of the more common ones is the shift from passive victimization to active identification with the aggressor. Although in therapy patterns of passive victimization are seen more frequently than aggressiveness, the latter is more often troubling to the patient, representing an ego-dystonic incorporation of hateful aspects of the predator. This aggressiveness can show up in fairly mild forms, however, and as such is easier for the patient to acknowledge precisely because major aggressiveness is not involved. In the following case, a patient acts out in therapy her struggle with power issues and identification with a dominant parent.

CASE 10

Ms. M is asked by her therapist to write a two-page essay on "Who am I?" When she hands in her assignment at the next therapy session, she asks the therapist to read the essay out loud so that they can use it as a basis for discussion. The therapist replies that he would prefer to read the essay at a later time, so as not to structure this particular therapy session. The patient puts on, as she has characterized it, a disappointed appearance, and repeats her request. The therapist again refuses, but then reverses himself and agrees. The patient smiles triumphantly and says, "I won. You backed down."

Ms. M characteristically perceives all interactions in terms of power. Most of the time this way of viewing relationships occurs automatically and is ego-syntonic. The moment-to-moment shifts of power in a relationship are not an extraneous perspective that the patient adds to her understanding of any interaction, but are integral to how she experiences the world of human relationships. Even if she does not self-consciously initiate or respond to an interaction with the power component in mind, she automatically includes it in her mental processing as any interaction proceeds.

Ms. M was raised in an abusive home in which power/powerlessness was recognized as the most important parameter of relationships. It defined vulnerability, with all the sadly predictable consequences. Power accrued to the person who was larger, stronger, faster, standing rather than sitting, possessing rather than importuning, willful rather than weak-willed, active rather than passive. Thus, the very act of requesting that her essay be reviewed in the therapy session carried with it, as indeed any other request also would, a testing of the power relationship between her and her therapist, especially since Ms. M's acquiescence in doing the assignment in the first place was itself seen as evidence of diminished power. The urgent request that the therapist read the essay aloud constituted an attempt to even out the power imbalance. The request, or almost demand, was a reworking of a very old and very important issue for Ms. M, although disguised as an ingenuous petition.

At the same time, the request involved some degree of treatment resistance, because it meant that the session would be structured in a way that would protect her from whatever associations might come up spontaneously in a less structured session. It is also likely that Ms. M wanted some recognition and praise for having completed the written assignment, certainly more acknowledgment than was given when the therapist unceremoniously dropped the essay on his desk. As in all situations in which several layers of meaning are present within a single brief communication, the therapist must quickly make a choice as to which theme initially to pursue.

The theme of power, focused in terms of who will get their way, appeared to be most critical and prominent at the moment. Although the triumphant comment, "I won," represents a continuation of Ms. M's interminable power struggle, it also indicated her willingness to examine the power issue, for she knew that in articulating the victory, which is a form of naming the process, she was giving up some of the power she had just acquired. In this sense, asserting her will over that of the therapist represents a replaying in therapy of old issues and an instance of acting-out, but by articulating the process immediately afterward, she moved the behavior out of the treatment resistance realm and made it available for examination.

Preoccupation with the power issue, calculation of the power ratio, and testing of the power balance are woven into the very tapestry of Ms. M's life. All relationships, including the therapeutic one, turn on the dual questions of will she win (or lose) and will she be permitted to win, this latter option in itself becoming a very tricky matter.

Variations of these two questions constitute one major theme that gets played out in Ms. M's therapy. When these themes are urgent and dominant, they overshadow all attempts at therapeutic work; when Ms. M is less threatened and more secure, she can hold the themes in abeyance in order to examine them and do other therapeutic work.

The first question, "Will I win?" represents a less complicated issue than the second. It involves a constant retesting of who has the power and who is vulnerable. The second question, "Will I be allowed to win?" is more heavily laden with complicated issues, for the concept of allowing someone to win carries with it conflicting implications of generosity and condescension. The very question acknowledges a dependency upon someone else's good feeling and sense of security. Ms. M was never allowed by an adult to win as a child, nor was she able to win by the use of straight power. The only semblance of being allowed to win was as a prelude to a seduction, in which her parent would temporarily plead and cajole for sexual accommodations. There was always a threat behind the plea, behind the charade that Ms. M was in charge and really had a choice. This memory, carried into the therapy situation, meant that any perceived "weakness" on the part of the therapist was seen either as true weakness, in which case he was held in contempt, or as duplicitous, in which case the therapist was presumed to have a corrupt hidden agenda. The corrupt agenda might be directly sexual, or it might just be emotional exploitation made possible by duping the patient to drop her vigilance and trust the integrity of the therapist.

The therapist may elect to ignore the power issue inherent in each interaction with Ms. M or choose to comment or even focus on it; the decision will be based upon an assessment of what task is most relevant at the moment. What is necessary, whatever the judgment, is the awareness that an old issue is being reworked in parallel to the other levels of interaction.

REPLAYING THE VICTIMIZATION THEME

While one of the goals of therapy is to bring to awareness the patient's patterns of replaying old issues, the matter is complicated when the pattern is one of victimization by others, because the theme of victimization is carried into the very process of discussing the pattern. The therapeutic problem is similar to those in working with the passive patient, in which any expectation, however indirect, for the patient to become more active may be met with compliance, thereby defeating the therapeutic intent. A further problem is that pointing out the pattern of victimization before one knows its source in the patient's life experiences comes across as a reproach, as one more criticism by a harshly judgmental adult.

CASE 11

Ms. B, finally rehospitalized after several months of escalating threats to kill herself with an overdose, berates her therapist for not having hospitalized her sooner, since everyone else but he realized that she had been feeling progressively worse. The fact that he finally agreed to her hospitalization only shows that, if he truly cared about her, he would have hospitalized her sooner and not let her go through so much pain. She berates him, however, only after first cautioning him not to get angry at her for what she is going to say.

Several themes emerge in this interaction. The first consists of the patient's giving stage directions, telling the therapist how he should respond. There are obvious control issues involved in such interactions, but calling them to the patient's attention in the past has not led to productive interactions. A second theme relates to the patient's anger at her therapist, which she deals with by anticipating and fearing his wrath. A third theme relates to replaying the motif of victimization, although only in a mild sense in this particular example. "Everyone disappoints me," the patient seems to be saying. The problem in flagging this issue as a repetitive one is that it tends to provide further justification for the patient to feel criticized and misunderstood. Practically any response of the therapist gets incorporated into the patient's twin perceptions that everything she does is wrong and that everyone disappoints her. Nevertheless, it would be a mistake for the therapist to respond to the content of the message by defending or explaining why he had not recommended hospitalization earlier.

In this particular case, Ms. B was an adopted child who may have been abused by her adoptive father. All themes fall back to the original rejection and original disappointment, which demonstrated for all time that Ms. B was unlovable and that the adult world would disappoint and/or victimize her. These themes have been intellectualized by Ms. B to the point where she can verbalize them, but she cannot connect them to the emotions surrounding events in the present time. Her sense of disappointment with the therapist is felt by her as justified by what he did and omitted to do, not as an exaggerated carryover from past injuries. Past injuries are independently acknowledged but their relevance to the present situation is denied. At issue here is that Ms. B does not frame the therapist's decision not to hospitalize her earlier as reflecting his concerned judgment of what is best for her, even if she disagrees with this assessment. Instead, she poses the issue in terms of whether he will join the long list of persons who have pretended to care about her, but in fact have ended up disappointing her.

Often several themes are crystallized into a single piece of acting-out. In the following case, the patient eroticizes the therapeutic relationship in a way that encompasses both victimization and aggression.

CASE 12

Ms. C is a 29-year-old married woman, working part-time and raising three children. She had been sexually abused by an uncle when she was five years old. As an early teenager, she had run away, which resulted in a gang-rape and brief experience with enforced prostitution, a series of events that she never reported. She is working in therapy on recovering memories of the childhood abuse by her uncle, which appears to be more extensive than she had previously realized. Therapy has been proceeding along on a twice-monthly schedule, but Ms. C calls up to ask for an extra appointment because she is upset about some emerging imagery. The therapist offers her a 6 p.m. appointment, since the earlier hours are booked. Ten minutes into the therapy session, Ms. C volunteers that she wishes to seduce the therapist and makes a move to begin unbuttoning her blouse. The therapist quickly tells her that sexual activity is out of the question and that he will terminate the therapy session, if not therapy totally, if she proceeds any further. He asks Ms. C to verbalize rather than demonstrate what this is all about. Ms. C, somewhat embarrassed, explains that she assumed that when the therapist gave her an after-hours appointment, he was signaling his sexual interest in her. She had given the matter considerable thought and this explanation made the most sense, fitting in with how she assumed most men felt about her, and about women in general. Since she had little value as a person, a man's interest in her could only be exploitative, and sooner or later, this would become manifest.

Such an overt invitation for the therapist to participate in acting-out with the patient is easy to spot and refuse. More subtle invitations to move beyond the customary boundaries in psychotherapy of sitting in an office and talking, often embedded in seemingly reasonable, not necessarily sexual, requests are more difficult to recognize and, therefore, more difficult to refuse, precisely because they initially appear reasonable. The basic technical principle remains the same, however. Although, in the case of a sexual invitation, the foremost reason for refusal to participate is an ethical one, the technical point remains that participating in acting-out with a patient renders that piece of behavior, and what underlies it, unavailable for therapeutic examination. What becomes important for therapy to explore in this particular example is Ms. C's basic sense that she has little value to men other than as an object of gratification. Scrutiny of this issue rapidly leads to her anger at men and at herself, and then to disdain of the men who have only a selfishly instrumental ethical code with no sense of deeper values. The occasion of a late appointment was reminiscent to Ms. C's childhood, when her parents would go out in the evening, leaving the patient with her uncle as a babysitter. These were the memories that led Ms. C to ask for the extra appointment in the first place. Acting-out the seduction with the therapist expressed Ms. C's opinion that somehow she must have seduced the uncle, and therefore was responsible for the ensuing sexual abuse. Yet Ms. C was also aware that, had the therapist succumbed, he would have been guilty of a gross violation of his responsibilities to her, just as her uncle had of the trust that had been placed in him. The two themes exist in parallel: the belief that she is irresistible to men as evidence of her own evil nature, and the belief that she is irresistible primarily because the man is corrupt. While it was not part of a thought-out plan, Ms. C realized, in discussing the incident with the therapist, that her anger at the therapist, had he participated in the seduction, would have led her to report him to the local professional board.

One finds in PTSD/borderlines contradictory patterns of replaying their victimization issues. One pattern is that of acting-out the fantasy of the seduction, of actively taking command of the initiation of sexual behaviors. Even here the fantasy of what follows bifurcates: in one direction toward avoiding harm by maintaining a more forceful stance, perhaps even assaulting the seduced collaborator either literally or through denouncement and public exposure; in the other playing out of the fantasy, so that the PTSD/borderline person loses control of the interaction and, in a reversal of aggression, becomes the victim of the other's violence. This risk is clearly present in those persons who become involved in prostitution out of a background of childhood sexual abuse and victimization. This latter fantasy, in which the patient as seducer becomes victim, was at times operative with Ms. C, who blamed herself for the gang-rape and enforced prostitution, by means of her impeccable logic that, if she had not run away, the ensuing assaults would not have occurred.

This second fantasy theme of the seduction that ends in victimization is also seen more directly in patients who play out the role of neediness or helplessness as a way of appealing to those perpetrators who are attracted to defenseless individuals in seeming need of assistance. The pattern is prominent with PTSD/borderlines, because it comes closest to repeating their childhood experiences of powerlessness. This is often seen in those individuals, usually women although not exclusively, who have a longstanding pattern of relationships with battering partners.

There are times when replaying old issues of victimization leads a patient to take an active initiative in setting up situations of enforced passivity and exposure to abuse.

CASE 13

Mr. N is a 26-year-old single man, employed part-time as an assembly line worker, with a history of severe emotional, physical, and sexual abuse. He was beaten and tormented during early childhood by his alcoholic father, who reportedly rubbed his face in chicken excrement under the rationale that, since this was what Mr. N was, he might as well learn to eat it. From ages five to fifteen, Mr. N was sexually abused by an uncle. Mr. N never told anybody about the sexual assaults, not only because his uncle blamed Mr. N for wanting to be raped, but also because the uncle threatened to kill him if he ever revealed their "secret." In addition, Mr. N was very certain that father, rather than protecting him, would have additional reasons to beat him.

Mr. N became suicidal in childhood, with a pattern of violent, self-destructive behaviors in public, such as throwing himself down a flight of stairs, driving his truck into a river, and attempting to cut his throat in front of his older sister. His most recent hospitalization was occasioned by his walking down a highway swinging an axe at oncoming traffic. Once in the hospital, Mr. N brightened up and showed no disturbed behavior for the first 24 hours. During the evening following admission, without obvious provocation, he went into his room and wrapped a bedsheet tightly around his neck. He was discovered and placed on close observation, but no further staffing action was initiated. An hour later, he grabbed a pool cue and started swinging it around, smashing several lamps and crockery pieces. He did not try to hurt anyone and was easily subdued by nursing staff, but when one arm was released, began banging his fist against his face. Mr. N was carried into the seclusion room and placed in loose four-point restraints. He wriggled one arm free and began punching himself in the face again. Staff then turned Mr. N over and placed him face down in tighter restraints. No further incidents occurred that night.

The following day, Mr. N revealed to his therapist the reasons for the sequence of behaviors the night before. On the night of admission, Mr. N had been told by a male therapy aide to leave the smoking room and try to sleep. This aide strongly reminded him of the uncle who had assaulted him repeatedly in childhood by first tying him face down in a bed and then raping him. Mr. N therefore became violent enough on the ward to ensure that he would be tied face down in the seclusion room during the night shift, fully expecting that the night therapy aide would come into the room and sodomize him. In fact, only female staff attended to Mr. N when he was in seclusion; the male therapy aide never entered the room.

This is a rather blatant example of a destructive pattern of reworking old traumas. The reenactment is driven by the fantasy of passivity, of being raped as one was in childhood. The dilemma for the therapist in such a situation is to achieve a suitable balance of supportive and exploratory work with the patient. The patient himself reports on the imagery that directs his actions, but is unaware of whatever dynamic issues may underlie his pattern of forcing others to tie him down. Yet the themes underlying this type of victimization pattern inevitably fall into several categories, some of which are more approachable than others. Mastery through repetition, in this case demonstrating that one can survive such assaults, is the most accessible and acceptable theme. Expiation of guilt by setting oneself up for humiliation and pain is also a motif that can readily be discussed with the patient. The question of what underlies the guilt is a much more difficult issue, since it involves, from the patient's viewpoint, themes of complicity and sexual arousal, both of which are intolerable for him to contemplate.

REPLAYING ISSUES OF BETRAYAL

I made reference earlier to a type of replaying old issues that begins with a request for special consideration in therapy. In such situations, the patient seeks not a single stereotyped pattern, but a somewhat open-ended acting-out, in which the action, depending on the responses of the therapist, can evolve in any of several directions. Inevitably, however, these reflect back to a core theme of disappointment or betrayal. The patient does not know in advance what will happen, and may hope at one level that this time her needs will be met and that a positive outcome will occur, but in fact such is rarely the case. In the following situation, it was initially the mental health clinic rather than the therapist who played the role of the emotionally abusive parent.

CASE 14

Ms. P is a 36-year-old ordained minister, divorced, and currently in conflict with her church board and parishioners. She has taken a leave of absence from her ministerial duties and is driving a school bus. After a rocky start in therapy due to conflicts with the clinic administration over billing procedures, she has reached the point where she feels she can trust her therapist, a male social worker in his mid-fifties. She has developed some amorous feeling for him, which she has not directly expressed yet.

Ms. P's parents divorced when she was six; the following year, her father died in a car accident. Two years later, her mother married a man who was sexually abusive to Ms. P and her younger sister. The abuse, however, was in the form of seductions, with the result that Ms. P was always deeply conflicted about her participation in these activities, which she knew to be wrong. At age 12, Ms. P confided in a girlfriend about the abuse, which started a process eventuating in the incarceration of stepfather. Ms. P, already humiliated by public exposure of her shame and guilty about her role in sending her stepfather to prison, was blamed by her mother for breaking up the family and was sent to live with relatives.

In therapy, Ms. P was grieving the loss of her idealized real father, which she considered the critical turning point in her life. The anniversary of her father's death was approaching and she asked the therapist if he could accompany her on a visit to the gravesite. She explained that she thought he would be better able to understand her emotions and turmoil if he was present with her on that occasion. The therapist was inclined to acquiesce with this request, which he saw as a reasonable one, but said that he would need to consider the request more fully. The therapist had previously been in conflict with his peer review treatment team, which tended to view him as having problems maintaining proper boundaries with his patients. He presented Ms. P's request at his peer review session and, as he anticipated, they strongly cautioned him against any interactions with her outside of the regular therapy setting. Angry, but reluctant to act directly in opposition to the team, he told Ms. P that he had discussed her request with his peer review team and that they recommended against it.

Ms. P was outraged. She had not realized that her therapist was discussing her personal problems at a team meeting. She did not even know who these people were who knew so many intimate details of her life. She had not given permission for her case to be discussed with anyone else. Furthermore, how could they make a judgment about what was best for her? She wanted to know the names and credentials of the members of the peer review team. She demanded to meet with the team, to find out what they knew, and to challenge their right to have any information about her. The peer review team refused to meet with Ms. P, stating that the entire situation was a transference issue to be worked out in therapy. They drew a parallel to the many angry meetings Ms. P had had with her church board, which ended unhappily with the board's recommendation that Ms. P take a leave of absence. Ms. P objected to this interpretation, citing it as an example of how the treatment team abused confidential material by using the information disclosed privately in therapy in a self-serving attack against her.

Whatever the initial motivation underlying Ms. P's request that her therapist accompany her to her father's gravesite, the situation quickly turned into a repetition of themes of personal betrayal, abuse of power, and overinvolvement by an uncaring authority structure. This antagonism between Ms. P and the clinic bureaucracy had been foreshadowed earlier in therapy, when the patient had conflicts with the agency about billing procedures and the therapist had intervened on Ms. P's behalf. But now the therapist, in Ms. P's eyes, became weak and ineffectual, unable to advocate for her. He was castigated by Ms. P with all the stored up anger that she had never allowed herself to experience consciously toward her father for leaving her and her stepfather for abusing her.

This is a complicated situation because, as is so often the case, the therapist has participated with the patient in acting-out a variation of an old pattern of misunderstandings and disappointment. The therapist's ready assent to his patient's seemingly reasonable request that he accompany her to father's gravesite meant that the significance of the request was never examined in therapy. The meaning to Ms. P of the therapist's agreement to have a special relationship with her, literally outside the boundaries of the clinic walls, was never explored. All of this was lost sight of in the storm that developed around the issue of betrayal of confidentiality.

It is not that Ms. P was inaccurate in her perceptions of her therapist's inconsistency or of the problem with confidentiality. There is, increasingly, a larger social issue regarding confidentiality in all psychotherapy situations. Third-party carriers are insisting on fuller descriptive justifications for continued approval of psychotherapy sessions beyond the 10 or 20 mandated by the terms of the health insurance policy. Case review, both by in-house overseers and managed care companies, are the rule rather than the exception. In view of this, Ms. P's vitriolic response must be viewed against a background of what the average informed consumer of psychotherapy can be expected to understand about the ubiquity of some kind of review process.

The technical difficulty in working out this kind of therapeutic morass is that the issues are contaminated by the therapist's poor judgment and overinvolvement, which serve to block a focused examination of how this interaction fits into Ms. P's pattern of being betrayed by the one she trusts, and tossed aside by uncaring others. Ms. P's therapist knew from previous conferences with his treatment team that they would not approve his accompanying his patient on a "field trip," but what he told Ms. P was that he had to think it over. He then set up Ms. P to fight his fight with the treatment team by trapping her in a classical splitting maneuver, in which he presents himself as good guy and the team as the bad guys. This only worked briefly, for Ms. P did not respond to the split, but correctly included the therapist among the betrayers. As a compromise response to Ms. P's demand that she be allowed to meet with the treatment team, a senior staff person met with Ms. P and her therapist. But the damage to therapy was already done. The perceived breech of confidentiality could not be reversed; other staff therapists knew details of Ms. P's life and used this knowledge to attack her. The therapist was unhelpful, gaining favor with Ms. P by agreeing with her that the clinic's decision was rigid and uncaring, but, in the process, presenting himself as a victim, much like Ms. P. In this situation, the therapist used the patient to express his grievances toward his clinic colleagues. The therapist was correct in consulting his colleagues regarding his patient's request for special consideration, but he should have presented his response to Ms. P as stemming from his own thoughtful decision, rather than stating that he wished to comply with Ms. P's request, but that his colleagues forbade him. The situation between therapist and patient was never resolved; therapy ended on a totally negative note.

It is a moot point whether such an ending was inevitable, whether in one way or another Ms. P's replaying of the issues of betrayal would have undermined therapy. There is no particular basis for this pessimism. A safer statement would be that, one way or another, Ms. P's problem areas around entitlement, trust, betrayal, and confidentiality would show up in therapy. All that this means is that the therapist has to be especially alert to subtle variations of the patient's important themes, and to respond to instances of requests for special consideration as a form of acting-out, as material to be examined, not as requests to be honored or as opportunities to engage his own clinic staff in an ongoing battle.

Is nothing safe? Must the therapist be forever on guard, suspicious of every statement made by the patient? Is this any way to relate to another human being? The answers are two yesses and a no, but I am not sure which questions get the yes and which the no. Certainly, a therapy relationship is both like and unlike any other relationship, or it ought to be. When it becomes too like other relationships, in terms of vagueness of boundaries, reciprocity of disclosure, and encroachments into exploitation, then it ceases to be a professional, therapeutic one. When it becomes too unlike other relationships, in terms of rigid stances, absence of warmth, and denial of shared feelings, then it also ceases to be a therapeutic relationship. The therapy relationship has to observe certain clear boundaries and standards of behavior without losing an essential component of humanness. The therapist does not have to be suspicious of every statement by the patient; suspicious is the wrong word with the wrong connotations. The therapist has to be aware that the patient has a different agenda, and that statements and requests have, in addition to the specific manifest content, a meaning in terms of transference issues. The therapist obviously also has to be aware of his own agenda.

The questions to be asked when Ms. P requests accompaniment to father's gravesite are, "What else is going on? What is the significance of my being asked to do this? What will be the meaning to Ms. P if I acquiesce, or if I refuse? How does the request fit into what else is going on in Ms. P's life at this time, and with what else is going on in therapy now? How do my own feelings toward Ms. P shape my understanding of these issues and my response to her request? How do I see myself as a therapist? How does my relationship to my colleagues at this clinic shape my response to the request? What else is going on in my life now?"

CONSTRUCTIVE PATTERNS OF REPLAYING OLD ISSUES

There is considerable opportunity for the therapist's participation in replaying the patient's old issues in healthy ways. Since these old issues come up either repeatedly or even continuously, much of the ordinary day-to-day operations of therapy consist of doing just this. There is nothing fancy or special about all this; I am merely giving labels to some routine procedures of psychotherapy that only become noticeable when they are absent.

Each time the patient is able to talk about painful memories, disturbing relationships, and impulses to hurt herself without giving into these impulses, then a therapeutic intervention has occurred. The process is given the fancy label of verbalization and catharsis, and much of therapy is about this very thing. One very important goal in the therapy of PTSD/borderlines is the elimination of self-injurious behaviors. When talk replaces action, progress has occurred. Cognitive repackaging is part of the talking process. Relabeling a disturbing, chaotic thought or image into something understandable enables the patient to be less upset about the content, or even just the presence, of the images. This is true not just for victims of childhood abuse, but for many types of PTSD sufferers. Many of the Southeast Asian refugees whom I see have significant PTSD symptoms. They come to the clinic seeking relief, and we give them antidepressant medications, group work, some individual counseling, and social service assistance. They still have intrusive imagery and nightmares. At that point, the best that we can do is acknowledge our limitations and explain that nightmares and flashbacks are the ways in which all humans respond to the experiences of combat, civilian violence, and torture, and that with time the intensity of the mental imagery will recede.

In a similar way, changing the borderline's diagnosis to PTSD is helpful in connecting what she is experiencing now by way of symptoms with the abuse experiences of childhood. We carry this cognitive repackaging into the details of the symptoms, into a demystification of dissociative episodes, panic symptoms, and intrusive imagery. I provide the expression "emotional flooding" or "emotional overload" to my patient as a way of designating the way a PTSD/borderline person becomes disorganized under stress, so that the experience of disorganization begins to make sense. Relabeling does not stop the phenomenon, but it moves the process out of a self-blame moralistic sphere into a more descriptive one. This shows up most clearly around topics of self-blame. Although, as I have stressed repeatedly, patients do not readily accept our telling them that they are not to blame for what was done to them in childhood, it is nevertheless important that they hear this from their therapists and others.

Since so many PTSD/borderlines were raised in situations where respectful boundaries were not observed, and since child abuse represents the ultimate example (short of death) of a boundary violation, the healthy replaying of this issue is a critical part of therapy. It does not take speeches and one need not hammer home the point to the patient about why the therapist must be very clear about respectful boundaries. This is one area where the therapist has to "act out" in a healthy way. I am not just speaking of the more obvious physical and sexual boundary issues, but also of psychological boundaries, of not infantilizing the patient, of not making decisions that the patient could make, of not assuming a familiarity or a knowledge of the patient that infringes upon the patient's privacy.

Along with this is the problem of locus of control. PTSD/borderline patients have experienced what it is like to have no control over what happens to them. This has often generalized into a sort of pessimistic fatalism that denies them the possibility of bringing about positive changes in their life. The patient will rework this issue with the therapist over and over again, oscillating between insistence that she is powerless to change things for the better and more subtle acting-out in which the therapist is won over to act upon the patient. The shift to an internal locus of control is a slow one, but it requires the quiet insistence of the therapist that the patient can do somewhat more for herself than she thinks she can.

The topic of locus of control in conjunction with themes of replaying old issues raises an important problem in the psychotherapy of borderlines that I had mentioned earlier. This is the basic incompatibility of a medical-psychiatric model that requires intrusive "parental" intervention into a patient's life decisions, at times overriding that patient's expressed wishes, and a psychotherapeutic model that requires minimal engagement into the real life of a person, especially beyond the temporal and geographical limits of the office. I had phrased this earlier as the conflict between the short-term goals of preventing self-injurious behaviors and suicide and the long-term goals of encouraging the patient's autonomy and inner locus of control. The very essence of a patient's drive to rework old issues in therapy is manifested in the patient's attempt to involve the therapist in stepping out of the therapeutic role and participating as a new and important actor in an old scenario. To the extent that the therapist is forced, or feels forced, to intervene actively in rescue attempts and to offer direct advice, psychotherapy as an exploratory process is compromised. I am not suggesting that active intervention should never occur, but only highlighting that, especially with PTSD/borderlines, it usually represents a collusion between patient and therapist in playing out an old issue in a somewhat new variation. I am suggesting, however, since I think that it is unseemly to equivocate too much, that therapists intervene too actively and too frequently, and that the burden of responsibility and control needs to be placed back onto the patient.

SUMMARY

The last two chapters have explored what I might call two meta-themes that recur throughout the therapy of PTSD/borderlines. Pursuit of gratification of needs and reworking of old issues constitute one level of conceptualizing and organizing a seemingly endless variety of specific transference behaviors that can be readily schematized in many other ways (e.g., forms of treatment resistance; PTSD patterns). There is heuristic value in using the two concepts (gratification of needs, working old issues) both in the way that the therapist thinks about the process of therapy and in the conduct of therapy itself, as a way providing the patient with recognizable labels for identifying destructive patterns of behavior. There are other models which can be used to organize one's thinking about therapy with PTSD/borderline patients. The last section of the book is devoted to developing yet another perspective on the effects of childhood sexual abuse on the course of psychotherapy.

SECTION III

Special Considerations in the Therapy of Abuse Victims

INTRODUCTION

We continue our examination of the processes whereby psycho-therapist and patient — in this case, a patient with an early life history of abuse — interact with each other. There is no definitive approach, no specific process, no single theory that encompasses the process. What we have instead is a succession of approaches from different angles, each offering a slightly different perspective by which to understand and proceed with the task. The different perspectives need to relate to each other in some broad sense; otherwise we end up with a hodgepodge of provisional approaches that represents eclecticism at its worst.

But it would be a mistake to try to provide too much closure to what are essentially open-ended systems. Our unifying viewpoint, bearing in mind the limitations and qualifications discussed in Chapter 3, is that the experiences of sexual abuse in childhood have been the major cause of the problems that bring this person to psychotherapy. This viewpoint, however, does not by itself dictate a particular therapy. We know that there are a variety of competing and complementary forms of therapy available for treating PTSD/borderlines, each of which fastens upon some prominent features of the condition and fashions a therapeutic regimen based upon a particular theoretical understanding of causal relationships and appropriate interventions. No approach as yet has demonstrated clear superiority over the others. Thus, while the hypothesis that childhood sexual abuse causes the PTSD/borderline response underlies therapeutic considerations in general, how we understand and address the specific issues presented to us in therapy is very much an open question.

Patient and therapist together, at times in concert and at times in struggle, define what the relevant issues are at the moment and what shall be ignored (but not forgotten or dismissed). The patient has an identity beyond that of patienthood. There are the external roles: child of two parents, oneself a parent, sibling to others sibs, worker,

179

student, friend, unemployed individual. There are the internal identities: hero or heroine, undiscovered genius, world explorer, hidden artist, underachiever, fraud, despicable person, potential murderer, ill-starred victim. Overlapping and underlying these public and private identities is the conglomeration of partial identities (whose center is the subject of this book) which threaten to submerge all the other possibilities such that the patient completely associates herself with this single aspect: the victim of childhood and adolescent sexual and physical abuse.

It is as if we were to ask the person, "Who are you?" and the answer would be, "I am a person who has been so deeply affected, so deeply scarred by the sexual abuse that I suffered that I am forever crippled—permanently damaged from what that little boy or girl might have grown up to be. All my thoughts, my emotions, my way of looking at myself and my world are colored, even dominated, by what I was made to experience, by what was done to me, by what I did."

This is treacherous territory for the psychotherapist. Who is to stand up and say that the patient is incorrect? Yet the therapist's task is to affirm as well as deny the patient's perspective of herself, and to do both simultaneously. Merely to affirm the patient's claimed identity as victim is to buy into all the suppositions and consequences of the notion of oneself as an irreparably damaged individual, deserving of special considerations. The therapist will be swamped in a morass of self-pity, pity, anger, and justifications. We are not speaking here of truth or falsity. The therapist cannot help the patient without accepting the actuality of the patient's abuse experiences. But equally, the therapist cannot help the patient in therapy if she accepts the patient's premises, on the patient's terms, of what and how the sexual abuse has affected her and of the inevitability of its effects. The therapist has to help lead the patient out of the mess that her life has become, and this involves stating, in whatever terms and behavior are true for the therapist, that the patient's life can be different, that the abuse experience has not irrevocably and totally damaged the patient, and that to think otherwise is to yield to the patient's demands to be treated as an entitled martyr or a depraved monster. To see only the sufferer in the patient is to go along from one's misguided sense of pity with providing everything that the patient demands, and to see these requests as reasonable expectations and reparations, in light of how the patient has suffered. The issue is not its reasonableness given the patient's premises, for who are we to judge in an ultimate sense what is reasonable or not? Rather, the therapist has to keep the focus constantly on the therapy, not on the miseries of the patient.

On the other hand, for the therapist to deny the patient's view of herself is to betray a lack of understanding and empathy that invalidates the therapist's claim to have something to offer the patient. The therapist has to accept the patient's perspective as the way the patient sees her life history and present situation. There is no need or basis to argue with the patient about her perspective, but equally, there is no need for the therapist to accept totally the patient's viewpoint.

The patient as an individual is more than the sum total of the abuse experiences. The patient may argue this point. The therapist has to not lose sight of the full totality (humanness) of the patient, but not to argue this out with the patient, just to respond to the patient in the fuller sense of what she is.

Yet, in this third section of the book, I am going to do the opposite of what I have just said. For the purposes of focus and discussion, this section will address those issues of the patient in therapy that relate most closely to the experience of abuse. There are several caveats that, as usual, I must make in reference to working with outlines and schemata. First, the focus on the patient as "one who has been abused" is just one aspect of the therapy, and needs to be integrated into the entirety of the process. Second, although the outline is in logical and sequential form, I have no illusions that this is the sequence in which the patient will bring up her issues about abuse or that this is how therapy actually proceeds, nor am I even suggesting that this is how therapy ought to proceed. I have tried to be as orderly and clear as possible in developing the outline on paper; in real life, any issue might emerge at any time in the course of therapy and will, of necessity, require its own scrutiny and response in terms of the variables at the moment—the patient's situation with respect to stability, self-injurious behaviors, external relationships—and the therapy situation with respect to nature of the transference, phase of the therapy, timing, and tolerance of the patient for working with difficult topics. Third, I am not suggesting that the listing is complete, or even that it is the best way to look at the issues, or that all the issues outlined here are relevant or will need to be addressed in any given therapy.

As I have thought about my work with patients, my supervision and peer discussions with other therapists, and my reading of the literature, the form and content of Table 3 has taken shape. These issues emerged, in various guises, in working with patients who have been abused in childhood and adolescence. The topics listed obviously overlap with the earlier discussions comparing patients' and therapists' goals, with the examination of the problems of pursuit of gratification of needs and replaying old issues. This is because the behaviors, conflicts, and therapeutic quandaries are the same ones discussed earlier, though we have changed the perspective and focus to gain a fresh outlook. In essence, Chapters 5 and 6 examined the process of therapy in terms of conflict between patient and therapist

TABLE 3

An outline of psychotherapy of the patient who has been abused

A. How to come to terms with the past
  1. Post-traumatic aspects
  2. Disillusionment aspects
  3. Conflict regarding complicity
  4. Resolution in forgiveness vs. acceptance of irreconcilability

B. How the past controls the present
  1. Dissociative episodes
  2. Self-hatred
  3. Mistrust of self
  4. Mistrust of others
  5. Seeking repetition of old (destructive) scenarios

C. How the past controls the transference
  1. Testing the therapist for rejection
  2. Testing the therapist for seduction
  3. Testing the therapist for victimization and exploitation

as the patient struggles to have the therapist provide gratification of her needs and the therapy serve as the forum in which old issues will be reworked. In the following chapters, we will look at the same interactions between patients and therapists, but focus in a more schematic way on the ways in which the experiences of childhood abuse influence the themes that come to dominate the content of therapy.

7

Coming to Terms with the Abuse of the Past

What is it about the past that one needs to come to terms with, and what does it even mean, "to come to terms with"? We have developed a variety of synonyms, such as "coping," "handling," "dealing with," and "managing," precisely because it is difficult to develop terms and concepts to convey and correspond to painful subjective experiences and interpersonal relationships. But synonyms only exchange one word with another. We are still left with needing to explain what is meant by the expression, "coming to terms with."

Coming to terms with the past, as it is used in this chapter, means accepting, in the fullest sense possible at the moment, that the events of childhood, including the assaults, betrayals, and warped family patterns, really did occur; that the impact upon my development, even if not comprehensible to myself or others, was profound in ways that I may never fully clarify; that memories of childhood may be forever incomplete and distorted; that painful memories, dreams, and intrusive imagery may always be with me; that I may have participated in the abuse and its cover-up differently at different stages of my childhood and adolescence and that I can accept this apparent fact without getting caught up in self-blame or pity; that, ultimately, I can embrace the brute facts of the past, certainly not joyfully and perhaps only grimly, in the realization that this is my past, however dismal, and that all that has happened to me has gone into making me the person I am today.

The first problem with such a formulation of what it means to come to terms with the past is that it sounds either inspirationally soupy or naively trite, or both. But this is what coming to terms with the past means. The second problem, of more practical importance, is that those very brute facts of the past, which I am being told to embrace, are themselves getting in the way of my accepting them. Those brute facts, to which we so casually refer, have made me into the kind of person who cannot accept my past, either what others have done to me or what I have done to myself. I cannot think of the past without shame and anger, and I cannot stop thinking about the past.

Presumably, this is where psychotherapy enters the picture. Psychotherapy offers something to the PTSD/borderline person who cannot come to terms with the past and whose past controls, in a destructive sense, the present. The PTSD/borderline person asks for another perspective, for a constructive helper to change the future by way of working on how the past affects the present.

What pieces of the past does one need to come to terms with? I have broken down the territory into four major components: post-traumatic aspects, disillusionment, conflict regarding complicity, forgiveness versus irreconciliability. As with all attempts to categorize human experiences, the four components are not mutually exclusive; they overlap in obvious ways. They make no claim of comprehensiveness; nature does not come compartmentalized into quarters. These four seem to be important themes that emerge repeatedly, although in different guises, in the psychotherapy of PTSD/borderlines. In therapy the themes come up chaotically, blending into each other; the topics do not come heralded or labeled. The value of laying the themes out in orderly sequence is strictly that we may examine them in detail. The danger is that the orderliness of the schema, as we have pointed out before, may convey the very false idea that psychotherapy itself is orderly and logical and sedate.

POST-TRAUMATIC ASPECTS

One of the legacies of having been abused in childhood and adolescence is that one's inner life, one's ongoing stream of consciousness, is forever changed. Memories of different sorts continue to come back and intrude themselves into the daily and nightly life of the person. These memories can be in the form of mental images that are fleeting or may constitute fully detailed and lengthy scenarios of past assaults or seductions to which additional horrifying or sado-masochistic fantasied elements are added. The memories may be partially blocked, with unreal imagery, as if one is witnessing a movie of a depersonalized or automaton-like small child or adolescent, either terrified before or devastated after the assault, with no imagery of the actual assault. The memories may be intellectually and visually unavailable, such that only visceral and emotional responses are present without distinct imagery: terror, anger, perplexity, panic, paralysis, overwhelming sadness, pelvic pain, gastrointestinal distress with nausea and vomiting. The memories may be of ostensibly neutral or "normal" family events in which the person nevertheless feels a sense of threat or intimidation or panicky anticipation, since life was irrevocably altered from the first moment of aggressive intrusion, however "subtle" it may have been. The memories may be of assaults by others in situations unrelated to the initial abuse, or the memories may be of routine daily events after the assaults, but in which the feeling-tone has been colored by the secret awareness of a double life.

The memories of childhood assaults may come of themselves, or be triggered by closely similar events or by events in which there is only a symbolic or formal resemblance, such as being criticized, or being stared at, or, as in therapy, being asked to reveal oneself. The memories can come day or night, but may be less intense or even absent when one is caught up in an absorbing task, and worse when one is alone, or in situations somehow reminiscent of past dangerous times; they are especially intrusive when one lies down to sleep and the stream of consciousness is free to take one where it will.

It appears to be a basic human trait that past events get replayed in our memories and imaginations. If the event is trivial, the replaying may be brief, even fleeting, and of low emotional intensity. As the event becomes larger in importance and impact, especially when it is of an intrusive, painful, and psychologically or physically violent nature, then we replay it over and over again, going over it in our minds in a driven manner that we seem powerless to oppose for more than a few moments. This is true of all of us. It is a quality we share in our humanness.

In essence, of course, we are speaking of post-traumatic stress responses. There is a sense in which all of our actions can be viewed either as avoidances of potential traumas or as a series of damage control maneuvers after life's many little (and occasionally large) difficulties and insults. While this position about life in general may be philosophically respectable from a particularly pessimistic perspective, it trivializes the types of post-traumatic responses to which we are referring. The value of acknowledging that all humans respond to the disasters of life by reworking these events in seemingly endless variations is that it places the extremes of human responses to the extremes of human traumas within a normal and understandable framework.

This brings us to the practical question of how psychotherapy goes about helping the patient come to terms with the past. In a very basic sense, the process begins the moment when the therapist redefines for the patient the name and nature of her ailment. Labels are enormously powerful in guiding our understanding and thinking about a process. Words matter. The borderline patient fully understands that borderline is a label of scorn; it is a judgment of character in a moral sense, suggestive of manipulation, willfulness, and undesirable excesses of many types. The label of PTSD in one stroke changes all this. Conceptualizing "borderlines" with abuse histories as primarily having a stress response syndrome provides the patient/ therapist dyad with an understandable etiological framework and a clear direction for therapy. It explains things in a way that the "borderline" tag, which essentially explains nothing, never did. Previously inexplicable symptoms and reactions become understandable. The patient realistically embraces this rediagnosis, and she is correct in doing so. The therapist, who is also often overwhelmed by the intensity and variety of the patient's symptoms and in need of a map or a direction manual, similarly grabs onto the rediagnosis since it promises to provide that map. Symptoms begin to make sense and therapy gains an approach and a direction.

But the relabeling of the abused "borderline" is a double-edged therapeutic sword. Exclusive and narrow emphasis on the centrality of the abuse experience leads to the neglect in therapy of other important developmental factors and to the expectation that catharsis will make the patient better. It suggests to many therapists that a sort of empathic and embracing reparenting of the patient will teach the patient that she is lovable and not to blame. Unfortunately, such an approach often leads to a regressive cycle in which the patient is encouraged in unrestrained reexperiencing of abusive memories (Haaken & Schlaps, 1991). Lengthy and repeated hospitalizations ensue, with major disruption of the patient's ongoing family relationships, schooling, and employment. In essence, once the sexually abused person enters into contact with mental health professionals, there is danger that the sexual abuse-PTSD model of borderline symptoms cues the patient in as to how persons who have been abused ought to behave. This is particularly the case when a simple straight-line linkage between abuse and symptoms is assumed, ignoring the complexity of development, the child's rich fantasy contributions to her responses to the abuse, the regressive pull of holding and hugging the patient when she dissociates, and the identification of the patient with precisely those vicious aspects of the predator that she hates the most.

The therapist needs to keep the connections between abusive experience and symptomatic outcome more fluid and open than does the patient. The therapist has to be able to continue reworking and recycling the connections into greater and greater complexity until the picture is a more accurate reflection of the depth to which the abusive experiences have been assimilated into the ongoing personality of the patient. The fact that there is considerable risk of oversimplification in linking childhood abuse to borderline symptoms does not overshadow the great gain that can be derived from this correlation. It is in this sense that the relabeling of the patient, or the process, from borderline to PTSD represents the crucial first step in coming to terms with the past.

The description of PTSD in DSM-III-R conveys a very accurate picture of the range of human responses to overwhelming trauma. The three major components are: (1) persistent reexperiencing of the traumatic event; (2) persistent avoidance of stimuli associated with the trauma and/or numbing of general responsiveness; and (3) persistent symptoms of increased arousal. Self-injurious behavior is not ordinarily considered part of the PTSD picture. This implies either that the "borderline" component adds something additional to the PTSD diagnosis or that, as Herman (1992a) suggests, the particular types of repetitive trauma and enforced passivity that are the hallmarks of sexual abuse in childhood cause this particular symptom picture (self-injurious behavior, other borderline features) to be added to the "regular" PTSD features listed in DSM-III-R. After all, there is no a priori reason why different forms of trauma should all lead to a single PTSD picture.

The clearest examples of adult PTSD are those seen in combat veterans, refugees, and survivors of natural disasters, in whom nightmares, intrusive imagery, and overreactivity appear as understand-able sequelae to the stressors. A more difficult conceptual problem arises when the traumas or stressors seem to be followed primarily by personality trait changes, such as aggressiveness or reclusiveness, rather than by discrete symptoms, such as an exaggerated startle response to sudden noises. What I am suggesting here is that the neat distinction that we try to make between PTSD as a collection of symptoms and PTSD as expressed in personality changes that sometimes follow chronic exposure to certain stressors is an artificial one. Chronic stress, most notably having to live under certain kinds of frightening or intimidating conditions from which there is no escape, can cause the development of compensatory or adaptive be-havior patterns indistinguishable from personality traits. This is es-pecially so in the case of children, because their personalities are less fixed than those of adults and because they are more helpless to improve their external circumstances. The best the child can do is to alter the perception and significance of reality, or his or her own responses to the reality as much as possible, or his or her state of consciousness such as through depersonalization and dissociation.

With the borderlines under consideration here, we can distinguish several types of developmental responses to growing up in a certain kind of unsafe environment. The first are those that occur automati-cally as part of the PTSD. These are the reexperiencing of the trau-mas, the flashbacks, intrusive imagery, and nightmares. The second are those maneuvers that one has largely developed as a way of coping with or diminishing these images, such as alcohol and drug abuse, avoidance of being alone, self-injurious behaviors, and dis-sociative episodes. The third are those complex stylistic adaptations of being-in-the-world, which more closely resemble or, in fact, are personality traits, such as victimization expectations and behaviors, self-hatred, interpersonal manipulativeness or indirectness, sexual-ization of relationships, and affective instability.

We are not speaking simplistically of assaults leading to symp-toms. We are speaking of the entire pathological environment in which the child lives. Sexual assaults of children do not occur in a vacuum. Not only are there pathological family patterns present in situations in which repeated seductions and assaults take place, which continue on well past the initial assault experience, but equally important, the child's total life experience is irrevocably changed.

Life is never the same. The threat, the violation of essential boundaries, the absence of safety and a sense of security, the secret shame,
the burden of maintaining a facade of family cohesion, and the
replaying of all this over and over again in one's inner thoughts are
forever present from the moment that the first assault occurred, or,
often, even before, if the actual event was preceded by months or
years of suggestive or intimidating behaviors on the part of the adult.

DISILLUSIONMENT

From a historical perspective, it is likely that most human eras
have looked upon their own time as particularly strife-ridden and
close to anarchy. Nevertheless, as products of our own particular
point in history, it is hard to avoid the conclusion that this past
half-century has been especially filled with violence inflicted by humans upon other humans. Rarely in human history, or so it seems,
have civilian populations been the target of systematic efforts of
extermination and annihilation. Rarely in human history, or so it
seems, has there been this degree of wanton expression of violence
upon helpless victims, ranging from child abuse to state-sanctioned
torture. It may be that media technology makes us more aware of
violence, or even glamorizes and encourages it, or that the break-
down of traditional family values and social structures in the West
lend fertile ground or, again, encourage such violence. Although a
historical perspective will not directly help the victims of child sexual
and physical abuse, other than as a reminder that violence of humans
upon humans is nothing new, it undergirds the observation that
the trauma done to humans by other humans is considerably more
damaging and enduring in its psychological effects than trauma done
by floods, earthquakes, tornadoes, and other impersonal acts of nature. It is not that natural traumas are trivial, but rather that there is
something about being hurt intentionally and gratuitously by other
human beings, about being treated as an object by another human,
that is particularly gripping in its destructiveness and demoraliza-
tion. It is only to human actions that moral concepts such as good
and evil can meaningfully be applied.

It is likely that the driving force in human evolution was the need
to adapt to the dangers posed by other humans, rather than by
animals or natural forces. The greatest macro-environmental risk

to survival, even in primitive humans once the acquisition of tools provided some means of defense against predators of other species, was attacks by other humans. The present arms race is merely a modern extension of a process of warfare begun millions of years ago. Simultaneously, our evolution has made us extraordinarily social creatures, dependent for our infant and childhood survival upon an emotional attachment to a nurturant caretaker and surrogate caretakers and, for most of us, dependent as adults upon a supportive social network. Since we have evolved as social animals and cannot really survive otherwise, it is understandable that the betrayal of our expectations of care and sociality by our own parents, kin, and social group is particularly traumatic and has such long-lasting effects.

Although the specific PTSD symptoms following childhood abuse are very dramatic and conspicuous in their presentation, it is the more subtle characterological aftereffects of abuse that developed within the context of disturbed family relationships that are so devastating to the ongoing life adjustment of the patient and that represent the much more difficult challenge in psychotherapy. When a caregiver becomes a predator, a source of hurt and danger to the child, then far-reaching consequences to the development of that child ensue. That the environment is no longer safe is the first obvious consequence. A gradual, and more conceptual consequence, one that must await a child's own maturation in terms of cognitive stages, is that of a progressive disillusion in the goodness of its caregivers and, of course, in its own goodness.

Although there are some borderline/PTSD patients in whom one finds a near-absolute anger and rejection of the assaultive parent or of the parent who failed to protect and nurture, the more common pattern is that of oscillations between hating and loving the parent, between wanting nothing to do with the parent and irrational need for the parent's love, or even just for the parent to be nice. The patient craves acceptance, still trying to please a parent who has been critical, rejecting, and often abusive throughout much of the patient's life.

As in much else of the patient's mental life, the patient has to do double bookkeeping. The memories of the abuse are too intense and pressing to keep from consciousness, but now seem remote and disconnected from this middle-aged or somewhat elderly and not too unkind parent. It is often as if the aggressive parent or kin who abused the patient in childhood bears little resemblance to the somewhat pathetic adult who is intermittently trying to be nice to the patient at the present time.

Patients who have been abused by parents or kin, often with abuse entailing a degree of sadism and violence that is out of all proportion to what would be needed merely to ensure passive compliance on the child's part, nevertheless were raised by these parents who, at other moments, acted in loving ways, if only in the presence of others. Acts of kindness and comforting and nurturance were often interspersed with, and may have been the prelude to, acts of incredible violence and degradation. One need not search very far for the origins of "splitting" in such situations. The child, now the adult patient, learned how to juggle images of aggressiveness and nurturance, and most remarkable of all, to do this against a background of unpredictability. From any perspective, these images are irreconcilable; they cannot be juxtaposed in any sane way such that the child can accept that the same parent who appears to give warmth and love can also be so sadistic. But if they are irreconcilable, the child cannot give up the memories, or the fantasies if there are no memories, of the warm parent. The images remain split — existing in parallel, but not touching each other. The patient is willing to keep the images split in order to maintain a connection to the loving parent. The therapist thinks that the patient needs to fuse these images, to recognize that one and the same parent was both nurturant and monster. The patient knows that this cannot be done. The acts were too monstrous ever to be reconciled with any notion of a loving parent.

The problem in therapy is that any effort to resolve the splitting, to merge the good parent with the bad parent, inevitably confronts the recognition of disillusionment. Fusing the good and bad parent includes recognizing in full consciousness the enormity of the betrayal by the person entrusted with nurturance and support. At that point, the pristine image of the good parent, an obviously unrealistic one that was maintained only by the mechanism of splitting, must be relinquished. Disillusionment is, literally, the loss of the illusion. Illusions are not easily given up.

The temptation in working on parental issues in therapy is for the therapist to take a protective stance toward the patient and attack the offending parent, verbalizing for the patient the outrage that the therapist thinks the patient ought to feel toward the abuser. Yet, often, the patient will have none of it. The patient feels called upon either to defend the parent from the therapist's attack or else to attack the therapist. The patient has been well taught in childhood about the importance of family cohesiveness. The situation once again represents the case where the therapist and patient do not have the same agenda. The therapist moves in with a seemingly common sense approach that completely ignores the complexity and depth of the patient's ambivalent attachment to the abusing parent. The patient is not ready for the disillusion that must accompany an accurate appraisal of the parent.

First, the patient has identified himself with the abusing parent. To criticize the parent is to criticize the part of the patient that is identified with the predatory parent. For the patient to agree with this criticism is the equivalent of the patient attacking himself. The point is not that the therapist becomes paralysed from action by awareness of this partial merging of the patient with the predator, but that the therapist has respect for the complexity of the issues and for the process of double bookkeeping used by the patient.

Furthermore, the patient's sense of self includes identification with the abusing parent; to reject the parent would be to feel incomplete and empty, to have a deficient sense of self. Finally, since the abusing parent is often the dominant or focal point in the family, to attack or reject the parent, if done openly, means to risk losing the entire family. This is especially the case since the patient firmly believes, usually based on good evidence although mixed with an exaggerated sense of the powerfulness of the parent, that the family will close ranks to defend the perpetrator and ostracize the patient. As several patients have told me, "Without my family, I am nothing."

Second, to the extent that the patient believes that she was instrumental, or at least a partner, in the abuse, then she cannot accuse the abuser without accusing herself. This will be more completely discussed when we consider complicity, but it does overlap here.

Third, the patient remains frightened of the parent and overestimates, as mentioned above, the power and importance of the parent — even when geographically separated. Fantasies of vengeful attacks by the parent give new nightmares to the patient. More realistically, concerns of alienating other family members, who will rally around the parent and deny the veracity of the charges of sexual abuse, continue to frighten the patient. Alternatively, fears of causing the death of the parent, such as bringing on a heart attack, or ruining the parent further inhibit the patient from expressing negative feelings about the parent. The therapist, in asking the patient openly to attack the parent, is asking the impossible.

Fourth, and conversely, the patient is often barely managing to contain her aggression and is terrified of losing control of her anger. It does not help to have the therapist (or therapy group) goad the patient prematurely to "get in touch" with anger, or to direct the anger toward the person who truly deserves it. This will occur in the course of therapy, but the early and artificial manipulation of emotions is not in the patient's best interests.

Finally, the emotion appropriate to disillusion is sadness. Coming to terms with the past means realizing what one has lost, feeling the disillusionment associated with the loss, accepting the fact that this person who should have given love has given pain. The degree to which this is accepted is up to the patient, and like everything else, cannot be forced. The risk in exposing sadness is that it too may overwhelm the patient — setting up thoughts of suicide or other escapes from a realization too painful to live with.

COMPLICITY

Of the entire devastating legacy of childhood sexual abuse, I think that the patient's sense of complicity, and all that follows in its wake, represents the most distressing ongoing feature to the patient and the most intransigent stumbling block to the therapy. Incest oriented psychotherapy has two clear cognitive goals: validation by the therapist that the abuse really occurred, and assurance that the patient was not to blame for the abuse. The first of these is relatively easy to accomplish, although occasionally the patient may seek repeated assurances that she is believed.

The second goal comes to grief under the very powerful conviction of the patient that she indeed was a full partner to the crimes, if not their initiator. Therapists, group members, friends, and incest books and magazine articles all tell the abuse victim the same message: that she, as a child, could not possibly be responsible for the predatory actions of an adult (or much older teenager); that the perpetrator is the culpable one, the victim is innocent. But the victim tenaciously holds to the belief that those who try to exonerate her are merely inventing a therapeutic myth, merely telling her lies to make her feel better. She knows that if they truly knew everything, they too would agree that she is to blame. The patient maintains this belief about her guilt even when she can tell you that other abuse victims whom she knows could not possibly have been responsible for the abuse that they suffered as children. Other children truly were exploited and victimized, but that does not apply to her. It is different in her case. She went along with, participated in, encouraged, perhaps seduced, maybe deserved, and even accepted benefits for the sexual abuse of her childhood.

As with much else that we have discussed, there always seems to be an element of double bookkeeping in the thinking of PTSD/borderlines. On the one hand, the patient is well aware that she was abused in the full sense of the word; on the other, she insists that she is guilty, and she proceeds to exact terrible punishment upon herself. What are we to make of this? What is the patient saying? Let us see what is involved in believing in one's complicity.

The issue is complex; there is enormous variation in the life story of each individual. But several central themes persist, all converging to lead the patient inexorably to the conclusion that she is to blame. We all know what the themes are, having heard them in one version or another from each PTSD/borderline patient. In fact, there are times when the patients' beliefs in their own guilt are so outrageously implausible that we have trouble believing that the patient is serious, that an intelligent person could come up with conclusions of self-blame given what we know about the circumstances under which the abuse occurred. Yet the patient confounds us by insisting, in words and deeds, that she is indeed serious, that she does blame herself for the sexual abuse that occurred in her childhood. These beliefs reflect an interplay between what the child has been told, usually by the perpetrator, and what the child has come up with herself, using developmentally age-appropriate logical and moral processes regarding causality, as she tries to explain to herself why the abuse is happening to her. What follows is an incomplete catalog of the complicity themes that abused persons believe about themselves.

Bad Seed Theories

In its simple version, there are two basic motifs here. The first is that the child has been told by the parent, or parents, that she has always been different, even from early infancy and perhaps in utero. This difference is usually described to the patient as an inability to be comforted, dislike of being touched, stiffening rather than moving toward mother when being hugged, refusal of the breast or bottle. The essence of the list reflects some disturbance in bonding from the earliest moments. I do not wish to get into issues of truthfulness or accuracy of memory here. There are several interesting research possibilities present, but retrospective research, especially when the subject of the study has already been declared deviant in some way, has too many pitfalls even to conjecture about accuracy and distortions. I would make just a few further comments about this. Even if some problem of early bonding is suggested by these "data," such descriptions are certainly in the minority in the histories of abused children, and the reported difficulties in bonding are as likely to be related to the *mother's* difficulties at that time as they are to the child's. Whatever "reality" may underlie the observations that "you always were different," what is relevant here is that the child was told this and uses it against herself as evidence that she, being different, brought the sexual abuse upon herself.

Second, since broken homes and blended families as so common nowadays, the child is often told that he/she is just like the parent who is no longer present in the family constellation. Usually this similarity relates to sociopathic personality behaviors and characteristics: irresponsibility, impulsivity and violence, sexual amorality and lustfulness, alcoholism and drug abuse. The child has ongoing fantasies about what the absent parent (or parents) were really like, and what life would have been like if that parent had raised the child; input from the present parent or caretaker does not control the fantasies, but it does influence how the child thinks about him/herself.

Child as Surrogate Mother

In some PTSD/borderline families, there was a role reversal in which the child became caretaker to the family. Again, there are variations to the particular pattern, but several central themes emerge.

In one variation, mother is childish, perhaps an incest victim herself and often a victim of the abusive male partner. The child protects this mother, and sometimes her younger siblings, by offering herself to the father; mother accepts her daughter's sacrifice or indeed may even have offered the child to the male predator. In such situations, the child does much more than take on a sexual role with the male adult in the family; the child often raises the younger children and serves as mother's confidante and nurse. I am not ignoring these important functions, but do not wish to wander away from the thread that we are following regarding complicity.

In another variation, the child is made to feel responsible for family cohesiveness, for holding the family together. One way of doing this is by accepting father's (or brother's or grandfather's) sexual overtures, because to refuse would lead to family divisiveness and perhaps to the departure of the abusing person. Once sexual abuse has occurred, the same logic prevents the child from revealing it. This is clearly seen in those cases in which the abused child, even as an adult, is blamed for breaking up the family, if disclosure of the incest secret has in fact disrupted the family integrity (a strange word to describe such families).

A third variation is one in which the mother appears to be overtly mentally ill. Often, in such situations, the mother is the abusive person or, at the least, a conspirator with the abusing father. The child's role here is especially difficult, for while she conscientiously attempts to be mother's caretaker, she must also protect herself from mother's aggressive, occasionally homicidal attacks. It is likely that most claims of victimization within satanic ritual abuse stem from this family constellation.

Although one might think that this overall pattern of child as caretaker and surrogate mother would contribute least to the child's sense of guilt, since in fact the child was protecting mother and younger siblings, nevertheless there are clear psychodynamic grounds for self-censure. These relate most directly to whatever satisfaction and benefits the child derived from replacing mother. It sullies the martyrdom that others are willing to bestow upon the PTSD/borderline person, who perceives herself as entering into the alliance with father, even if under duress, voluntarily and, from her point of view, profitably. So even a situation in which the child acted altruistically and to her clear-cut detriment is turned upside down by the PTSD/borderline person into cause for guilt.

Child as Wanton Woman Who
Deserved What She Got

If ever there were a case demonstrating male chauvinistic rationalizations, it is here; yet the abused child places the entire burden upon herself. This is not accidental, of course, since she has usually been brainwashed by the perpetrator into thinking that she is the prime mover and he is passively compliant in gratifying her wishes and giving her what she really wants or deserves. The themes and variations proceed as follows:

> I was precociously sexual and, in a variety of ways, tempted the man to desire me sexually. Since I am irresistible, perhaps magically, the man could not resist. Therefore he cannot be blamed; all blame falls on me. I was willful; at worst, he was weak.
>
> Furthermore, I tempted the man because I wanted him to be sexual with me. I know this because he told me, "You've been wanting this a long time, and now I'm going to give you what you've been wanting."
>
> Still further, I am guilty because I enjoyed aspects of the sexual abuse. Even when I thought I hated it, I felt myself getting aroused. I am depraved.
>
> Finally, and proof of my essential perversion, I accepted bribes and favors. I took candy and toys; I took money and spent it at the store. My siblings did not get such presents. I went on special trips with daddy. I know what such women are called who trade sex for payment. I sold myself. I did whatever he wanted me to do sexually. I am a prostitute. That is what my father told me I am, and he is right.

Compounding this overwhelming sense of complicity is the patient's perception, reinforced by the perpetrator, that having complied even once, no matter what the realistic duress, the child is a full partner in crime and cannot reveal the secret without totally implicating herself. The child has been told either that no one will believe her or that everyone will believe that she really wanted and initiated the sex.

As with many of the other examples of double-bookkeeping, the

PTSD/borderline person had to ignore a lot of discrepant messages at the time, such as father saying that he would kill her if she ever told anybody, and throughout her adolescent years, as she slowly came to realize that the abuser was to blame. She continues to discount or excuse any information that might take blame away from herself. The PTSD/borderline remains steadfast in resisting all attempts of others to relieve her guilt and to place it where everyone else thinks it belongs: on the perpetrator and those who permitted or tolerated the abuse.

What is it the patient thinks she knows that we do not?

The patient has looked into the heart of evil and saw herself there. Either she was evil in the first place, attracting and perverting those about her, including the abuser, or evil has permeated her very being as a result of her participation, however passive, in the abuse. She knows this with an immediacy that is more powerful than the weak apologetics of her therapist and others. What this means is that the therapist's continued reassurances and arguments that the victim is not to blame do not convince the victim. The therapist must be willing to hear out, without arguing, all that the patient has to say about her own complicity, if she is willing to go into the details. Furthermore, since the legacy of abuse is in part a residual of anger and violence and, at times, sadism within oneself, the patient must also come to terms with that part of herself that most resembles the abuser. Some abuse victims go on to be abusers, sometimes of children, sometimes in their adult intimate relationships; others feel the anger and impulses and resist them, but nevertheless are aware of their potential for violence. Some despair of ever trusting themselves enough to risk having their own children, for fear that they will repeat the cycle of child abuse. This area of concern is a particularly devastating one for many abuse victims, for it brings home to them how very far reaching and encompassing are the effects of what the abuser did to them.

Such are the long-term consequences of childhood abuse that need to be dealt with in therapy to whatever extent the patient wishes and can sustain. It is for these reasons that patients will not accept bland reassurances of innocence, even though we on the outside fully believe that they are innocent, no matter what the facts of complicity may be.

RESOLUTION IN FORGIVENESS VS.
ACCEPTANCE OF IRRECONCILABILITY

I am least comfortable with this topic, probably because of the complexity, when one begins to think about it, of the notion of forgiveness. Furthermore, forgiveness is often assumed to belong to the domain of religious beliefs and practices. To the extent that this is so, the psychotherapist may have no special expertise or qualifications to offer opinions or work on forgiveness with patients.

As a concept, forgiveness touches upon basic issues of morality, justice, pardon, love, suffering, and reconciliation. On the one hand, forgiveness is one of the basic tenets of Christianity, held up as an ideal stance to take toward those who have damaged us. On the other hand, forgiveness has entered the self-help books (Smedes, 1984), especially those directed toward victims of sexual abuse, in such a general way as to dilute the very strong meaning of the term. In this latter sense, abuse victims are given activities and exercises by which they can work toward forgiveness of themselves, including their body parts that have been violated. Since the processes of forgiving oneself and forgiving one's trespassers appear to be very different entities, I will restrict the use of the term "forgiveness" in this discussion to a change in attitude of how I feel about the other person. The notion of forgiving oneself has already been examined under the topic of coming to terms with the past.

An interesting literature has developed in the past two decades on the topic of forgiveness. Some of this literature is primarily out of a pastoral and religious tradition (Brandsma, 1982; Cunningham, 1986), some from a philosophical viewpoint (Downie, 1965; Lewis, 1980; Murphy & Hampton, 1988), and some directed primarily to the issue of forgiveness as it surfaces, or might have relevance, in psychotherapy (Bergin, 1988; Enright, Santos, & Al-Mabuk, 1989; Enright & the Human Development Study Group, 1991).

Consensus on what does and does not constitute forgiveness is hard to come by, leading to considerable disagreement among writers about what forgiveness is and whether it is even desirable as a goal in psychotherapy. Is forgiving the perpetrator of childhood sexual abuse ultimately necessary for complete healing of the damaged individual or is it an essentially inauthentic (i.e., contrived) resolution, the attainment of which asks of the injured person both the realistically unattainable and the psychologically undesirable? For those who hold to a spiritual perspective, forgiveness is an important objective, because the harboring of anger will ultimately interfere with one's relationship to God. Will the incest victim be healthier if she can forgive her trespassers or, conversely, if she holds on to a modicum or more of justifiable anger and resentment, providing that it does not dominate her very being? This latter question may be an empirical and researchable rather than a strictly moral one, if we can ever come to agreement on how to define "healthier," "forgiveness," "modicum," "resentment," "dominate," and "being." If one approaches the subject with the assumption that refusal or inability (the language of volition versus compulsion again) to forgive inherently diminishes the person, then there can be no debate about whether one ought to forgive; the only issue is a practical one of whether it can be done and, if so, what specific means would best accomplish this?

But if one does not make that assumption, if one comes to the problem with a degree of philosophical and psychological skepticism, then not only are the answers quite unclear, but also there is no single answer that would be true for all abused persons. Some will be better off if they could forgive, some would be better off not forgiving. For many, the process of working on forgiveness may be what is most helpful psychologically, whatever the ultimate resolution in forgiveness there might be.

What are the components of forgiveness? Although there is considerable disagreement as to what is entailed in forgiveness, leading to disputes as to whether a particular act of forgiveness really constitutes forgiveness or something else, such as pardon or justice, the following factors are generally thought of as the elements required for forgiveness to have taken place. I would only note at this point that, since the notion of forgiveness encompasses, to a large extent, a subjective attitude as well as external behavior, there is bound to be a gap between the words we use to describe someone's mental events and how the forgiving person is truly feeling and thinking.

1. Acknowledgment that I have been damaged in some way by an offender. This seems to be the starting point; without offense, there is no question of forgiveness.

2. The sense that the other person is not necessarily deserving, by anything he has done, of my forgiveness. This is an important point, since it severs any relationship between my decision to forgive and the offender's statements about regrets, apologies, penitence or, on the other hand, his continued justification of why he offended me. Forgiveness cannot be ordered, owed, or demanded; it can only be freely given, with no conditions or expectation of the other. Softening of my attitude toward the offender that is conditional upon the contrition of the offender is usually considered pardon rather than forgiveness.

3. In forgiving, I freely give up my anger and, with it, any claims, moral or material, that I may have against the offender. The offender is no longer obligated to me because of what he has done to me. I release the offender from any hold I had over him because of his misdeeds against me.

4. Some theorists add that a feeling of love for the offender must replace the feeling of anger in order for it to be true forgiveness. I personally find this unreasonable and elitist. It not only asks for a degree of sainthood that few can reach, thereby diminishing whatever accomplishments I may have achieved at giving up my anger, but seems to intrude an additional requirement that does not appear to be essential to my forgiveness. The expectation that I should feel love toward my offender stems from a particular religious tradition and may not have a universal claim on me. At a practical level, it is not clear that loving my offender will improve my mental health. I may be willing to forgive and to do this in a sincere way, replacing anger with neutrality, but not with affection or love. To demand that I have love for my abuser in order for my effort to be considered true forgiveness may only serve to diminish my hard struggle to forgive at all. It is possible that what the theorists are referring to as the component necessary for complete forgiveness is compassion, not love, but this is not clear in the writings. The many nuances, subtleties, and subjective judgments involved as we consider forgiveness brings back my earlier reticence to discuss the topic. But the subject is too important to sidestep. I cannot claim that I am correct in how I view or

practice or fail at forgiveness, but can only present it as it best makes sense to me.

What are the benefits that accrue to the forgiver? Is forgiveness a proper subject for psychotherapy? At a most basic level, we have seen people in therapy, and elsewhere, who are consumed by their anger, who scatter their anger all about them, even to those who love them, and who appear miserable with that anger. One does get the sense that they cannot move on in life until some of the anger is abandoned. But even here I must qualify my comments by pointing out that, miserable as the person appears, it is possible that holding on to the anger is an important piece of his "selfhood" and that the emotional costs of giving up the anger and resentment are greater than the benefits. Nevertheless, conventional wisdom and common sense seem to tell us that, if the person could give up some anger in a manner that would not represent a defeat, she would have a better life. I only wish to insert here the usual skeptic's warning about not taking too many "common sense" aphorisms for granted.

Furthermore, it is possible to work with patients in therapy on themes related to their anger without necessarily bringing in the more difficult or, at times, irrelevant goal of forgiveness. But forgiveness may be both relevant and helpful, and the therapist should be open to the patient's interest in the possibility, or may properly inquire whether the patient is interested in thinking and talking about forgiveness. The dangers in doing this are that it may appear to the patient, merely by the therapist's raising the issue of forgiveness, that the therapist is siding with the offender or trivializing the offenses, as if suggesting to the patient that she is wrong in being so angry and that she ought to forgive the offender. It is the therapist's duty to be sensitive to this issue in both directions, including whatever personal biases, religious beliefs, and countertransference issues the therapist may have about forgiveness in general or the role of the patient's anger in particular. Since we have talked earlier about the importance of the therapist's validating the patient's rights to the feelings she is feeling, we need to keep in mind that any casual discussion about anger and forgiveness may have a critical and judgmental tone from the patient's perspective; further, I am not suggesting here that the patient would be incorrect.

In addition to the possibility that work on forgiveness may help the patient with anger, a further benefit may be that a discussion of forgiveness will get at the equally troublesome sentiment of entitlement. A sense of entitlement is a powerful factor in driving the patient into a variety of destructive behaviors, designed either to obtain that to which one feels entitled or to demonstrate by self-injurious behaviors how much one has been hurt; one feels, in essence, entitled to hurt oneself in response to injuries inflicted by others. Forgiveness entails, along with much else, giving up my claims to entitlement. Nothing more is owed to me from the offender or anyone else. Since entitlement is often a core theme, relinquishing it, even partially, is a significant personal accomplishment. If work on forgiveness can lead in this direction, then it is a fruitful area to consider.

It may be that forgiveness is just not possible, that the person is not interested in forgiving, or sees it as unattainable at this time, or even thinks that it is incorrect for her, that it would represent a defeat and a loss. A therapist should not be judgmental about the patient's attitude regarding this, even if he/she truly believes that improvement is impossible without forgiveness. If the therapist can agree to follow the patient's lead in this area, then the alternative to forgiveness is acceptance of irreconciliability.

This leads back to my earlier observation that the process of working on forgiveness in therapy may be most helpful psychologically, whatever the ultimate resolution. Approaching the sexual abuse and its aftermath from many perspectives, including that of forgiveness, enables the patient to examine at some remove the evolution of her responses to the abuse. Murphy (Murphy & Hampton, 1988) argues strongly that resentment under circumstances of injury is an essential component of self-respect and that, conversely, forgiveness too easily embraced signifies a lack of self-respect. Therapeutic work on forgiveness entails an examination of what injury beyond the physical, although this is not inconsequential, was done to the patient, and what attitudes the patient wishes to maintain toward the perpetrator. The perpetrator treated the patient as an object to be used for personal gratification; does forgiveness of the perpetrator entail agreement with this view of oneself? On the other hand, it is possible that forgiveness is a way of saying to myself that I have emerged undefeated, although damaged, and that I have grown to the point where I can forgive and get on with my life.

I personally think that the additional expectation of feeling love in place of resentment toward the perpetrator, which may make sense from some religious frameworks, is psychologically naive in terms of the complexity of the relationship between perpetrator and victim. I also recognize that, of course, the very essence of the requirements of charity and forgiveness is that they are most difficult to achieve. A moral precept that asked the easy responses of us would hardly be much of a precept. Virtues must be encouraged precisely because they go against our selfishness and worldly self-interests. Nevertheless, since the relationship between victim and perpetrator was often one of extreme closeness and dependence, such as parent-child, in which the very notion of love has been totally subverted from any normal meaning of the word, then in what sense of "love" should the victim be asked to love the abuser? To love the abuser as a parent should be loved? To love the abuser as one adult to another? To love the abuser as one human to another, or as one Christian to another? The terms need to be clarified before expectations are placed upon the patient.

I am going into these details because it is clear that the therapist's personal values will be critical here and because a fair amount of psychotherapy and abuse work is done under church sponsorship and by pastoral counselors. This represents an interesting area of overlapping and shared responsibilities, which the topic of forgiveness so well highlights. From my viewpoint as a secular therapist, I would suggest that the essential task of the therapist is to prevent intrusion of one's own values and attitudes about forgiveness, in order to explore and work with the patient in the direction that is consistent with the patient's values and psychological necessities. It is an open question as to whether the therapist should make his/her own value systems clear to the patient. As usual, I would avoid a doctrinaire approach to this very delicate subject. I emphasize this precisely because forgiveness overlaps so fully with religious and spiritual attitudes, areas in which the therapist ordinarily holds no special expertise. But cautiousness about an area is not the same as avoidance. Since forgiveness is a topic that is of concern to many patients, the therapist must be prepared to allow it into therapy and work with it. The therapist may wish (or ought to wish) to obtain consultation from professionals who have given more thought to the matter or who hold a common faith with the patient. But then again, consultation in general, while working with PTSD/borderlines, is always a good idea.

SUMMARY

The tasks of the patient who has been sexually abused in childhood involve a lifetime operation, only a small portion of which occurs in the therapy office. Although each patient's life history is unique, there nevertheless are sufficient areas of commonality as to make the emergence of certain themes fairly predictable within the course of psychotherapy. Coming to terms with the abuses of the past is one such general area that may mean different things to different people, but which must, by the very nature of human memory and reactivity, figure prominently in treatment. Working on "coming to terms with" also implies a positive direction, a sense of a future that can be different from the past. There are undoubtedly many ways to conceptualize just which issues of the past one needs to come to terms with. I have suggested four broad areas that seem to encompass many of the particular issues raised by PTSD/borderlines. The following chapter shifts the focus from the past to the present, although recognizing the fact that past, present, and future are always combined, in different proportions, in our consciousness.

8

How the Past Controls
the Present

The danger for patients, a danger encouraged by therapists and the general climate of the times, is that patients will come to define themselves as victims, as if their whole being takes on meaning only to the extent that they identify themselves as victims. An entire industry has arisen in the late 20th century around victimology. The industry encompasses the media (TV shows, movies, books and magazines), mental health (therapists and counselors, group therapists, workshop leaders, specialized inpatient and outpatient treatment programs), and the law (litigation lawyers who coach patients regarding what symptoms to display).

At the center of the industry is the victim. Having once been literally a victim, the victim, now designated a survivor, is especially susceptible to several kinds of distortion of the present moment, two of which are important here: to create and perceive present situations as replicas of the past in which he/she will once again be exploited, and to be vulnerable to the suggestions of others that encourage the survivor to maintain victim status by reframing present events as new examples of exploitation.

While recognizing that I appear to be overstating the case and to be insensitive to the suffering that patients have endured, I still must emphasize that we do our patients a disservice by glorifying the victim role to heroic proportions. The media — and this is entirely their prerogative since they are not bound by therapeutic constraints — have sensationalized victimhood. For example, Stephen King's latest horror novel, *Gerald's Game*, is about a woman who, because she was sexually abused as a child by her father, allows her husband to handcuff her to a bedpost in an isolated house. When the husband promptly dies of a heart attack, the woman, trapped by her past, is once again in the predicament of the victim's role. In a similar vein, Brian De Palma's movie, "Raising Cain," depicts child abuse within the context of a man with multiple personality disorder, one of whose personas is a murderous psychopath. The sensationalism involved in these depictions contributes to the public misperception of these conditions, but also serves as the template for how troubled persons are expected to behave.

The mental health field, driven by a zealotry that conveniently finds common interest with market forces to maintain full clinic enrollment, encourages persons to explore and find symptoms of PTSD attributable to past injuries, a process that culminates in the creation and fortuitous discovery of multiple personalities and the establishment of profitable multiple personality and dissociative disorder clinics throughout the country. Coincident with this, lawyers have vociferously advocated the viewpoint that everyone has a claim and that someone is to blame.

One need only pick up practically any daily newspaper in any large city in the U.S. in order to find a story about a claim of PTSD-like damages resulting from a variety of events, specious or otherwise. For example, one story carries the claims of a 29-year-old male lawyer, a former aide to a woman city council member, that the councilwoman sexually harassed him during a 20-month period that ended with his resignation one year ago. Except for a brief consultation job, the ex-aide, a lawyer himself, has been unemployed since then. The ex-aide claims that, as a result of the councilwoman's outrageous conduct, he "has suffered and continues to suffer severe emotional distress, depression, sleeplessness, humiliation, embarrassment, pain and suffering, and lost wages and benefits" (*Minneapolis Star-Tribune*, August 25, 1992). He is seeking more than $150,000 in damages from the councilwoman and the city. For her defense the councilwoman is entitled to retain a private attorney at $130 per hour at city expense. By early December 1992, the councilwoman's lawyers had billed the city $30,000, and this was just for the initial factfinding and legal motions phase of the suit. The case is not expected to come to trial for at least six months (*Minneapolis Star-Tribune*, December 3, 1992). I wonder if the money will come from a school children's hot lunch program, a housing program for homeless adults, or salaries for two case managers for the disabled.

I wish to differentiate between sexual harassment in the workplace, which we know occurs (although I personally have my doubts in this particular case), and the magnitude of the claims of personal injury brought about such harassment. Not every interpersonal conflict and bruised sensitivity need produce chronic insomnia, nervousness, inability to find employment, and entitlement to hundreds of thousands of dollars of damages. There is a terrible cost to the public from this type of lawsuit. One would think that it would be possible to pursue a grievance regarding workplace harassment without resort to the well-publicized list of PTSD symptoms. The concept of PTSD, clearly intended to describe reactions to severe stressors that are outside the usual range of human experiences, has been extended to cover all unpleasant events in which there is a possibility of financial gain and personal revenge. Such situations diminish appreciation of the real trauma suffered by true victims of childhood sexual abuse and similar chronically abusive environments.

The essential problem is one of balance as we think about cases in which a patient has been damaged by childhood abuse. The essential solution is damage assessment, damage control, and debatedly, damage reparations. What has happened instead is that the patient has been told, directly and indirectly, that, as a result of having experienced childhood abuse, she is a victim who is expected to have certain psychological symptoms that effectively eliminate taking responsibility for present behavior. The culmination of this trend occurs when the mental health professionals divide the person up into little parts, called personas or inner children, most of whom are stuck somewhere back in the abusive years of childhood and adolescence, and therefore cannot be expected to behave responsibly or to cooperate with the psychotherapy. These "personas" may self-mutilate, hide themselves under blankets, become promiscuous, fail to function as wage-earner or family member, or use alcohol and drugs, but no one can be held responsible because the action is always done by someone else, i.e., by a different and usually elusive persona. Defense attorneys, never ones to avoid trying out and exploiting the latest fad, increasingly employ the multiple personality claim for an insanity defense in criminal trials (Perr, 1991).

I do not wish to focus solely on multiple personality disorder. The broader notion of PTSD, of which MPD is only an egregious example, has become the latest category by which to describe and explain most psychiatric entities and emotional troubles other than major affective disorders and schizophrenia. Mental health professionals and lawyers, each bearing their own unique gifts, descend upon every fresh disaster (mudslide, flood, tornado, shooting spree, shipwreck, operation Desert Storm), looking for budding cases of PTSD and generating business for themselves in the process. Whether the benefit of such early "identification" and treatment of PTSD outweighs the harm of establishing expectations of long-lasting PTSD symptoms in the context of traumas, accidents, and disasters for which compensatory payments may be involved is not clear. The efficacy of psychological trauma services has not been demonstrated (Solomon, Gerrity, & Muff, 1992). What is clear is that the number of people who suffer from PTSD, including the number who stand to benefit materially if such suffering can be documented and litigated, as well as the percentage of people in each disaster who go on to develop PTSD, has risen greatly in the past decade (Sparr & Boehnlein, 1990).

There is no doubt that people do suffer from PTSD, and that PTSD was long ignored or even derided. Our belated awareness that many "borderlines" developed their symptoms in the context of childhood trauma testifies to the importance of recognizing the existence and acknowledging the relevance of symptoms of PTSD. The basic issue, nevertheless, is one of balance, of not getting caught up in a fashionable social movement that encourages embellishment of symptoms, attribution of blame, and diminished responsibility for oneself in the wake of life's misfortunes.

Perhaps it needs to be reemphasized that reworking traumatic events in one's head, experiencing physiological arousal when thinking about or in situations reminiscent of the events, and attempts to avoid thinking about the trauma, do not in themselves constitute a disorder (Chrousos & Gold, 1992). These are normal and universal responses to life-threatening experiences of all types and represent part of the normal process of human adaptation. No animal species would survive if it did not learn rapidly, even with a single trial, to identify and respond, via fight or flight, to life-threatening situations. The physiological and psychological response to trauma does not in itself require treatment, although for a variety of reasons our society may choose to make it available. The stress-response syndrome is self-limiting in most cases. For precisely this reason, DSM-III-R added a time-duration criterion that the symptoms must be present for more than one month before a diagnosis of PTSD is made. Davidson and Foa (1991), co-chairs on the DSM-IV subcommittee on PTSD, comment that the distinction made in DSM-III between acute and chronic PTSD was dropped in DSM-III-R, partly because acute PTSD symptoms could be viewed as a normative response to an abnormal event. This being the case, Davidson and Foa suggest that PTSD should not be uncritically applied as a psychiatric diagnosis, noting that more than 50% of rape victims recover from the psychological trauma within three months. One proposed solution would be to introduce a V code to denote uncomplicated post-traumatic stress reactions, a step that would emphasize the difference between the normal response to trauma and PTSD.

The closest analogy to this distinction is the relationship of uncomplicated bereavement to depression. Bereavement, the response to loss of a loved one, is not an abnormal response, nor does it necessarily require treatment, even though, in its early stages, it may fully resemble major depressive disorder. Our society may choose to offer grief counseling to replace other, more traditional forms of comfort that are less available in our modern age. Our society may also choose to support pharmacological treatment for the insomnia or anorexia that accompanies grief, but neither bereavement nor traumatic stress response, no matter how intense in the acute phase, constitute psychiatric disorders. This perspective is fully compatible with the observation that a certain number of persons suffering from bereavement and traumatic stress responses will progress to conditions that are chronic, maladaptive, and disabling. Somewhere along the time and severity line between initial normal response and chronic maladaptive response, we, by convention, call the response a disorder. The exact point on the continuum is somewhat arbitrary, similar to most definitions that separate health and illness. I am not suggesting that preventive intervention is not possible or desirable in some early cases. The main caution is that we not too readily medicalize normal human responses and, specifically in the case of trauma, we not turn distress into disorder by reinforcing development of new or exaggerated symptoms.

In this discussion about the effects of the traumatic past on the present, I shall focus on how these issues emerge as themes in the process of psychotherapy, paying particular attention to the role that therapy can play in encouraging or discouraging proliferation of symptoms. Underlying this discussion is the awareness of a basic dilemma in the therapy with PTSD/borderlines: The short-term therapeutic interventions designed to decrease the immediate likelihood of self-injurious and suicidal behavior are often at odds, because they may play into the patient's pathological goals of gratification of needs and reworking old issues, with the long-term goal of decreasing the use of self-injurious and suicidal threats as symptomatic ways of dealing with stressful situations that stir up old abuse reactions. To the extent that the therapist feels compelled to intervene with rescue attempts and other interventions that shift focus away from examining what is driving a patient's particular symptomatic response at the moment, therapy will likely reinforce rather than discourage continuation of such symptomatic behaviors.

DISSOCIATIVE EPISODES AND NUMBING

Dissociation is often considered one of the hallmarks of PTSD, especially of the PTSD/borderline syndrome that follows in the wake of childhood sexual abuse. It is commonly accepted that the abused child learned to dissociate during the abuse as a way of distancing herself from what was being done to her, and that the ability and tendency to dissociate then generalized to become a characteristic way for the PTSD/borderline person to deal with many sorts of stress and emotional arousal.

There is an interesting problem, however, that makes this direct causal linkage from abuse to childhood dissociation to adult dissociation somewhat puzzling. In neither DSM-III nor DSM-III-R is dissociation even mentioned as a symptom of borderline personality disorder. What are we to make of this? In Gunderson's 1984 book on BPD, dissociation is mentioned briefly in five places, either in reference to depersonalization and derealization, as a component of transient psychotic episodes, or as necessitating residential treatment if dissociation is prolonged. The only mention of dissociation in Stone's 1980 book is in a reference to Benjamin Rush, the founder of American psychiatry and a signer of the Declaration of Independence. Stone's 1990 book on his follow-up studies of BPD refers to dissociation only in passing in a two-page discussion of multiple personality disorder, which itself lies buried in the back of the volume in an Appendix entitled "Unusual Syndromes." Kernberg's 1975 book does not list dissociation in the index and his 1984 book refers briefly to dissociation as a subspecies of splitting, in the context of dissociated or split-off aspects of the self. Clearly, Kernberg is referring to the psychological defense of splitting and not to dissociative episodes. In Druck's (1989) discussion of therapeutic approaches to the borderline patient, dissociation is not listed in the index.

In my 1988 book on BPD, I make several references to dissociative episodes as a form of self-induced trance states, occurring primarily in response to memories of abuse or as a prelude to self-injurious behaviors. But in general, none of the above-mentioned authors focus particularly on dissociative episodes. The DSM-IV subcommittee on Axis II disorders, commissioned with the revision of the diagnostic criteria for BPD, has recommended the inclusion of a ninth criterion in recognition of the importance of cognitive disturbances seen in BPD. Specifically mentioned in the proposed new criterion are "transient, stress-related psychotic-like experiences, e.g., paranoid ideation, depersonalization, derealization, hypnogogic illusions." Dissociative episodes, however, are not included in this description and thus will not appear as part of the diagnostic criteria recommended for BPD in DSM-IV.

As I look back to my own work with borderline patients from 1968 to 1988, I do not recall that dissociative episodes were particularly prominent. Neither, apparently, did Gunderson, Kernberg, Druck, or Stone find them so. In my clinical experience, dissociative episodes were certainly present, but they did not dominate the clinical picture, as they appear to now. What has happened? Is it another example of men being blind to women's anguish? I cannot believe that patients were dissociating as obviously as they are today, and that we all missed it. I realize that this may sound like a self-serving rationalization, since obviously we missed a fair amount of sexual abuse histories. But there is a difference. A patient, if not directly asked, may not volunteer a history of sexual abuse, or may even deny it when an inquiry is made, but there is no missing the dissociative states that we have begun to see in the past few years. It is not that we are seeing more borderlines nowadays. In 1979, some of my nurses went on strike because they said I was admitting too many borderlines. This was not true, of course, since the ward was a residency-run service and I personally was not staffing the emergency room nights and weekends admitting borderlines, nor was I encouraging the psychiatric residents to admit borderlines. Borderlines were coming to the emergency room with symptoms severe enough to require hospitalization. Many borderlines were seen and admitted to psychiatric wards 20 years ago, but they did not have nor report prominent dissociative episodes.

The best conclusion that I can reach to explain the apparent increase in prevalence and prominence of dissociative symptoms in borderlines is that the psychiatric profession has coached patients in what symptoms they are expected to display. This is not surprising or unusual; we know that culture shapes many psychiatric symptoms and syndromes. In the present situation, the therapists have not invented dissociative episodes; dissociation was there, but only as one among many symptoms, and less prominent than self-injurious behaviors, stormy interpersonal encounters, and angry, dysphoric moods. The major controversy ten years ago was whether BPD was a variant of affective disorders, since mood disturbances and instability appeared so prominently in the symptom picture of borderlines. This focus on affective symptoms has receded and now we see the more prominent presentation of PTSD symptoms.

Just as some patients were trained and/or learned, if they wished to be admitted to hospital, to talk of suicide or homicide, or of flashbacks and nightmares if involved in a lawsuit for disaster damages, so dissociative symptoms have been shaped by the mental health profession's and the media's extraordinary fascination with dissociative episodes and the multiple personas that are the logical consequences of extreme dissociation. One hundred years ago, physicians were intrigued by patients who had hysterical seizures, paralyses, and paresthesias; now we are intrigued by disorders of states of consciousness.

There is at present controversy over whether PTSD should be placed under the anxiety disorders, where it now resides, or moved to the dissociative disorders, as was recommended by the DSM-III-R advisory committee on dissociative disorders (Brett, Spitzer, & Williams, 1988). The consensus wisely has been to keep it within the anxiety disorder category, since dissociation forms only one cluster of symptoms seen in PTSD. One can see where the irrepressible logic of such a lateral transfer would go: BPD is a form of PTSD which is a form of dissociative disorder. The interplay of territorial and market forces in the professions seems clearly at work in these considerations. The following is a case in which the child abuse/PTSD-borderline-multiple personality disorders are confounded, to the detriment of the patient.

CASE 15

Ms. Q is a 29-year-old, presently unemployed dental hygienist, married, with one young child. She was functioning well as worker, mother, and wife until she became depressed one year ago following her mother's death. As the depression worsened, she also developed anxiety symptoms and some vague recollections of childhood sexual abuse by an uncle living nearby. She was referred for psychotherapy in order to work on the abuse issues. She became increasingly upset as her memories returned. She joined a group of abuse survivors and began reading several books on victims of sexual abuse. A suicide attempt by tricyclic overdosage precipitated hospital admission.

In the hospital, Ms. Q started to have increasingly vivid imagery of abuse, initially by the uncle and then by a vague group of men and women clustered about her in a barn. She went into trance states while experiencing these imageries, feeling as she did at the time of the abuse. Nursing staff, in working with Ms. Q, labeled these as flashbacks and encouraged her to "get into the memories" and to talk about them. As Ms. Q began to have more and more trouble "returning" from the trance states, and spoke in a little girl's voice during the episodes, or screamed and cried about what she was remembering, the staff spoke reassuringly to her, held her hand, cradled her head in their laps, and asked for the name of the little girl who seemed to emerge from the distraught young lady. Fourteen somewhat distinct personalities were discovered and named during the next six weeks, with several of the personas engaging in increasingly vicious self-injurious behaviors while in the hospital. The trance and self-injurious behaviors never occurred when her husband and child were visiting her. One year later, she was still spending more time in the hospital than out, dissociating and hurting herself as staff continued to encourage more memories and more presence of the many personas.

This has been a one-sided case presentation. I assume that success stories of psychotherapy with patients who dissociate can be found with equal ease. Nevertheless, I use this case report to raise an obvious point that has troubled many therapists. What is the proper response to dissociative episodes? Once again, I think that a middle course is most responsible. The therapist can acknowledge that dissociative episodes are occurring and can label them as such for the patient. The patient can be told, without going into a wordy explanation, that dissociative episodes represent a psychological response to extreme emotional arousal and danger, and that the patient has begun to use this mechanism for more and more situations that are less and less threatening.

It is the patient's task to begin to look at imagery and events that trigger dissociation and to begin to verbalize these mental processes in therapy. Some trance states are clearly self-induced and, like any other activity, practice improves the speed and depth with which the trance state is induced. Furthermore, we know, as discussed in Chapter 4, that dissociative patients are highly susceptible to "remembering" and elaborating memories based upon suggestions of what might have occurred in the past. This is especially true when the therapist encourages the patient, during a dissociative episode, to recover forgotten memories. I would see it as the therapist's responsibility to help the patient move out of the dissociative state and then process what had just occurred, rather than encourage further immersion into dissociation.

The therapist only reinforces dissociative states by telling the patient that she is not responsible for actions performed during these states and has no control over the rapid shifting of states of consciousness. We are not talking of a court of law in which a therapist has to prove an assertion beyond a reasonable doubt, nor are we talking about obviously psychotic illnesses. We are talking about therapy and the stance that a therapist takes with regard to a patient's actions. Is it just a convenient fiction to tell a patient he/she is responsible during dissociative episodes? The fact is that there is no objective way to decide this; responsibility and control are defined by the two parties involved in therapy, as they struggle to examine and change today's response to yesterday's trauma. What has happened to the patient in childhood is very sad. What will happen to the patient in the future will be even sadder if responsibility is sloughed off onto putative personas.

We have to examine what the therapist conveys to the patient about dissociative episodes. Are we saying: "We agree that you are flooded with very distressing imagery and thoughts. We agree that you cannot control yourself. Therefore, WHAT? . . . " Therefore, we will step in and rescue you. The problem is how completely do we step in? What specific interventions do we apply? How can we tell who really needs taking over and when? How much do our fears of litigation and our need to be omnipotent rescuers lead us into some very untherapeutic maneuvers?

The therapist has to deal with the patient as a single person, speaking of and even to the various personas as aspects of a single personality. This may be particularly difficult with the patient who has been reinforced and rewarded for dissociative episodes and displays of multiple personas. The pay-off in terms of high drama, intense interpersonal involvement, and license to act-out while disowning responsibility are not things that will be given up readily. The therapist does not have to argue with the patient, or insist that the patient give up any personas, or do anything that he/she does not want to do. The therapist has to maintain the integrity of his/her own position. The therapist cannot tell the patient how to act; the therapist can only tell the patient how he/she (the therapist) will act and respond to the patient's dissociations.

SELF-HATRED

The victim of childhood sexual abuse maintains a very interesting inversion of causal reasoning. She claims that she is responsible for what was done to her in childhood, but that she is not responsible for what she does now. This is an incredible assertion, a reversal of common sense and all that the psychology of child development tells us. The therapist must maintain somewhat the opposite stance from the patient. Taking into account that it sounds as if I am speaking in absolutes when I am actually thinking in terms of relative values and nuances, the therapist comes from the position that the child was the innocent victim caught in the craziness of the adult world, but that the patient, now an adult, has some choices, however constrained and influenced by the past, about what happens to her and how she behaves, including her work in therapy.

The task of the therapist is thus at odds with a major belief system of the patient. As mentioned earlier, therapists are rarely able to convince a patient that she is not to blame for having been victimized. The patient's sense of complicity in the abuse is one major reason for the immutability of her contempt for herself. But other psychological factors are also important here, one of which is that the person feels the same aggression stirring within her as she experienced from the abuser. Even minor pieces of violence or expressions of anger by the patient are seized upon as proof that she is as vile and dangerous as her abuser. It is this thought, that she carries within her the same potential for violence as did her abuser, that propels many PTSD/borderlines into self-destructive behaviors.

A third factor contributing to the patient's self-hatred is her incorporation of the criticisms leveled at her by her abuser, usually verbalized within the context of the abuse itself. She accepts that she is a bad girl, an ungrateful and disobedient daughter, a prostitute, a willful bitch, and that as such she deserved and, more importantly, continues to deserve, severe and fitting punishment. Some of these themes are present in the following case.

CASE 16

Ms. R is a 26-year-old part-time student whose sexual abuse by her mother ended only when she ran away from home at age 16. As a child, she was made to drink large quantities of water and then sit in the middle of the kitchen without being allowed to go to the bathroom. Mother said it was to teach her self-control. After several hours of increasing agony, she would wet her pants in an explosion of anguish and humiliation. Mother would drag her upstairs, screaming vituperatively at her, rip off her clothing under a scalding shower, and then sexually abuse her. Ms. R now feels that she cannot truly hate her mother because her mother had to be sick to do all that. On the other hand, Ms. R not only hates herself for what she "allowed" mother to do to her, but has also adopted as her own value system mother's blame and contempt, which were heaped on her in childhood. She has scorn for herself for having lost control of her bladder, cried, gagged, become frozen in fear, and purchased life for herself by cooperating with the abuser. She should have refused to sit in the kitchen until she thought she would burst; she should have either run to the bathroom or else urinated immediately in the kitchen.

Ms. R frequently cuts her arms and legs. During hospitalizations, she claims inability to urinate, necessitating twice daily catheterizations by nursing staff. Weaning Ms. R off catheters has been a very difficult process. She is aware that she is now, as an adult, demonstrating the bladder control that she could not have done as a child. She also takes pleasure in defeating the staff, who eventually give in and catheterize her; she can hold out longer than they. But her awareness of the significance of this power struggle does not enable her to give it up; it only adds another reason for her to hate herself.

Each component of the self-hatred has to be worked on separately and yet jointly, because each component is related to all the others. A particularly recalcitrant piece, as exemplified in the case cited above, is the contempt that Ms. R feels for that little girl who whined and cried and "gave in." This is a fairly common theme in PTSD/borderlines, who cannot permit themselves to feel sympathy or pity for their own depersonalized childhood.

There is no simple therapeutic answer here, but rather a slow hearing-out of the patient's story, going back again and again to the same events and the same misperceptions about blame and responsibility. Self-hatred is a lifetime issue for PTSD/borderlines. It cannot be resolved within the time-frame of most therapies and it need not be resolved. It needs to be worked on to the point where the patient stops hurting herself directly and, eventually, indirectly. By this I mean that working on limiting or ceasing the behavioral acting-out of the self-hatred represents an earlier therapeutic goal than the more long-range and improbable goal of self-love or even self-respect. It is not that these latter objectives are unimportant; it is, rather, that they will come along slowly as part of the package. Self-respect will be the result of constructive action on the part of the patient, as well as a reflection of the respect given the patient by the therapist.

MISTRUST OF OTHERS

The central position of trust as a goal in therapy has been exaggerated. Since the outcome of many of the patient's important relationships has been betrayal at many levels, there is no reason for the patient to be very trusting, and good reason to be cautious about trust. The patient does not have to trust the therapist, certainly not initially, for therapy to begin. In fact, too early an expression of trust should make the therapist wonder about the emergence of transference themes of idealization, ingratiation, and victimization. It should also alert the therapist to questions of countertransference, in terms of whether the therapist has his/her own issues about being liked or trusted or idealized, which have been picked up and responded to by the patient. Campbell (1992) has commented that the therapeutic maneuver of encouraging patients to see their past and present environments as primarily hostile has the countertherapeutic result of having the therapist become the only positive figure in the patient's life, thereby further alienating the patient from potentially supportive relationships in the present time.

As therapy proceeds, questions of trust will arise naturally and should be processed just as other emerging issues about the therapeutic relationship are. Problems with trust do not have a special place in therapy, nor do they occur in isolation of transference/countertransference issues or strategies of treatment resistance. The following case vignette illustrates this.

CASE 17

Ms. S has increased her self-injurious behavior lately. She acknowledges this, but has steadfastly refused to discuss it any further. The therapist has the impression that the cutting involves more than just arms and legs, but he is not sure. He tells Ms. S that he assumes that the reason she cannot discuss the cutting is that she is too ashamed of what she is doing. Ms. S agrees that she is ashamed of the cutting and all that is implied in it, but adds that shame is not the only reason why she will not speak of it. She does not fully trust what she anticipates the therapist's response will be. The therapist is surprised to hear this, since he had narrowed his vision about the cause of the patient's reluctance to speak of cutting to what he assumed was her overwhelming sense of shame. Ms. S goes on to say that she is afraid that if the therapist were to hear the details of the self-injurious behavior, he would feel that hospitalization was necessary and that, one night, there would be a knock on the door and the police would be there with commitment papers signed by the therapist. She is aware that he has never indicated that he thought Ms. S should be in the hospital and that, in fact, he has expressly stated that hospitalization should be avoided in her case. Nevertheless, ever since he told her pointedly that he wanted her to have no doubts that he is opposed to her cutting herself, she has been worried that he will force her into a hospital. She came to this conclusion because the therapist had not spoken so strongly about any of her other behaviors. She no longer felt that she could trust the therapist to restrain his need to take charge of her life, even though she could acknowledge that he might believe that he would be doing it for her own good.

Ms. S linked her present fear that the therapist would take over to a previous hospitalization when her father forced her into a hospital following her suicide attempt, bullied the doctors into medicating her with high-dose antipsychotics, and then signed her out of the hospital against medical advice. He sexually assaulted her at home the following day.

Although I have brought this case up in the context of trust, it is clear that, as always, many things are going on simultaneously. If anything, the trust issue is the easiest to understand in this context. The basis of the patient's mistrust was not just that she had had a disastrous experience with hospitalization and its aftermath in the past, but that it seemed entirely possible that her therapist and her father, although seemingly very different from each other, might share the same sadistic male need for power and control. Although the therapist had not given any evidence that he wanted to take decision-making away from Ms. S, this was no guarantee for the future, nor was Ms. S willing to take the risk by giving the therapist evidence that he could possibly use against her.

The other issues here relate to whether Ms. S "really" wanted to be in the hospital, both because she did not feel safe at that time outside the hospital and because of a drive to repeat old victimization scenarios. The stated fear of hospitalization also contained within it the ambivalent wish that the therapist would take over for her in a positive way when she felt that she could no longer control her self-injurious behaviors. This possibility touches on the theme of the mother who failed to step in to protect the patient from the incestuous father. The therapist is being given the opportunity to show concern for Ms. S's well-being in a way that mother never did.

My discussion of these counter-themes, of unstated themes expressing the contrary of that which has been verbalized by the patient, should be taken as hypotheses to think about, not as certainties to act upon. Therapists too readily assume the accuracy and correctness of the psychodynamic verity that, in expressing a fear, a person is really revealing a wish. We have no basis to assume this as a universal axiom. In recognition of human complexity, however, it is plausible to question whether certain statements of patients also contain opposite sentiments, as long as we remember that our hunches are hypotheses to be examined.

Therapy consists of talking about these issues—in this particular case, of trust—rather than acting on them. There is no need for the therapist to try to convince the patient that he is trustworthy, or that he is different from father, who was abusive, or from mother, who was neglectful. The patient already knows this at some level. The specifics of what trust means in this particular context between these two people, against the background of their individual life experiences, becomes a topic of focus, rather than a discussion of trust in the abstract. Trust moves in and out during therapy; it may decline when the therapist makes mistakes, which are bound to happen, or when the patient sees a connection between a present situation and a previous one of betrayal. The trust level, so to speak, can be examined when trust issues arise. The therapeutic goal of "building trust" is something that may be written on an insurance form to satisfy a quality control or managed care audit; it is an acceptable shorthand notation for a much more complex process, but should not be taken too literally or too seriously.

On the other hand, if the trust issue is raised too often by the patient, the therapist has to inquire whether it is serving as treatment resistance, as a way of avoiding difficult therapeutic work. It is not that trust is not an issue; it is rather that therapy cannot wait for trust to be there in order for therapy to proceed. Similar to the therapeutic alliance, the development of trust is not a prerequisite for therapy; it is one piece of evidence that therapy is proceeding. The PTSD/borderline should be in no hurry to be trusting.

SEEKING REPETITION OF OLD
DESTRUCTIVE SCENARIOS

I am stuck again between active and passive verbs, between the language of volition and that of determinism. Saying that the patient "seeks" old destructive scenarios sounds like the old game of blame the patient. If only she would not get herself into the same old pickles, her life (and her therapy) would go much better. Alternatively, taking the patient out of the center of action, as if behavior occurs without motivation or involvement, as if the patient is an automaton living out a bad script written from a desperate childhood, seems to eliminate the vital core of the person herself.

CASE 18

Ms. T tells her therapist that on the way to a part-time job, she feels an overwhelming urge to cut herself. She gets off the bus, goes to a drug store to buy a razor blade, returns home and cuts. Ignoring for the moment all the usual therapeutic considerations, such as, what was the patient experiencing while on the way to work, what else was going on in her life, what else was going on in therapy, and focusing just on the volitional aspects of what ordinarily is called "impulsive" or, interestingly, "compulsive" behavior, what are we to make of her action? Did she get off the bus because she wanted to cut, or because she had to cut? Perhaps she just did not want to go to work? I recognize that there is no answer, but the question is important because it touches on the topic of what can be expected of the patient.

Ms. T's present life appears to be powerfully shaped in a destructive direction by her past. Shall we speak with her in the language of volition or compulsion? The phrasing of the chapter title, "how the past controls the present," sounds as if there is little volition involved. But words are treacherous. As earlier, I do not raise this dilemma with the thought to resolve it, but to indicate that there is an ongoing struggle within the psychotherapy as to how to conceptualize the influence of past on present. However each of us may accommodate this issue, the fact remains that, although in an obvious sense, everyone's past profoundly influences the present, the past is much more intrusive and uniformly destructive in the present life of PTSD/borderline patients. It is this gross intrusiveness that forms the key issues in therapy and that also make therapy so very difficult and painful.

The patient expects people in the present to have motivations and actions similar to persons in the past. The patient also has, more or less, a fairly limited repetoire of initiatives and responses, also based on her past experiences, to persons in the present. Part of the task of the therapist is to point out when behaviors in the present seem to be repeating patterns from the past.

CASE 19

Ms. O is a 38-year-old married woman with two children from her present marriage. She has been battered by her husband almost the entire 14 years of her marriage. She has sustained a broken nose, broken wrist, and innumerable bruises and soft tissue injuries. He has held a gun to her head and a knife to her throat. She has never pressed charges against him. She previously moved out once for four days, but he sweet-talked her into returning. She has finally moved out with her two children to a shelter and appears more determined in her resolve to stay away from her husband than previously.

Therapy issues have focused on a few central themes, the first being a complex of ideas and feeling derived from her childhood abuse experiences, the second related to giving up her children from her first marriage at the time of dissolution of that marriage. The net result of both experiences, one in which she was the victim of her stepfather's abuse and the other in which, from her point of view, she abandoned her children, merged into an overwhelming sense of sadness and self-blame. When she had been abused as a child, she made up stories to herself about what a wonderful mother she would be to her children. The shattering of these cherished daydreams, which sustained her through many awful periods, left her with a conviction that no amount of punishment would ever cancel out the wrongs she had done. Contributing to this was her knowledge that her own alcohol and drug abuse in the first marriage led to the loss of custody of the children. It confirmed for her the suspicion that she must have been to blame for the childhood abuse. Although Ms. O recognized that her husband was sadistic and "not normal," she felt she had no right to complain or to get out of the marriage. It was only when her daughter reached age 12 and she realized that her husband was starting to take an interest in and threaten this girl that she sought therapy with the goal of leaving him.

The therapist in this situation had the benefit of the leverage provided by Ms. O's concern for her daughter. Ms. O also knew that if she did not take steps to protect her daughter, the therapist would be obliged to report any child abuse, if it did occur. Ms. O effectively set up a situation in which, although she would not be the one actually to report her husband, her husband still would be reported. She and the therapist talked about this as an issue in therapy, with the therapist agreeing to share some responsibility with Ms. O in seeing to her own and her daughter's safety. The therapist's willingness to take an active role in protecting Ms. O allowed Ms. O to take an active role in protecting her daughter.

The stakes were particularly high, with the possibility of moving into a third generation of abused women in this family. Ms. O's own sense that she deserved to remain a victim kept her in a brutal marriage. In therapy, a combination of positive transference, with the therapist fulfilling the role of the idealized protective mother, and the realization that her daughter did not deserve the abuse she was almost certainly going to receive, allowed

Ms. O to begin to question her own assumptions about her blameworthiness. While not exculpating herself by any means, she was able for the first time to take positive steps for her children's welfare.

It is clear that replaying old issues carries with it the potential to rework one's previous behaviors in a new and more positive manner, as well as the potential to reinforce further one's own self-hatred and victimization. The initial task of therapy is to point out the pattern of repeating past traumas. This moves the therapeutic work into an examination of the driving forces behind the pattern and gives the patient a better opportunity to change her participation in recreating the past. Naming the process usually serves to interrupt it.

SUMMARY

Far from forgetting the past, the PTSD/borderline patient is often at the mercy of memories of a past that constantly intrude into the present. Styles of cognitive processing, such as dissociative episodes, and important feeling-tones about oneself and one's environment, such as self-hatred and mistrust of others, present themselves in the therapy hour as well as in the rest of the patient's life. This provides the therapist with the opportunity to work on these issues with the patient within the immediacy of therapy. This opportunity is not without risk that the therapist will influence the patient to conform her memories and cognitions according to the therapist's theoretical persuasions. While this risk is always present in psychotherapy, the long-term consequences of childhood abuse, especially self-hatred and a need to please an authority figure, leave the PTSD/borderline patient particularly vulnerable. There is no ready answer for this, especially since the psychotherapy field has become polarized around the complex issue of the accuracy of early memories. My thoughts specifically in regard to working with patients on themes relating to the past intruding into the present are to focus primarily on present maladaptive patterns, with nominal or cautious weaving in of past material.

9

How the Past Shapes
the Transference

Transference is a central concept in psychotherapy. It hypothesizes that the manner and style in which a patient relates to the therapist and the therapy situation are strongly influenced by the nature of the relationships and experiences that the patient had with significant others in the past. When stated in this general way, the notion of transference phenomena in psychotherapy has gained sufficient acceptance that it is not considered controversial. Indeed, the belief that most, if not all, of our present responses in life in general are deeply determined by our past experiences is a cornerstone of modern popular psychology. In the present discussion of transference and PTSD, the contribution of genetic factors to human behavior will be ignored, because it becomes intrusive to end every sentence with a reminder that life experiences alone cannot account for the way we are, that there is always an interplay between genetic endowment and life experiences. I trust that the reader will add this unstated ending to the relevant sentences as we proceed.

The concept—that what we are is shaped by what kinds of experiences we have encountered in our lives—finds particular focus in PTSD. Since we have hypothesized that transference is the coloring of the therapeutic relationship by the patient's past experiences and relationships, then it follows that the effects of childhood sexual abuse experiences will strongly determine the transference reactions of PTSD/borderline patients. This helps us to understand why the psychotherapy of PTSD has been so complicated and difficult. Transference, by definition, is an integral component of therapy with all patients, but with the PTSD/borderline patients in particular, the intensity and intrusiveness of past conflicts bring heightened emotionality and acting-out into the relationship between patient and therapist.

Once we accept rather than debate the fact that transference reactions form an intrinsic part of all interactions in therapy, then the critical technical issue in therapy becomes an examination and determination about what to do with the transference. Should transference be ignored, confronted, interpreted? Never, sometimes, always? We know that the recognition, or mere suspicion, that we are witnessing and participating in a patient's transference reaction does not in itself tell us how to respond, although we assume that we are better off recognizing it than not.

All interactions between therapist and patient have both transference and reality components. On any given interchange, there may be several different levels of transference and reality meanings occurring simultaneously, all of them to some degree accurate (and therefore to some degree inaccurate) and all of them to some degree important. Given this multiplicity of realistic and symbolic meanings at every moment in therapy, the therapist, and the patient, must constantly make decisions about what seems important and what seems like a distraction. The task is complex and circuitous, because "important" themes and topics do not come labeled as such, and our judgment that a particular transference theme seems most relevant at this given moment does not imply that the other themes that we let slide by are therefore unimportant. For example, we may decide that a particular direction a patient is taking is a distraction, but we may then decide that this seeming wandering off the point is an important theme in therapy for this very reason, because the patient may specialize in distractions.

CASE 20

Ms. U discusses in therapy two related issues, her marital problems and her fertility difficulties. She has just learned that she is again pregnant, but because of various endocrine complications another miscarriage is predicted by her obstetrician. The following week, Ms. U discusses in great detail her marital problems and appears to work productively on how father's desertion during her childhood may have set up a foundation of anger toward men.

About two-thirds through the session, the therapist asks Ms. U about the pregnancy. "Oh," Ms. U replies, "I miscarried the day after I saw you last week." "How come you did not mention it today?" her therapist, a middle-aged woman, inquires. Ms. U smiles gamely, "It did not seem that important." "Not important!" exclaims her therapist, "I could not think of anything more important." Ms. U is flooded with silent tears. The therapist asks Ms. U whether she had planned to mention the miscarriage at all, if the therapist had not inquired; she also asks what Ms. U would have thought had she (the therapist) not expressed concern about the pregnancy.

What ensued was not just a discussion of the pain and despair involved with each new pregnancy, but also an acknowledgment of Ms. U's ability in all her relationships to deflect topics away from what really matters to her. In this example, it was important for the therapist to recognize that a distraction (disguised as an intellectual analysis of her marital problems) was occurring, discuss the content (another miscarriage) that was being avoided, and then shift to the process, which reflected a style of interaction that Ms. U had developed successfully. Ms. U was aware that, in social and work situations, her skill in getting people to talk about themselves enabled her to avoid revealing much about herself. In the therapy session, Ms. U continued to use this style, at times purposely, such as in this vignette, but mainly because it had become her basic way on interacting socially. It was not that she made small talk in the therapy situation; her discussion about her marital problems was real enough and was important, but it did not have the urgency of what she was avoiding, which was the miscarriage.

Regarding the last issue raised by the therapist — what Ms. U would have thought of the therapist if she (the therapist) had not asked her about the pregnancy — Ms. U denied that she would have thought anything special. It is important to note that in asking about Ms. U's pregnancy, the therapist was not just signaling the relevance of this topic for therapy, but also expressing a personal concern and empathy, as one human to another, for Ms. U's sadness. Her inquiry reflected both a therapy concern and a personal concern. She was letting Ms. U know, role modeling in a sense, that their professional relationship does not prevent the therapist from having genuine personal concern for her. This is a complicated issue and one which obviously can lead to nontherapeutic intrusions into a patient's life. However, the fact that an interaction, if bungled, can lead to complications does not mean that one need be too rigid about boundaries.

Ralph Greenson (1968), in his book on psychoanalytic psychotherapy, has a very sensitive discussion about a fledgling analyst who is unable to deviate from "orthodox" analytic technique in order to ask his patient how her young son, who was critically ill, is faring. In Greenson's case, the patient leaves the therapy, telling the analyst that he needs analysis more than she does.

As this example illustrates, patient and therapist must decide whether it is important to stay with the content, or whether the process is of overriding concern, such that the topic is to be put aside for the moment. Tracking of one issue entails ignoring perhaps ten other issues; in once-a-week therapy of one-hour duration, this means that many potential issues will never even be acknowledged, let alone examined. Given these limitations externally imposed by the very structure of psychotherapy, the critical task in therapy is not to acknowledge in some vague fashion that such and such must be transference, but to decide which of the many transference issues within the therapy situation reflect the important themes in the patient's life, what the nature of these transference issues is, how workable the transference issues appear to be at the moment, and what specific approach one will need to take in regard to each transference phenomenon.

CASE 21

Ms. V tells her therapist, whom she sees on a monthly basis, that, in her weekly women's group, the group therapist had Ms. V sit in her lap and hugged her for a few minutes. Although Ms. V wanted this very much, she also felt uncomfortable about it, wondering if the hug was sexual as well as maternal. She feels that the individual therapist will disapprove of her getting a hug from the group therapist and, more to the point, that the therapist will disapprove of her (the patient) setting up the situation so that the group therapist offered to have Ms. V sit on her lap. Ms. V knows that hugs now do not compensate for mother's coldness in childhood, but does not wish to forego the immediate warmth of the hugs.

There are several topics and transference issues here, all in this little interchange. The content of the individual therapy session relates to the patient's narrative about sitting in the therapist's lap during group therapy and the complex reactions that were stirred up at that time. Past and present are intertwined, as immediate yearnings and partial gratifications bring forth even stronger memories of pain and despair in the past. Therapist and patient can profitably work on these issues at length. But there are also the process issues. A patient is choosing to tell her therapist about her interactions with another therapist. Furthermore, although Ms. V states that she expects his disapproval, she tells the therapist the story anyway. Does one pursue content (her conflict about getting hugs from the group therapist) or process (her decision to tell the present therapist about this)?

The therapist chooses process because he judges that the transference reaction embedded in the therapy process is the critical issue here. He asks Ms. V what she thinks about her telling him about another therapist. The query is more pointed than a general, "Why are you telling me this?" "Why" questions often come across to patients as implying a criticism, seemingly calling upon patients to defend themselves. They are also unfocused, which at times is desirable, in terms of not preselecting the initial direction of the patient's response. Given the limited time available, however, the therapist wants to cover some of the more obvious features of the exchange. Ms. V states that she is not sure, but thinks her choice of what to talk about in therapy may relate somewhat to wanting the male therapist to disapprove of the female group therapist. The therapist agrees with Ms. V, pointing out that she was, in essence, tattling on her group therapist. Ms. V says that she is annoyed with the group therapist; she (Ms. V) wants even more hugs from the group therapist than she has received and, furthermore, the group therapist has not answered her telephone call for an extra individual appointment, something that the group therapist occasionally schedules for members of the therapy group. She smiles as she states that she is telling the good daddy about the bad mommy. In her real life, her daddy was not a "good daddy." She trusts the male therapist because he has refused her request for a hug. She is aware that in telling him about the other therapist's hugs, she is also inviting him to hug her, repeating the incestuous themes from childhood. Yet she knows that, had the therapist hugged her, he would no longer be safe. As much as she wants his hug, she counts on his ability to maintain secure boundaries. She also wants his approval of her as a good patient, one who does not seek out repetitions of destructive relationships.

In line with wanting her male therapist's approval, there is a component of projection to this multilayered transference episode. Ms. V assumes that the therapist will disapprove of her, not for wanting hugs, which she believes he would accept as a normal human desire, but for actually arranging in group therapy to get the hugs. She anticipates this negative reaction even before speaking to the therapist, although she did have some indication from her previous efforts to get him to hug her. Nevertheless, the assumption that the therapist will not approve of her must reflect her own ambivalence about the propriety of being hugged by and sitting in the lap of her group therapist. It also reflects her wish to please her therapist by behaving in ways that she assumes he values.

In tracking the process issues involved in this complicated transference reaction, other themes, such as the patient's difficulties in childhood with an emotionally unavailable mother, are briefly acknowledged, but not developed within the therapy hour. They probably will surface again, or Ms. V may well work on them on her own, or even in group therapy. The focus on the process issues in this case did, of course, touch upon the content of her childhood experiences, especially in developing the notion of splitting raised by Ms. V's complaints to the male therapist about the female therapist. In this example, the therapist judged that it was important to work with the transference themes and relatively to neglect the content themes.

One last aspect of this case requires brief comment, because it is a fairly common occurrence. The patient is in two therapies simultaneously, an individual therapy and a group therapy. In this particular situation, therapy was by design reduced to monthly sessions once the patient joined the women's therapy group. There is gain and risk to this type of arrangement, and no guide book to determine what the proper mix of therapies, if mix at all, is optimal. In point of fact, many women, particularly with childhood sexual abuse issues, find a women's group very helpful, although I share a concern expressed in the psychotherapy literature, which was reviewed in Chapter 3, that false memories of incest can be created in patients in some of these groups. Once again, the possibility of misuse of a therapeutic modality does not invalidate the usefulness of that treatment. The significant issue that I discussed above is merely the need for the different therapists to be aware of the potential complications, such as splitting, that can occur with such an arrangement.

TESTING THE THERAPIST FOR REJECTION

Patients often test for rejection in relatively subtle ways, carefully scrutinizing the therapist's face, voice, demeanor, or responses to find evidence of dislike, disgust, disapproval, and other negative judgments. Usually this occurs without acknowledgment that an important test is in progress; the therapist finds out about it only later on, when he discovers that he has failed (or, occasionally, passed) the test. This also occurs, for example, with special requests and telephone calls. The content of the telephone call may or may not be important, but the question of whether the telephone call will be returned, and within what time-frame, often overrides the stated purpose of the call.

There are other times when it appears painfully obvious that the patient is setting up such impossible conditions that rejection is inevitable. Interpretations, direct labeling of the test conditions, and attempts at validation short of total acquiescence are often to no avail.

CASE 22

Ms. W is a 32-year-old single woman, working full-time in a retail shop. She has a background of non-aggressive sexual exploitation by a stepfather from age four to twelve, at which time a divorce between the parents removed the stepfather permanently from Ms. W's life. Ms. W was attached to this man and grieved his departure, especially since she was blamed for the abuse and ensuing divorce, and rejected emotionally by her mother. Ms. W's interpersonal relationships throughout adolescence and young adulthood were marked by a dependent, clinging quality that ultimately pushed people to seek greater distance from her. Ms. W was seen by a succession of therapists, usually quitting each one when her conditions of therapy could not be met. In the particular situation under consideration here, Ms. W had set up a power struggle three weeks in a row by refusing to leave the therapy room at the end of the therapy hour. Therapy sessions usually consisted of an almost uninterrupted hour of complaints by Ms. W about how shabbily people in her life, including the therapist, were treating her. The following is a letter addressed to her therapist, a psychologist, who tried to provide a supportive, nonrejecting environment.

Carol,

I don't understand how you could intentionally refuse me the support I so desperately need. I still think about cutting and suicide every day, because perhaps, as you and your staff show me by your recent actions and/or lack of actions, that this is the very reality I have to accept. That no matter how hard I always try to prove that I'm a good person and have something to contribute to this world, that maybe none of that is true. Perhaps I am just an unacceptable human being. You know that I need therapy. But if you and your staff are just interested in confirming my worst fears that I described above (that I am not acceptable the way I am), then I do not see how I can benefit from therapy. I only feel worse about myself afterwards.

You cannot realistically expect me to repress all my emotions just because the clock on the wall demands that I leave. My feelings deserve better respect than that. If you see value in me as a human being who deserves to be helped and does not have to live feeling this intense emotional pain, then I would like to meet with you again. However, I work from 7:45 a.m. until 4:30 p.m., as you know. I ask you to respect my time, as you wish me to respect yours.

Sincerely,

Ms. W

Some cases are helpful for discussion because they illustrate very ordinary events; other cases are helpful because the extraordinary events they illustrate stand out so sharply that we can gain a better perspective about what is at stake with the ordinary cases. Ms. W was requesting, in a begging, pleading, wistful yet aggressive manner, that her therapist should agree to see her beyond ordinary clinic hours (the regular five o'clock slots were all filled) at six o'clock, which the therapist was willing to consider for an occasional appointment, but also that the session should last well beyond the usual one hour, until she reached an undefinable point each time when she felt ready to leave. In the previous three sessions, the therapist had finally walked out of the therapy room, with the patient still in it, after an hour and 15 minutes. The patient sat in the empty room until the housekeeping staff told the patient she would have to leave because the clinic was being locked at eight o'clock. At the last of these three sessions, the therapist told the patient that there would be no further appointments until the patient agreed to leave at the end of each one-hour session, something the patient was not willing to do.

Whatever it was that the patient had in mind in seeking therapy, obtaining conventional psychotherapy was not high on her list. We could speak in motivational terms of seeking gratification of needs and of replaying old issues, but not in terms of examining her own dynamics and behaviors, or even of changing her maladaptive patterns, at least not too readily. Of course, a therapist working with such patients has to expect some acting-out or dramatic transference behaviors, but certain prerequisites must be present for therapy to proceed. The tragedy in this situation is that the script is written so clearly, but appears unalterable within the boundaries of therapy as ordinarily conceived. The patient tells the therapist that all her life she has been rejected and she begs the therapist not to become one more name in a long list of individuals who have rejected her. Yet even as she says it, the outcome is in sight. Since she has set up unfulfillable requirements as proof of acceptance, all, including Ms. W, know that rejection, that which she claims to fear, will come. The drive to replay old issues in this case wins out. Ms. W is stuck in a rut; the old way does not work, except to bring about a repetition of old failures that confirm her vision of herself and her world. But she does not know any other way and she is too frantic even to consider what others are saying to her.

We can hypothesize a variety of reasons why this is so. From a psychodynamic conflict theory point of view, several themes might be operating here: a need to maintain the perception of herself as the martyr; a sense of entitlement such that only heroic measures could compensate for all the past hurts; the belief that she would be rejected anyway even if she were not obnoxious, so that this way she can attribute rejection to her obnoxiousness; a sense that life is only meaningful when she can engage others in a struggle. From an ego deficit point of view, other dynamics might be at play: Ms. W lacks those ego structures, especially of object constancy, which would enable her to tolerate temporary abandonment, bind the anxiety of not knowing how someone feels about her, and sustain her from one appointment to the next without the ongoing presence of the therapist. These are hypotheses about what might underlie Ms. W's desperate behavior. Interventions of a supportive nature based upon such hypotheses, as well as gentle acknowledgment of the struggle occurring between Ms. W and the therapist, were not successful in this instance in calming Ms. W sufficiently that she would tolerate the restrictions of the therapy situation.

I have to clarify that I have used this case to illustrate problems centering about testing the therapist for rejection. I do not have any clever solutions or magic words that would suddenly enable Ms. W to achieve some distance from the urgency of her needs or convince her to lower the intensity of her demands in order to give therapy a chance. There are limits to what the therapist may technically and ethically do to keep a patient engaged in therapy. Statements of positive regard, of interest in working with Ms. W and developing a relationship with her within the confines of psychotherapy, interpretations of what the issues might be, and clarification of what therapy can provide and not provide were puny in comparison to the intensity of Ms. W's verbal onslaught and refusal, or inability, to relinquish a very maladaptive style of interacting in therapy.

TESTING THE THERAPIST FOR SEDUCTION

Several of the cases discussed earlier in this book have centered about the core theme of seduction of the therapist. This is hardly surprising, given the complex dynamics that develop as a consequence of childhood sexual abuse. The desire to seduce the therapist, the perception that the therapist is sexually interested in the patient, the belief that the pure love of the therapist will heal her distrust of others, the suspicion that the adult world holds only exploitation of her, and the drive to debase the therapist are themes that are present in various combinations in the psychotherapy of the PTSD/borderline patient. The patient may offer herself directly, proposing a sexual liaison with the therapist as being the most therapeutic act that he could do for her, or else she may present to the therapist a picture of profound helplessness and despair that only physical comforting will alleviate.

There is a large and increasing literature on therapist-patient sexual relations (Applebaum & Jorgenson, 1991; Bouhoutsos et al., 1983; Gabbard, 1991; Gartrell et al., 1986; Gutheil, 1991; Herman et al., 1987; Pope, 1990 a & b; Pope & Vetter, 1991; Schoener & Gonsiorek, 1988). There is also increasing public awareness and outrage at such relations, even to the point where the possibility of a patient's active pursuit of and participation in sexual relations with a therapist are denied because the nature of the psychodynamics of the victim within the transference situation is thought to preclude free and informed consent. This latter argument is misguided, infantilizes patients by suggesting that they are not capable of desiring a sexual relationship, and confounds several important distinctions. The issue of intent or consent on the patient's part is totally irrelevant to the matter of the therapist's fiduciary relationship to the patient. Strasberger, Jorgenson, and Randles (1991) provide a clear discussion about this issue; it is the duty of the therapist to attend to the needs and well-being of the patient, which, whatever the rationalizations of the therapist, specifically excludes sexual relationships.

The fact that psychodynamic conflicts or forces, even if at an unconscious level, drive the patient to want or acquiesce to sexual relationships with the therapist, however, does not remove the patient's consent or volitional behavior, any more than such an argument from a therapist about his own deep-seated countertransference neurosis would remove his responsibility for exploiting a patient. It is in this sense that it may be helpful to view the patient's seductive behavior as a form of testing the therapist, similar to other types of testing of the transference. Such a formulation places the seductive behavior within the larger framework of replaying old issues within the transference, circumventing a futile quasi-political discussion about free will and the victim mentality.

The way for the therapist to pass the test, specifically in terms of seduction, is not to take the seduction personally and not to be seduced. We all know this. In addition to the fundamental ethical issue involved, which expressly forbids a sexual relationship between therapist and patient, "sexual relationships in therapy" is really an oxymoronic phrase; it has stopped being therapy. If ever there is an example in which gratification of a patient's wish by a therapist blocks examining what the wish is all about and what lies behind it, acting out sexually with the patient is it. Complicity of the therapist in this sort of acting-out also conveys the message that the therapist has no idea what therapy is all about and what is important to the patient's recovery. It may be that the therapist is openly sociopathic and exploitative, in which case he should not be doing therapy. Hopefully, it is more likely that the therapist has failed to appreciate the ethical and technical essentials of therapy, such that he does not know what to do and not do in therapy and has somehow managed to convince himself of the therapeutic legitimacy of his actions. It may also be that the therapist knows that he is wrong, but has already proceeded to encourage seduction in its less obvious forms and now lacks the strength of character to resist the "ultimate" temptation. I realize that this last formulation is couched in moralistic terms, but that is the nature of what we are dealing with.

I have no statistics, but I think that many cases of sexual involvement of therapist and patient develop out of the therapist's quandary of how to proceed in therapy, leaving the path open to the rationalization that physical closeness and comforting of the patient will help her get over her emotional pain, sexual mistrust, and social isolation.

CASE 23

Ms. Y, a married woman in her mid-thirties, discusses in therapy her life with an alcoholic husband. He is inattentive to her except when drunk, then demands sexual relations. Ms. Y has learned to comply with these demands, but longs for a romantic relationship of mutual respect and affection. The therapist, a middle-aged pastoral counselor, offers to meet with Ms. Y's husband to try to alter this pattern of behavior, but Ms. Y thinks that would do more harm than good. The therapist is moved by Ms. Y's despair, yet talking in therapy does not seem to help either her situation or her loneliness. He tells Ms. Y how concerned he is about her and wonders if there is anything he can do to comfort her. She is not sure of what he can do. At the end of one particularly painful session, the therapist is moved by compassion and reaches out to make contact. The embrace is warm but fleeting. At the next session, Ms. Y is silent, but then tells the therapist how the memory of his hug comforted her throughout the long week. She admires his strength and stability. The therapist begins to perceive Ms. Y in a different light, as a person with so much to offer, but damaged by unfortunate life experiences. At the end of the session, when Ms. Y moves to embrace him, he holds her tightly and reassures her of what a good person she is. Over the course of the next few months, there is a slow and cautious progression of physical expressions of respect, longing, and desire that stop short of sexual intercourse. The therapist begins to have second thoughts about the direction that therapy has taken, but judges that Ms. Y is too vulnerable to rejection for him to change what has been happening. Ms. Y, however, has her own second thoughts about the sexualization of therapy and, during the therapist's vacation, consults another therapist who convinces her to report the therapist to the state attorney's office.

This case illustrates the problem of a therapist responding to a patient's emotional distress with attempts to provide physical comfort and closeness. It is inevitable that a patient caught in an unhappy marriage will make comparisons between all that the therapist appears to be and all that the spouse is not. Ms. Y's childhood fantasies of being rescued from her desperate situation become realized in the person of the therapist. She has wanted to believe that, somewhere, she will find a man who cares for her and does not exploit her. This is never articulated in therapy, but is acted out in conjunction with the therapist, who initially tells himself that adding a soothing, comforting hug at the end of the therapy hour will help carry his patient through a difficult period. It is a mutual seduction in which temporary alleviation of distress is purchased at the cost of more arduous and painful therapeutic work. It is a betrayal of Ms. Y for the therapist to suggest that the therapeutic response to her marital problems is to demonstrate in action that she really is a desirable and worthwhile woman.

TESTING THE THERAPIST FOR VICTIMIZATION AND EXPLOITATION

This category represents a large class of problems seen in the therapy of PTSD/borderline patients, of which seduction of the therapist is just one part. Victimization, the perception of oneself as a victim, the corresponding perception of life's experiences as basically exploitative, and the acting in such a way as to become victimized, is a core feature of many persons who have been sexually abused in childhood. The essential ingredient is that the patient plays out a situation in which she is vulnerable and the therapist abuses his power by denying her something that she needs or by demeaning her.

CASE 24

Ms. I is a 32-year-old single part-time aide in a nursing home. She has a history of sexual abuse by her stepfather. She begins a new psychotherapy with a psychiatrist, telling him that she has filed grievances against her three former therapists for unprofessional conduct. She recognizes that he may not want to take her on as a patient with this history, but she really is quite depressed, although she does not wish to take medications, and she has been told that he is a good therapist. With some hesitation, the psychiatrist agrees to begin therapy with Ms. I.

After six months of weekly therapy, no untoward incidents have occurred, but Ms. I is appearing more depressed and begins to speak more seriously about suicide. The psychiatrist strongly recommends that she begin taking antidepressant medication, but Ms. I adamantly refuses. That weekend, she goes to the local emergency room and is given a prescription for a few days of antidepressant medication. On Monday, she shows up at her psychiatrist's office, requesting a refill of the prescription started at the emergency room. The psychiatrist has a full schedule and cannot see her immediately. Ms. I screams at the receptionist, knocks over a lamp, and abruptly departs. She goes back to the emergency room and requests a refill of her antidepressant medication. The emergency room doctor telephones the psychiatrist, who informs her of Ms. I's behavior in his office, and suggests that, in view of Ms. I's impulsiveness, he cannot recommend giving her more medication without a full evaluation. Ms. I then telephones her psychiatrist, berates him for speaking about her to the emergency room doctor without informed consent, and quits therapy.

This situation combines many of the typical difficulties that develop in the treatment of PTSD/borderline patients. There is a history of previous problematic therapeutic encounters, a beginning period of serious work together, and then an eruption of acting-out that usually pulls in other mental health professionals. Often the patient is successful in splitting the professionals, finding someone who will agree that the former therapist was callous or unfair, reinforcing the patient's perception of herself as victim. There is no absolute way to avoid this type of testing of the therapist or of succumbing to the test. The therapist has to be alert to the possibility that victimization themes lie behind seemingly casual requests, statements, and interactions, but excessive vigilance on the part of a therapist is not conducive to therapy.

SUMMARY

Transference, by definition, is an integral part of psychotherapy. If a dominant theme in a patient's life is victimization, then this will show up as a dominant theme in a patient's therapy. The therapist cannot completely avoid falling into some interactions with the patient that are less than optimal. These may be interpreted by the patient as evidence of victimization or emotional exploitation on the part of the therapist. The therapeutic response at that point has to involve some attempt to process the previous interactions in terms of victimization themes, and to do so without blaming the patient.

10

Countertransference Issues

A girl one month shy of her 16th birthday attends a high school program on sexual assault presented by two workers from the County Sexual Assault Treatment Program. After the program, she tells the two sexual assault counselors that she had been abused at age nine by a police officer who had escorted her to the dog pound several times. The authorities are notified and an investigator from the Sheriff's Department interviews the adolescent, who narrates that the police officer swung her under his legs, holding her by the crotch; that he asked to see down her pants and top; that he rubbed her shoulders, chest and leg; that he pulled down her shirt once and offered her a soda if she would take off her pants. The investigator also informed the girl's mother, who had some memory of wondering about her daughter going to the dog pound with the police officer. The police officer is questioned and he, too, remembers the trip to the pound, but his memory of the events is obviously different. He denies wrongdoing, but offers to apologize to the girl if he had made her feel uncomfortable. The county attorney decides not to prosecute because the girl's memories "were not clear and hard to substantiate" after a seven-year interval. The two sexual assault counselors arrange a meeting, in their presence, between the police officer and the girl. The girl's mother is not informed of the meeting. At the meeting, the police officer apologizes for any pain he had caused her.

Six months later, the girl files a lawsuit against the policeman, his employer (the town), and, surprisingly, the two sexual assault counselors and the mental health agency for which they work. The suit alleges that the girl was traumatized by the meeting between herself and the policeman, that she had had nightmares and flashbacks and tried to kill herself several times. After one of the suicide attempts, she was hospitalized and diagnosed with borderline personality disorder. One of her lawyers is quoted as saying, "The prognosis for this young lady is very, very poor. She was very, very severely traumatized, and she's going to have a hell of a time getting rid of the scar tissue" (Twice a victim?, 1992).

This report can serve as the basis for an entire sociological analysis of one aspect of life in America as we approach the 21st century. It is filled with human drama, conflict, ambiguity, power differences in relationships, personal and institutional clashes of methods and motives, and finally, what seems to be the only and inevitable recourse in America to expressing one's dissatisfaction, the lawsuit. As such, this complicated incident touches on many of the themes discussed previously in this book. Yet I want to use it here primarily to highlight the last topic left for discussion, that of countertransference. The case does not involve psychotherapy as it is ordinarily conceived, but the behavior of the two assault counselors suggests a loss of perspective and proper distance from the needs of the teenage girl, mirroring similar difficulties seen in ongoing therapy situations.

What has happened here that the advocates of the adolescent are blamed and sued for trying to help the young lady work through a single episode of sexual abuse that occurred seven years earlier? Although I think that the "facts" of the case are now irrevocably contaminated by the involvement and coaching by lawyers, we can try to reconstruct the advocates' original viewpoint and intent. The advocates worked from a frame of reference that they knew what was best for the young girl. They assumed that an early confrontation with the policeman, and his apology to the girl, would allow her to get over any buried and unresolved issues resulting from the abuse incident. They decided that they, not the girl's mother, were the proper ones to provide support to the girl during the confrontation. They belittled the mother's potential role in helping her daughter, thereby adding to whatever difficulties the teenage daughter and mother might have been having. They bullied the young girl and the policeman to have the meeting, neither of whom appeared very eager for the confrontation, and they wrote the agenda. It is not clear whether there was much if any debriefing or counseling for the teenager in the days and weeks following the meeting.

It is the power differential in counseling and therapy situations that converts countertransference phenomena into countertransference problems. Otherwise, there would only be two (or more) individuals, each with his/her own transference problems. This is the ordinary situation in life. Each of us relates to others out of our own life experiences and whatever else influences us. It is only when we speak about a therapy arrangement that one of the participants in the interaction, the therapist, the one with the authority, is said to have countertransference rather than transference reactions. This is an acceptable convention, emphasizing, quite properly, not the differences in origin of each's transference, but the differences in impact and influence of each's transference on the other. The therapist's transference only becomes a countertransference problem when the therapist begins to fashion therapeutic interventions and behaviors based upon his/her personal issues rather than what is best for the patient.

In the case presented above, the teenage girl tells a brief story to two adult experts, who bring to the situation their very own life experiences, biases, theoretical understandings and misunderstandings, zealotry, and notions of fairness and right and wrong. The issue is not just that they lost sight of the needs and vulnerabilities of the teenager, but that they were in a position of authority to take over decision-making for the girl. It is ironic that this is the very charge that they were incensed about in regard to the policeman. The offenses here are worlds apart, but the formal symmetry of working out one's issues on a person with less autonomy and power is clearly present.

In a sense, the entire therapy section of this book involves a consideration of countertransference. Countertransference is the reciprocal concept to transference; it is the influence of the therapist's personality and life experiences on her responses to the patient in therapy. It is always present, even when not obviously intrusive in the process of therapy. Countertransference problems show up differently in the therapy of different types of patients. Much attention is paid to it in the therapy of PTSD/borderline patients because the intensity and prominence of their self-destructive behaviors, acting out, and transference reactions stir up strong responses from the therapists. But I would emphasize that the anger that arises in working with a difficult obsessional patient or the rejection that therapists direct toward their passive-dependent patients are just as important countertransference intrusions into therapy as are the feelings that get stirred up in the treatment of PTSD/borderlines. It is likely that the dynamics of victimhood and idealization/devaluation that permeate the transference of PTSD/borderline patients provide too convenient a set-up for the countertransference problems of the therapist, especially with the traditional match-up of somewhat older male therapist and younger female patient. Just think for the moment of trying to influence an obsessional patient, whose very core consists of resistance to suggestion and contrariness. I am sure it has happened, but I am not aware of any allegations of sexual abuse between therapist and obsessive-compulsive patient.

As usual, I need to circle back to clarify a few points. The patient with a history of childhood sexual abuse is going to bring certain very intense reactions and attachments to the therapy. She will be caught in the grip of replaying old issues and seeking gratification of her needs, and the therapist is the interactional focus of all this. At the same time, the therapist, pulled into a more active role than he usually is with other therapy patients, finds that he has to fall back upon his own personal judgment because the demands for his involvement seem so different from what is usually encountered in therapy. This is not the patient's "fault," and the patient is not responsible for what the therapist does. To say that the therapist is responding to the patient's provocations is not to blame the patient or to take ownership of the actions away from the therapist.

If the patient's provocations are not recognized as transference reactions, then it is likely that the therapist will take them personally and respond to them based upon his countertransference issues, which, by definition, will involve a component of exploitation of one sort or another. While the patient may encourage mutual acting-out, and try to elicit personal, as opposed to therapeutic, responses from the therapist, the therapist may not legitimately encourage or participate in the patient's acting-out. There is a different onus on the therapist, a different expectation of behavior.

I merely present this as the ideal, the goal. In actuality, the therapist is a real person, not a therapeutic mannequin, and so we see in therapy the sum of the therapist's personality and therapeutic persona. Countertransference responses are inevitable; they are part of the territory, but need to be scrutinized as much as possible. What I am interested at this point are the subtle and everyday influences of countertransference, rather than the dramatic and devastating ones. These are what we deal with within ourselves from day to day.

CASE 25

Ms. Z, a 28-year-old divorced and presently lesbian woman, tells her therapist that she finds herself becoming increasingly aggressive in the early sexual relationship with a fairly new partner. She is concerned because the partner is important to her and she does not want to ruin this relationship. The therapist suggests that Ms. Z consider a two-week moratorium on sexual activities with her partner, in order for her to think about what is behind the aggressiveness. The moratorium would also give Ms. Z and her partner a chance to consolidate the relationship a little further without the stresses of sexual intimacies. At the next appointment, Ms. Z tells the therapist that his instruction had the opposite effect; she had begun to think compulsively about sex with the partner. She had initiated sexual relations and hit the partner a few times, who promptly declared a moratorium on the relationship with Ms. Z.

The countertransference issue here showed up in the therapist's rapid move to give advice to Ms. Z. He perceived her as particularly vulnerable to rejection at this time and wished to protect her from what he saw as the inevitable outcome of her aggressive behavior in the new courtship relationship. But his advice had the opposite effect, although we cannot be sure that Ms. Z would not have pursued an aggressive course with her lover even if the therapist had not made any comments at all. Nevertheless, her perception of the therapist's advice as a command rather than merely as advice was a red flag in her face, challenging her autonomy. In thinking that he could protect Ms. Z from rejection, the therapist ignored the special relationship that he had with her and the influence that this would have on her perceptions of any suggestions that he would offer in the therapy situation. At least in part, his countertransference issue regarding protecting the patient, and her transference issue about not being told what to do, distracted the therapy from an examination of what was underlying Ms. Z's aggressiveness with her girlfriend.

Other countertransference issues might be at work here, suggested by the content of the therapist's recommendation that Ms. Z tone down a lesbian relationship. Undertones of jealousy and/or disapproval can be disguised by advising celibacy and sexual continence for the good of the patient.

There are no data on the prevalence, presentations, and impact of countertransference, and it is difficult to imagine how one would even go about researching such a vague yet ubiquitous phenomenon. I get the sense that the major countertransference difficulties that show up with therapists in the treatment of PTSD/borderlines are in the general direction of positive rather than negative attitudes. It is likely, although by no means universal, that those therapists who are openly antagonistic to borderlines do not continue to see many in their practices. Although there is always considerable leeway for anger and open rejection of the patient based upon a therapist's countertransference issues, it would appear that the difficulties that show up most dramatically relate to the rescuing, caretaking, and sexually exploitative problems of the therapists. We are all too psychologically sophisticated not to be able to suggest that there may, or must, be considerable hostility underlying these seemingly "positive" countertransference postures, but such reasoning, accurate at times, only gets us into a hall of mirrors. It is always possible that an expressed or acted-out emotion contains within it the opposite sentiment too, and certainly a degree of hostility appears to be present in many cases of sexual exploitation of the patient by the therapist.

I am trying to make a more mundane point, that the day-to-day therapeutic errors that are attributable to countertransference usually emerge as the expression of positive and warm feelings for the patient. These are usually caretaking and/or sexual feelings. As a result of acting on these feelings, the therapist becomes directly involved in the patient's life, at the minimum in terms of advice, suggestions, and directions, and at the maximum in terms of rescue operations, fighting the patient's battles for her, and sexual relationships of one sort or another.

There is no simple remedy for avoiding acting-out on the basis of countertransference forces. Somewhat by definition, these forces are out of conscious awareness. The human ability to rationalize what one does, to keep from oneself a recognition of one's more personal and selfish motivations, is truly unlimited. Yet some therapists do, and most do not. Are the differences only circumstance, luck, not happening to meet up with the wrong patient (wrong being the patient who pushes our countertransference buttons) at the wrong time (wrong being a time of increased vulnerability for the therapist)?

The remedies are generic and, at best, will help only to avoid major disasters, and perhaps to change the tone of ordinary interactions. The therapist has to study himself/herself at least as carefully as the patient, without taking the focus off the patient. The therapist has to scrutinize and evaluate the process of what is occurring between the two participants in the therapy. All actions, verbal and

especially behavioral, have to be judged in terms of how they conform to the most conventional, staid, and traditional rules of psychotherapy.

The problem, of course, is that there is no book of rules to cover
all the possible variations of clinical interactions and situations.
PTSD/borderlines, particularly, seem to have needs that are so special that they require one to bend the rules, to do the unusual and
unconventional. The patients require personal revelations from the
therapist so they will feel accepted and be able to trust and reveal in
turn; they require physical contact from the therapist so they will
know that they are not outcastes; they require being told what to do
because they are so easily confused and misled; they require exqui-
sitely careful phrasing of observations because they are so sensitive
to rejection; they require special handling on holidays and vacations
because they are so dependent upon the therapist; they require endless affirmation because their self-esteem is so fragile.

PTSD/borderlines are and are not all of these things. They are
sensitive and fragile and have low self-esteem and needs special to
their life experiences. But the therapist does not have to lose all
therapeutic perspective just because the patient is vulnerable. The
therapist just has to be thoughtful and careful, pray a lot, act re-
spectfully, and avoid special handling of the patient. Doing things
that are not ordinarily done in therapy by most reasonable therapists
is a very good sign of two things: the first is that the therapist does
not understand the patient or the principles of psychotherapy, and
the second is that the therapist is acting under the strong influence
of countertransference problems. I would recommend peer supervision and staff conferences, in which therapy cases are regularly reviewed and discussed, as probably the soundest way to stay on track
and out of trouble with one's patients.

Is there no room for innovation, creativity, imaginativeness in
therapy, especially the therapy of PTSD/borderlines? Like the good
skeptical fox that I am, the answer is yes and no. The main answer
is YES, there is little room for innovation, etc., if by that we mean
thinking that everyone else is a fool and does not understand PTSD/
borderlines as well as we do and that we know better. The other
answer is a small no, if by that we mean the ability to think through,
without action, a complex situation and arrive at a better understanding of it and a creative way of presenting it to the patient for

the patient to think about. This is nothing personal, but most therapists, and I absolutely include myself, are getting by with difficult patients with great difficulties, and do not need to add to the patient's difficulties by the conceit that we have discovered something special. What patients need from us is stability and good judgment and a little bit of help; we can save our brilliance for our personal friends.

11

Concluding Remarks

It has been six years since the writing of my previous book on borderlines. The changes between then and now, while somewhat predictable from social trends at the time, are nevertheless startling. One domain of change, anticipated from events in the last half of the '80s, has been the drastic cutbacks in insurance reimbursements for certain types of "softer" psychiatric care, primarily treatment programs such as psychotherapy that aim at quality of life issues rather than the more easily circumscribed "major mental" illnesses.

A second domain of change, also seemingly responsive to the progression of a broad social movement, has been the expansion of the concept of PTSD as it applies to persons who have experienced a variety of adverse life circumstances, especially childhood sexual abuse. As with the factors that influenced the original DSM-III configuration of borderline personality disorder, it is not difficult to recognize ideological and market considerations connecting the adverse and competitive atmosphere for reimbursement of psychotherapy with the resultant scramble among therapy providers to define (and possibly create) a new category of severe mental disorders for which the only effective treatment is long-term psychotherapy. Carol Tavris (1993) has commented on this in a front page article in the *New York Times Book Review*, as follows:

> As individual works of confession and advice, abuse-survivor books are often reassuring and supportive. They encourage victims of childhood molestation to speak up, to understand that they are not alone and to find help. The problem is not with the advice they offer to victims, but with their efforts to *create* victims—to expand the market that can then be treated with therapy and self-help books. To do this, survival books all hew to a formula based on an uncritical acceptance of certain premises about the nature of memory and trauma. They offer simple answers at a time when research psychologists are posing hard questions.

A needed reaction to the extravagant claims of the sexual abuse/ dissociative disorders/PTSD lobby is indeed in place. I emphasize needed because there is considerable evidence that some patients and families are being damaged by a form of therapy that convinces a patient that he/she has had certain dreadful life experiences, explains all present problems as stemming from these unremembered events, and then offers an expensive cure for these problems.

However, the fact that some circles present exaggerated claims should not have us lose sight of the significance of sexual abuse and its very real consequences. Many good studies have documented the fact that childhood sexual abuse is overrepresented in the psychiatric population, especially in the broad category of borderline patients. In some sense, the linkage of borderline personality disorder with a history of childhood sexual abuse has simplified psychotherapy by giving it a focus and a mission. The risk of this, as with all simplifications, is that the focus becomes unduly narrow, ignoring both other important developmental issues and perspectives in the life of the patient, and the manner in which abuse and victimization issues can be used in therapy by patients and therapists alike as a way of distorting and avoiding difficult therapy problems.

It is these latter concerns that call for a scrutiny of technical issues in psychotherapy. By "technical," I refer to the formal aspects rather than the particular subject matter of any given moment in therapy. Given that a patient has a history of childhood sexual abuse and symptoms referable to that abuse, how shall that knowledge guide my choices of when to respond and when to remain silent, of when to be supportive and when confrontive, of when to say, "I think you better be in the hospital?" How does the patient's particular history of childhood sexual abuse affect his/her motivations, expectations and participation in psychotherapy, and the therapist's theoretical formulation and practical responses to the patient?

The first half of this book was devoted to examining clinical models and research findings that have direct relevance to how we think about our work with PTSD/borderlines, including whether the entity of PTSD/borderline itself makes sense. There is often a chasm between the results of clinical studies and the application of psychotherapeutic technique. Frankly, it is as if the routine practice of psychotherapy goes its merry (or troubled) way, totally ignoring research findings which can bring important information to the clinician. To date, these findings fall into two areas. The first, gleaned primarily from follow-up studies, tell us which factors are and are not associated with good and poor outcomes. It is important to know suicide rates, suicide risk factors, and other prognostic features because such knowledge ought to guide our actions, even while we recognize that it is often impossible to apply statistical information to specific decisions at a crisis point with an individual patient.

Literally as I write these lines, I receive a message to call a patient who is at home thinking of cutting herself. She has not cut for five months. I wonder, as I return her call, whether my knowledge that cutting is negatively correlated with suicide will be helpful in my interaction with the patient and with whatever immediate decisions I will make. If not, how can I pretend to tell other therapists how to think about therapy? I think my knowledge will be useful, in the sense that I am less likely to swing into injudicious action based upon my anxieties over her safety. But all this is relative, for if she appears to raise the stakes during our telephone conversation, will my rereading Chapter 2 help me, or should I have reread Chapter 5 and decided not to return the call? Fortunately, we have a fairly positive discussion. I do not become intrusive, and I return to this writing with some peace of mind, however temporary.

The other research area that I think has been ignored by clinicians has been that relating to suggestibility and the whole business of true versus false versus distorted memory. Again, we cannot transpose the clinical and experimental research findings about memory distortions onto an individual patient's life history, but we certainly can be more aware of the problem areas relating to human recall.

Armed, so to speak, with our up-to-date research findings, which provide us with an aerial map of the battleground, we still need to get into the trenches and slug it out with our patients. Grand theories will not help, and even the reigning model that links sexual abuse to borderline symptoms does not dictate a particular course of action or a particular therapeutic modality. From my point of view, the keys to solid therapy consist of scrupulous adherence to the basic principles of psychotherapy combined with attention to the key themes and motifs that operate in the lives of PTSD/borderline patients. Despite individual variations, the common experience of childhood sexual abuse in these patients produces certain relatively similar symptoms and behaviors in therapy. Strongly shaping the transference patterns is the fact that the patient's motivation for "getting better" is overshadowed by the drive to bring about or sustain a certain kind of relationship (caretaking; argumentative; abusive; sexualized; admiring) with the therapist. The task of therapy is to help the patient identify maladaptive patterns, make some sense of their origins, and find new and more helpful patterns for coming to terms with the past and getting on in life. Fundamental to working with the patient is the necessity to steer clear of joining the patient in acting-out his/her transference issues.

Such a simple statement runs the risk of glossing over some very difficult and painful times for patient and therapist. This is the opposite of what I have tried to convey, and why I wish to avoid theories that tend to intellectualize and sanitize the therapeutic relationship. The schemas and models that I discuss in the last half of the book are presented as rough and incomplete maps of what one will most likely find in the psychotherapeutic territory. Whichever model the therapist loosely adheres to, I have been impressed with the value of peer supervision, or at least collegial discussion, of difficult cases and would informally recommend this to psychotherapists working with PTSD/borderline patients.

Bibliography

Adler, G. (1985). *Borderline psychopathology and its treatment*. New York: Jason Aronson.

AMA Council on Scientific Affairs (1985). Scientific status of refreshing recollection by the use of hypnosis. *Journal of the American Medical Association, 253,* 1918–1923.

AMA Council on Scientific Affairs (1990). Medical and non-medical uses of anabolic-androgenic steroids. *Journal of the American Medical Association, 264,* 2923–2927.

Appelbaum, P.S., & Jorgenson, L. (1991). Psychotherapist-patient sexual contact after termination of treatment: An analysis and a proposal. *American Journal of Psychiatry, 148,* 1466–1473.

Apter, M. (1992). *The psychology of excitement*. Evanston: Northwestern University Press.

Barnier, A.J., & McConkey, K.M. (1992). Reports of real and false memories: The relevance of hypnosis, hypnotizability, and context of memory test. *Journal of Abnormal Psychology, 101,* 521–527.

Beatrice of Nazareth (1991). (R. De Ganck, Trans. and ed.). Kalamazoo: Cistercian Publications.

Beck, J.C., & van der Kolk, B. (1987). Reports of childhood incest and current behavior of chronically hospitalized women. *American Journal of Psychiatry, 144,* 474–1476.

Benedict (1975). *The rule of St. Benedict* (A.C. Meisel & M.L. Del Mastro, Trans. and eds.). New York: Doubleday.

Bergin, A.E. (1988). Three contributions of a spiritual perspective to counseling, psychotherapy, and behavioral change. *Counseling and Values, 33,* 21–31.

Berlin, I. (1986). *The hedgehog and the fox*. New York: Simon and Schuster.

Bernstein, E.M., & Putnam, F.W. (1986). Development, reliability, and validity of a dissociation scale. *Journal of Nervous and Mental Disease, 174,* 727–735.

Billig, N. (1991). Deceptions in psychotherapy: Case report and considerations. *Canadian Journal of Psychiatry, 36,* 349–352.

Blumenthal, S.J., & Kupfer, D.J. (Eds.). (1990). *Suicide over the life cycle*. Washington, DC: American Psychiatric Press.

Bonaventure: The soul's journey into God; The tree of life; The life of St. Francis (1978). (E.H. Cousins, Trans.). New York: Fordham University Press.

Bouchard, T.J., Lykken, D.T., McGue, M., Segal, N.L., & Tellegen, A. (1990). Sources of human psychological differences: The Minnesota study of twins reared apart. *Science, 250,* 223–228.

Bouhoutsos, J., Holroyd, J., Lerman, H., Forer, B.R., & Greenberg, M. (1983). Sexual intimacy between psychotherapists and patients. *Professional Psychology, 14,* 185–196.

Bowker, J. (1970). *Problems of suffering in religions of the world.* Cambridge: Cambridge University Press.

Bradley, R. (1984). Julian of Norwich: Writer and mystic. In P. Szarmach (Ed.), *An introduction to the medieval mystics of Europe* (pp. 195–216). Albany: State University of New York Press.

Brandsma, J.M. (1982). Forgiveness: A dynamic theological and therapeutic analysis. *Pastoral Psychology, 31,* 40–50.

Brett, E.A., Spitzer, R.L., & Williams, J.B.W. (1988). DSM-III-R criteria for post-traumatic stress disorder. *American Journal of Psychiatry, 145,* 1232–1236.

Briere, J., & Zaidi, L.Y. (1989). Sexual abuse histories and sequelae in female psychiatric emergency room patients. *American Journal of Psychiatry, 146,* 1602–1606.

Brown, G.R., & Anderson, B. (1991). Psychiatric morbidity in adult inpatients with childhood histories of sexual and physical abuse. *American Journal of Psychiatry, 148,* 55–61.

Brown, J.E. (1971). *The gift of the sacred pipe.* Norman: University of Oklahoma.

Bryer, J.B., Nelson, B.A., Miller, J.B., & Krol, P.A. (1987). Childhood sexual and physical abuse as factors in adult psychiatric illness. *American Journal of Psychiatry, 144,* 1426–1430.

Burgess, A.W., Hartman, C.R., & McCormack, A. (1987). Abused to abuser: Antecedents of socially deviant behaviors. *American Journal of Psychiatry, 144,* 1431–1436.

Campbell, T.W. (1992). Therapeutic relationships and iatrogenic outcomes: The blame-and-change maneuver in psychotherapy. *Psychotherapy, 29,* 474–480.

Carmen, E.H., Rieker, P.P., & Mills, T. (1984). Victims of violence and psychiatric illness. *American Journal of Psychiatry, 141,* 378–383.

Centers for Disease Control (1991). State tobacco prevention, control activities: Results of 1989–1990 Association of State, Territorial Health Official Survey — Final Report. *Journal of the American Medical Association, 266,* 3105–3108.

Charlton, W. (1988). *Weakness of will: A philosophical inquiry.* Oxford: Basil Blackwell.

Christianson, S-A. (1992). Emotional stress and eyewitness memory: A critical review. *Psychological Bulletin, 112,* 284–309.

Chrousos, G.P., & Gold, P.W. (1992). The concepts of stress and stress system disorders. *Journal of the American Medical Association, 267,* 1244–1252.

Chu, J.A. (1991). The repetition compulsion revisited: Reliving dissociated trauma. *Psychotherapy, 28,* 327–332.

Chu, J.A. & Dill, D.L. (1990). Dissociative symptoms in relation to childhood physical and sexual abuse. *American Journal of Psychiatry, 147,* 887–892.

City's bill for attorney fees hits $30,000. (1992). *Minneapolis Star-Tribune,* December 3.

Claridge, K. (1992). Reconstructing memories of abuse: A theory-based approach. *Psychotherapy, 29,* 243–252.

Conn, L.M., & Lion, J.R. (1983). Self-mutilation: A review. *Psychiatric Medicine, 1,* 21–33.

Cousins, E.H. (1983). Francis of Assisi: Christian mysticism at the crossroads, In S.T. Katz (Ed.), *Mysticism and Religious Traditions* (pp. 163–190). Oxford: Oxford University Press.

Craine, L.S., Henson, C.E., Colliver, J.A., & MacLean, D.G. (1988). Prevalence of a history of sexual abuse among female psychiatric patients in a state hospital system. *Hospital & Community Psychiatry, 39,* 300–304.

Crits-Christoph, P. (1992). The efficacy of brief dynamic psychotherapy: A meta-analysis. *American Journal of Psychiatry, 149*, 151–158.

Cunningham, B.B. (1985). The will to forgive: A pastoral theological view of forgiving. *Journal of Pastoral Care, 39*, 141–149.

Davidson, J.R.T., & Foa, E.B. (1991). Refining criteria for posttraumatic stress disorder. *Hospital & Community Psychiatry, 42*, 259–261.

Dawson, D.F. (1988). Treatment of the borderline patient: Relationship management. *Canadian Journal of Psychiatry, 33*, 370–374.

de Cantimpre, T. (1986). *The life of Christina of St. Trond* (M. King, Trans.). Saskatoon: Peregrina.

de Cantimpre, T. (1987). *The life of Lutgard of Aywieres* (M. King, Trans.). (p. 79,42). Saskatoon: Peregrina.

De Ganck, R. (1991). *Beatrice of Nazareth in her context*. Kalamazoo: Cistercian Publications.

Dodge, K.A., Bates, J.E., & Pettit, G.S. (1990). Mechanisms in the cycle of violence. *Science, 250*, 1678–1683.

Downie, R.S. (1965). Forgiveness. *Philosophical Quarterly, 15*, 128–134.

Druck, A. (1989). *Four therapeutic approaches to the borderline patient: Principles and techniques of the basic dynamic stances*. Northvale, NJ: Jason Aronson.

Enright, R.D. and the Human Development Study Group (1991). The moral development of forgiveness. In W. Kurtines & J. Gewirtz (Eds.), *Moral behavior and development* (Vol. 1, pp. 123–152). Hillsdale, NJ: Erlbaum.

Enright, R.D., Santos, M., & Al-Mabuk, R. (1989). The adolescent as forgiver. *Journal of Adolescence, 12*, 95–110.

Favazza, A.R. (1987). *Bodies under siege*. Baltimore: Johns Hopkins University Press.

Favazza, A.R. (1989). Normal and deviant self-mutilation. *Transcultural Psychiatrists Research Review, 26*, 113–128.

Finkelhor, D. (1986). *A sourcebook on child sexual abuse*. Beverly Hills, CA: Sage Publications.

Flanagan, S. (1988). *Hildegard of Bingen 1098–1179: A visionary life*. London: Routledge.

Frances, A., Clarkin, J., & Perry, S. (Eds.). (1984). *Differential therapeutics in psychiatry: The art and science of treatment selection*. New York: Brunner/Mazel.

Friedman, L. (1988). *The anatomy of psychotherapy*. Hillsdale, NJ: Analytic Press.

Frischholz, E.J., Lipman, L.S., Braun, B.G., & Sachs, R.G. (1992). Psychopathology, hypnotizability, and dissociation. *American Journal of Psychiatry, 149*, 1521–1525.

Furst, P.T. (1977). "High states" in culture-historical perspective. In N.E. Zinberg (Ed.), *Alternate states of consciousness* (pp. 53–88). New York: Free Press.

Fyer, M.R., Frances, A., Sullivan, T., Hurt, S.W., & Clarkin, J. (1988). Suicide attempts in patients with borderline personality disorder. *American Journal of Psychiatry, 145*, 737–739.

Gabbard, G.O. (1989). On 'doing nothing' in the psychoanalytic treatment of the refractory borderline patient. *International Journal of Psycho-Analysis, 70*, 527–534.

Gabbard, G.O. (1991). Psychodynamics of sexual boundary violations. *Psychiatric Annals, 21*, 651–655.

Gardner, D.L., & Cowdry, R.W. (1985). Suicidal and parasuicidal behavior in borderline personality disorder. *Psychiatric Clinic of North America, 8*, 389–405.

Garmezy, N. (1981). Children under stress: Perspectives on antecedents and correlates of vulnerability and resistance to psychopathology. In A.I. Rabin et al. (Eds.), *Further explorations in personality*. New York: Wiley.

Garmezy, N., Masten, A.S., & Tellegen, A. (1984). The study of stress and competence in children: A building block for developmental psychology. *Child Development, 55*, 97–111.

Gartrell, N., Herman, J., Olarte, S., Feldstein, M., & Localio, R. (1986). Psychiatrist-patient sexual contact: results of a national survey, I: prevalence. *American Journal of Psychiatry, 143*, 1126–1131.

Gibbs, M. (1989). Factors in the victim that mediate between disaster and psychopathology. *Journal of Traumatic Stress, 2*, 489–514.

Goff, D.C., Brotman, A.W., Kindlon, D., Waites, M., & Amico, E. (1991). Self-reports of childhood abuse in chronically psychotic patients. *Psychiatry Research, 37*, 73–80.

Goldstein, R.B., Black, D.W., Nasrallah, A., & Winokur, G. (1991). The prediction of suicide. *Archives of General Psychiatry, 48*, 418–422.

Goodwin, J.M., Cheeves, K., & Connell, V. (1990). Borderline and other severe symptoms in adult survivors of incestuous abuse. *Psychiatric Annals, 20*, 22–32.

Green, B.L., Lindy, J.D., & Grace, M.C. (1985). Posttraumatic stress disorder: Toward DSM-IV. *Journal of Nervous and Mental Disease, 173*, 406–411.

Green, J. (1985). *God's fool: The life and times of Francis of Assisi*. New York: Harper and Row.

Greenson, R.R. (1967). *The technique and practice of psychoanalysis*. New York: International Universities Press.

Gunderson, J.G. (1984). *Borderline personality disorder*. Washington, DC: American Psychiatric Press.

Gunderson, J.G., Frank, A.F., Ronningstam, E.F., Wachter, S., Lynch, V.J., & Wolf, P.J. (1989). Early discontinuance of borderline patients from psychotherapy. *Journal of Nervous and Mental Disease, 177*, 38–42.

Gunderson, J.G., Kolb, J.E., & Austin, V. (1981). The diagnostic interview for borderline patients. *American Journal of Psychiatry, 138*, 896–903.

Gutheil, T.G. (1989). Borderline personality disorder, boundary violations, and patient-therapist sex: Medicolegal pitfalls. *American Journal of Psychiatry, 146*, 597–602.

Gutheil, T.G. (1991). Patients involved in sexual misconduct with therapists: Is a victim profile possible? *Psychiatric Annals, 21*, 661–667.

Haaken, J., & Schlaps, A. (1991). Incest resolution therapy and the objectification of sexual abuse. *Psychotherapy, 28*, 39–54.

Hawton, K. (1990). Self-cutting: can it be prevented? In K. Hawton & P. Cowen (Eds.), *Dilemmas and difficulties in the management of psychiatric patients*. Oxford: Oxford University Press.

Henderson, J. (1978). The Flagellant movement and flagellant confraternities in central Italy, 1260–1400. In D. Baker (Ed.), *Religious motivation: Biographical and sociological problems for the church historian* (pp. 147–160). Oxford: Oxford University Press.

Herman, J.L. (1992a). *Trauma and recovery*. New York: Basic Books.

Herman, J.L. (1992b). Complex PTSD: A syndrome in survivors of prolonged and repeated trauma. *Journal of Traumatic Stress, 5*, 377–390.

Herman, J.L., Gartrell, N., Olarte, S., Feldstein, M., & Localio, R. (1987). Psychiatrist-patient sexual contact: Results of a national survey, II: psychiatrists' attitudes. *American Journal of Psychiatry, 144*, 164–169.

Herman, J.L., Perry, J.C., & van der Kolk, B.A. (1989). Childhood trauma in borderline personality disorder. *American Journal of Psychiatry, 146*, 490–495.

Herman, J., Russell, D., & Trocki, K. (1986). Long-term effects of incestuous abuse in childhood. *American Journal of Psychiatry, 143*, 1293–1296.

Herman, J.L., & Schatzow, E. (1987). Recovery and verification of memories of childhood sexual trauma. *Psychoanalytic Psychology, 4*, 1–14.

Hildegard of Bingen (1986). *Scivias* (B. Hozeski, Trans.). Santa Fe: Bear & Company.

Hill, D. (1989). On states of consciousness. In E.H. Reynolds & M.R. Trimble (Eds.), *The bridge between neurology and psychiatry* (pp. 56–71). Edinburgh: Churchill Livingstone.

Horowitz, M.J. (1974). Stress response syndromes: Character style and dynamic psychotherapy. *Archives of General Psychiatry, 31*, 768–781.

Horowitz, M.J. (1987). *States of mind: Configurational analysis of individual psychology* (2nd ed.). New York: Plenum.

Horowitz, M., Wilner, N., & Alvarez, W. (1979). Impact of event scale: A measure of subjective distress. *Psychosomatic Medicine, 41*, 209–218.

Howard, K.I., Davidson, C.V., O'Mahoney, M.T., Orlinsky, D.E., & Brown, K.P. (1989). Patterns of psychotherapy utilization. *American Journal of Psychiatry, 146*, 775–778.

Human Development Study Group (1991). Five points on the construct of forgiveness within psychotherapy. *Psychotherapy, 28*, 493–496.

Jacobson, A. (1989). Physical and sexual assault histories among psychiatric outpatients. *American Journal of Psychiatry, 146*, 755–758.

Jacobson, A., Koehler, J.E., & Jones-Brown, C. (1987). The failure of routine assessment to detect histories of assault experienced by psychiatric patients. *Hospital and Community Psychiatry, 38*, 386–389.

Jenny, C. (1988). Adolescent risk-taking behavior and the occurrence of sexual assault. *American Journal of Diseases of Children, 142*, 770–772.

Julian of Norwich (1978). *A book of showings to the Anchoress Julian of Norwich* (Vols. 1–2). (E. Colledge, & J. Walsh, Eds.). New York: Paulist Press.

Kallman, F.J. (1946). The genetic theory of schizophrenia: An analysis of 691 schizophrenic twin index families. *American Journal of Psychiatry, 103*, 309–322.

Kashani, J.H., Daniel, A.E., Dandoy, A.C., & Holcomb, W.R. (1992). Family violence: Impact on children. *Journal of the American Academy of Child and Adolescent Psychiatry, 31*, 181–189.

Kernberg, O.F. (1975). *Borderline conditions and pathological narcissism*. New York: Jason Aronson.

Kernberg, O.F. (1984). *Severe personality disorders: Psychotherapeutic strategies*. New Haven: Yale University Press.

Kieckhefer, R. (1984). *Unquiet souls: Fourteenth century saints and their religious milieu*. Chicago: University of Chicago Press.

Kisch, J. (1992). Utilization of mental health services: Attrition versus aggregation. *HMO Practice, 6*, 33–38.

Koretzky, M.B., & Peck, A.H. (1990). Validation and cross-validation of the PTSD subscale of the MMPI with civilian trauma victims. *Journal of Clinical Psychology, 46*, 296–300.

Kreitman, N., & Dyer, J.A.T. (1980). Suicide in relation to parasuicide. *Medicine, 39*, 1827–1830.

Kroll, J. (1988). *The challenge of the borderline patient*. New York: Norton.

Kroll, J., Carey, K., & Sines, L. (1985). Twenty year follow-up of borderline personality disorder. In C. Shagass (Ed.), *Biological psychiatry*. New York: Elsevier.

Kroll, J., & De Ganck, R. (1986). The adolescence of a thirteenth century visionary nun. *Psychological Medicine, 16*, 745–756.

Kroll, J., & De Ganck, R. (1990). Beatrice of Nazareth: Psychiatric perspectives on a medieval mystic. *Cistercian Studies, 24*, 301–323.

Kroll, J., Habenicht, M., Mackenzie, T., Yang, M., Chan, S., Vang, T., Nguyen, T., Ly, M., Phommasouvanh, B., Nguyen, H., Vang, Y., Souvannasoth, L., & Cabugao, R. (1989). Depression and posttraumatic stress disorder in Southeast Asian refugees. *American Journal of Psychiatry, 146*, 1592–1597.

Kullgren, G. (1988). Factors associated with completed suicide in borderline personality disorder. *Journal of Nervous and Mental Disease, 176*, 40–44.

Kullgren, G., Renberg, E., & Jacobsson, L. (1986). An empirical study of borderline personality disorder and psychiatric suicides. *Journal of Nervous and Mental Disease, 174*, 328–331.

Lambert, M.J. (1989). The individual therapist's contribution to psychotherapy process and outcome. *Clinical Psychology Review, 9*, 469–485.

Landecker, H. (1992). The role of childhood sexual trauma in the etiology of borderline personality disorder: Considerations for diagnosis and treatment. *Psychotherapy, 29*, 234–242.

Lawrence, C.H. (1984). *Medieval monasticism*. London: Longman.

Levin, A.P., & Hyler, S.E. (1986). DSM-III personality diagnosis in bulimia. *Comprehensive Psychiatry, 27*, 47–53.

Lewis, M. (1980). On forgiveness. *Philosophical Quarterly, 30*, 236–245.

Life of Juliana of Mont Cornillon (1990). (B. Newman, trans.). Toronto: Peregrina.

Linehan, M.M., Armstrong, H.E., Suarez, A., Allmon, D., & Heard, H.L. (1991). Cognitive-behavioral treatment of chronically parasuicidal borderline patients. *Archives of General Psychiatry, 48*, 1060–1064.

Lives of the Desert Fathers (N. Russell, Trans; B. Ward, Intro.). (1980). London: Mowbray.

Luthar, S.S., & Zigler, E. (1991). Vulnerability and competence: A review of research on resilience in childhood. *American Journal of Orthopsychiatry, 61*, 6–22.

Margo, G.M., & McLees, E.M. (1991). Further evidence for the significance of a childhood abuse history in psychiatric inpatients. *Comprehensive Psychiatry, 32*, 362–366.

Masson, J.M. (1984). *The assault on truth: Freud's suppression of the seduction theory*. New York: Farrar, Straus and Giroux.

Matas, M., & Marriott, A. (1987). The girl who cried wolf: Pseudologica phantastica and sexual abuse. *Canadian Journal of Psychiatry, 32*, 305–309.

McDonnell, E.W. (1954). *The beguines and beghards in medieval culture*. New Brunswick: Rutgers University Press.

McGlashan, T.H. (1986). The Chestnut Lodge follow-up study: Long-term outcome of borderline personalities. *Archives of General Psychiatry, 43*, 20–30.

Meehl, P.E. (1977). Specific etiology and other forms of strong influence: Some quantitative meanings. *Journal of Medicine and Philosophy, 2*, 33–53.

Merskey, H. (1992). The manufacture of personalities: The production of multiple personality disorder. *British Journal of Psychiatry, 160*, 327–340.

Minnesota Statute Annotated (1992). Section 169.974, Subdivision 4. St. Paul: West Publishing Company.

Mohl, P.C., Martinez, D., Ticknor, C., & Appleby, J. (1989). Psychotherapy refusers. *Comprehensive Psychiatry, 30*, 245–250.

Morrison, J. (1989). Childhood sexual histories of women with somatization disorder. *American Journal of Psychiatry, 146*, 239–241.

Mullen, P.E., Romans-Clarkson, S.E., Walton, V.E., & Herbison, G.P. (1988). Impact of sexual and physical abuse on women's mental health. *Lancet, i*, 841–845.

Murphy, J.G., & Hampton, J. (1988). *Forgiveness and mercy*. Cambridge: Cambridge University Press.

Ogata, S.N., Silk, K.R., Goodrich, S., Lohr, N.E., Westen, D., & Hill, E.M. (1990). Childhood sexual and physical abuse in adult patients with borderline personality disorder. *American Journal of Psychiatry, 147*, 1008–1013.

Ornstein, R. (1986). The organized systems: Changing consciousness. In R. Ornstein (Ed.), *The psychology of consciousness* (pp. 181–200). New York: Penguin.

Palmer, R.L., Chaloner, D.A., & Oppenheimer, R. (1992). Childhood sexual experiences with adults reported by female psychiatric patients. *British Journal of Psychiatry, 160*, 261–265.

Paris, J. (1990). Completed suicides in borderline personality disorder. *Psychiatric Annals, 20*, 19–21.

Paris, J. (1991). Personality disorders, parasuicide, and culture. *Transcultural Psychiatric Research Review, 28*, 25–39.

Paris, J. (Ed.). (1992). *Borderline personality disorder: Etiology and treatment*. Washington, DC: American Psychiatric Press.

Paris, J., Brown, R., & Nowlis, D. (1987). Long-term follow-up of borderline patients in a general hospital. *Comprehensive Psychiatry, 28*, 530–535.

Paris, J., Nowlis, D., & Brown, R. (1988). Developmental factors in the outcome of borderline personality disorder. *Comprehensive Psychiatry, 29*, 147–150.

Paris, J., Nowlis, D., & Brown, R. (1989). Predictors of suicide in borderline personality disorder. *Canadian Journal of Psychiatry, 34*, 8–9.

Paris, J., & Zweig-Frank, H. (1992). A critical review of the role of childhood sexual abuse in the etiology of borderline personality disorder. *Canadian Journal of Psychiatry, 37*, 125–128.

Perconte, S.T., & Goreczny, A.J. (1990). Failure to detect fabricated posttraumatic stress disorder with the use of the MMPI in a clinical population. *American Journal of Psychiatry, 147*, 1057–1060.

Perr, I.N. (1991). Crime and multiple personality disorder: A case history and discussion. *Bulletin of American Academy of Psychiatry & Law, 19*, 203–214.

Perry, S. (1989). Treatment time and the borderline patient: An underappreciated strategy. *Journal of Personality Disorders, 3*, 230–239.

Plakun, E.M. (1991). Prediction of outcome in borderline personality disorder. *Journal of Personality Disorders, 5*, 93–101.

Plakun, E.M., Burkhardt, P.E., & Muller, J.P. (1985). Fourteen year follow-up of borderline and schizotypal personality disorders. *Comprehensive Psychiatry, 26*, 448–455.

Pope, H.G. Jr., Frankenburg, F.R., Hudson, J.I., Jonas, J.M., & Yurgelun-Todd, D. (1987). Is bulimia associated with borderline personality disorder? A controlled study. *Journal of Clinical Psychiatry, 48*, 181–184.

Pope, H.G. Jr., & Hudson, J.I. (1992). Is childhood sexual abuse a risk factor for bulimia nervosa? *American Journal of Psychiatry, 149*, 455–463.

Pope, K.S. (1990a). Therapist-patient sexual involvement: A review of the research. *Clinical Psychology Review, 10*, 477–490.

Pope, K.S. (1990b). Therapist-patient sex as sex abuse: Six scientific, professional, and practical dilemmas in addressing victimization and rehabilitation. *Professional Psychology, 21*, 227–239.

Pope, K.S., & Vetter, V.A. (1991). Prior therapist-patient sexual involvement among patients seen by psychologists. *Psychotherapy, 28*, 429–438.

Powers, W.K. (1977). *Ogala Religions*. Lincoln: University of Nebraska Press.

Pribor, E.F., & Dinwiddie, S.H. (1992). Psychiatric correlates of incest in childhood. *American Journal of Psychiatry, 149*, 52–56.

Rich, C.L. (1990). Accuracy of adults' reports of abuse in childhood. (letter). *American Journal of Psychiatry, 147*, 1389–1390.

Rigotti, N.A., & Pashos, C.L. (1991). No-Smoking laws in the United States. *Journal of the American Medical Association, 266*, 3162–3167.

Roy, A. (Ed.) (1986). *Suicide*. Baltimore: Williams and Wilkins.

Runeson, B., & Beskow, J. (1991). Borderline personality disorder in young Swedish suicides. *Journal of Nervous and Mental Disease, 179*, 153–156.

Russ, M.J. (1992). Self-injurious behavior in patients with borderline personality disorder: Biological perspectives. *Journal of Personality Disorders, 6*, 64–81.

Russell, D.E.H. (1986). *The secret trauma: Incest in the lives of girls and women*. New York: Basic Books.

Sansone, R.A., & Fine, M.A. (1992). Borderline personality disorder as a predictor of outcome in women with eating disorders. *Journal of Personality Disorders, 6*, 176–186.

Scarr, S. (1992). Developmental theories for the 1990s: Development and individual differences. *Child Development, 63*, 1–19.

Schoener, G.R., & Gonsiorek, J. (1988). Assessment and development of rehabilitation plans for counselors who have sexually exploited their clients. *Journal of Counseling and Development, 67*, 227–232.

Schroeder, S.R., Schroeder, C.S., Smith, B., & Dalldorf, J. (1978). Prevalence of self-injurious behaviors in a large state facility for the retarded: A three year follow-up study. *Journal of Autism and Childhood Schizophrenia, 8*, 261–269.

Scull, A. (1992). *Social order/mental disorder*. Berkeley: University of California Press.

Sederer, L.I., & Thorbeck, J. (1986). First do no harm: Short-term inpatient psychotherapy of the borderline patient. *Hospital and Community Psychiatry, 37*, 692–697.

Selzer, M.A., Koenigsberg, H.W., & Kernberg, O.F. (1987). The initial contract in the treatment of borderline patients. *American Journal of Psychiatry, 144*, 927–930.

Sexual harassment accusation. (1992). *Minneapolis Star-Tribune*, August 25.

Shay, J.J. (1987). The wish to do psychotherapy with borderline adolescents — and other common errors. *Psychotherapy, 24*, 712–719.

Shearer, S.L., Peters, C.P., Quaytman, M.S., & Ogden, R.L. (1990). Frequency and correlates of childhood sexual and physical abuse histories in adult female borderline patients. *American Journal of Psychiatry, 147*, 214–216.

Shore, D., Anderson, D.J., & Cutler, N.R. (1978). Prediction of self-mutilation in hospitalized schizophrenics. *American Journal of Psychiatry, 135*, 1406–1407.

Simeon, D., Stanley, B., Frances, A., Mann, J.J., Winchel, R., & Stanley, M. (1992). Self-mutilation in personality disorders: Psychological and biological correlates. *American Journal of Psychiatry, 149*, 221–226.

Skodal, A.E., Buckley, P., & Charles, E. (1983). Is there a characteristic pattern to the treatment history of clinic outpatients with borderline personality? *Journal of Nervous and Mental Disease, 171*, 405–410.

Smedes, L.B. (1984). *Forgive and forget: Healing the hurts we don't deserve*. San Francisco: Harper and Row.

Soloff, P.H. (1992). Pharmacological therapies in borderline personality disorder. In J. Paris (Ed.), *Borderline personality disorder: Etiology and treatment*. Washington, DC: American Psychiatric Press.

Solomon, S.D., Gerrity, E.T., & Muff, A.M. (1992). Efficacy of treatments for posttraumatic stress disorder: An empirical review. *Journal of the American Medical Association, 268*, 633–638.

Sparr, L.F., & Boehnlein, J.K. (1990). Posttraumatic Stress Disorder in tort actions: Forensic minefield. *Bulletin of the American Academy of Psychiatry and Law, 18*, 283–302.

Sroufe, L.A., & Fleeson, J. (1986). Attachment and the construction of relationships. In W. Hartup & Z. Rubin (Eds.), *Relationships and development* (pp. 51–72). Hillsdale, NJ: Erlbaum.

Stevenson, J., & Meares, R. (1992). An outcome study of psychotherapy for patients with borderline personality disorder. *American Journal of Psychiatry, 149*, 358–362.

Stone, M.H. (1980). *The borderline syndromes*. New York: McGraw-Hill.

Stone, M.H. (1990). *The fate of borderline patients*. New York: Guilford.

Strasburger, L.H., Jorgenson, L., & Randles, R. (1991). Criminalization of psychotherapist-patient sex. *American Journal of Psychiatry, 148*, 859–863.

Surrey, J., Swett, C. Jr., Michaels, A., & Levin, S. (1990). Reported history of physical and sexual abuse and severity of symptomatology in women psychiatric outpatients. *American Journal of Orthopsychiatry, 60*, 412–417.

Swett, C. Jr., Surrey, J., & Cohen, C. (1990). Sexual and physical abuse histories and psychiatric symptoms among male psychiatric outpatients. *American Journal of Psychiatry, 147*, 632–636.

Szasz, T.S. (1974). *The myth of mental illness* (rev. ed.). New York: Harper and Row.

Taube, C., Goldman, H., Burns, B., & Kessler, L. (1988). High users of outpatient mental health services, I: definition and characteristics. *American Journal of Psychiatry, 145*, 19–24.

Tavris, C. (1993). Beware the incest-survivor machine. *New York Times Book Review*, January 3, p. 1.

Terr, L.C. (1991). Childhood traumas: an outline and overview. *American Journal of Psychiatry, 148*, 10–20.

Twice a Victim? *Minneapolis Star-Tribune*, Sept. 19, 1992.

van der Kolk, B.A., Perry, J.C., & Herman, J.L. (1991). Childhood origins of self-destructive behavior. *American Journal of Psychiatry, 148*, 1665–1671.

Vita of Ida of Louvain (1886). AASS April 2 (D. Papebrouck, ed.). Paris.

Wakefield, H., & Underwager, R. (1991). Sexual abuse allegations in divorce and custody disputes. *Behavioral Science and the Law, 9*, 451–468.

Waldinger, R.J., & Gunderson, J.G. (1984). Completed psychotherapies with borderline patients. *American Journal of Psychotherapy, 38*, 190–202.

Waller, G. (1991). Sexual abuse as a factor in eating disorders. *British Journal of Psychiatry, 159*, 664–671.

Wallerstein, R.S. (1986). *Forty-two lives in treatment: A study of psychoanalysis and psychotherapy*. New York: Guilford.

Weekes, J.R., Lynn, S.J., Green, J.P., & Brentar, J.T. (1992). Pseudomemory in hypnotized and task-motivated subjects. *Journal of Abnormal Psychology, 101*, 356–360.

Weinstein, D., & Bell, R. M. (1982). *Saints and society: The two worlds of western christendom, 1000–1700*. Chicago: University of Chicago Press.

Westen, D., Ludolph, P., Misle, B., Ruffins, S., & Block, J. (1990). Physical and sexual abuse in adolescent girls with borderline personality disorder. *American Journal of Orthopsychiatry, 60*, 55–66.

Widom, C.S. (1991). Avoidance of criminality in abused and neglected children. *Psychiatry, 54*, 162–174.

Wilson, J.D. (1988). Androgen abuse by athletes. *Endocrine Review, 9*, 181–199.

Wilson, J.P., & Walker, A.J. (1990). Toward an MMPI trauma profile. *Journal of Traumatic Stress, 3*, 151–168.

Winchel, R.M., & Stanley, M. (1991). Self-injurious behavior: A review of the behavior and biology of self-mutilations. *American Journal of Psychiatry, 148*, 306–317.

Winfield, I., George, L.K., Swartz, M., & Blazer, D.G. (1990). Sexual assault and psychiatric disorders among a community sample of women. *American Journal of Psychiatry, 147*, 335–341.

Zanarini, M.C., Gunderson, J.G., Marino, M.F., Schwartz, E.O., & Frankenburg, F.R. (1989). Childhood experiences of borderline patients. *Comprehensive Psychiatry, 30*, 18–25.

Zweig-Frank, H., & Paris, J. (1991). Parents' emotional neglect and overprotection according to the recollections of patients with borderline personality disorder. *American Journal of Psychiatry, 148*, 648–651.

Index

absolution of guilt, 152
abuse, *see* sexual/physical abuse in childhood
acceptance, 111
acknowledgment, and forgiveness, 201
acting-out, 157–61
  case examples of, 115–16, 165–66, 239
  complicity of the therapist in, 236, 243, 245
  of self-hatred, 219
Adler, G., 20, 129
adverse life circumstances, and PTSD, 248
affective disorders, 10, 11, 214
  borderline personality disorders as, 31
  and childhood abuse, 47–48
  risk of suicide in, 135–36
affirmation
  boundaries as an aspect of, 114–20
  in therapy, 112–13, 21–23
  and self-injurious behavior, 95
agenda of patients and therapists, 172–73, 193
aggressor, identification with, 161–63
alcohol abuse
  case example, 224
  among incest victims, 55
  and suicide rates, 26
alcohol ingestion, social view of, 84
AMA Council on Scientific Affairs, 67, 83

anger
  and forgiveness, 202
  and negative transference, 20
  and relationship to God, 201
  replaying, 170
  and self-hatred, 218
  validation of, 118–20, 194
anoretics, reported abuse of, 48
antidepressants, effect in borderline conditions, 27
antisocial personality disorder
  among incest victims, 54
  and suicide rates, 26
anxiety disorders
  and hypnotizability, 66
  among incest victims, 55
  PTSD as, 214–15
Appelbaum, P. S., 235
Apter, M., 84
asceticism, 90
  see also medieval ascetics
average expectable environment, 75, 152

Bachrach, B., 8
bad seed theories of guilt, 196
Barnier, A. J., 66
Beatrice of Nazareth, 92–93
Beck, J. C., 37
Beck Depression Scale, 68
behavior modification, 93
Benedict, 91
bereavement and depression, 211
  see also grief
Bergin, A. E., 200
Berlin, I., xvi

Bernstein, E. M., 42, 68
betrayal, replaying issues of, 169–73
Billig, N., 63
biological components of SIB, 88
biological theory of BPD, 31
blame, and volition, 104
Blumenthal, S. J., 135
bonding, 196
borderline personality disorder
  association with childhood abuse,
    49–53
  comparison with depression, 51–52
  diagnosis of, and childhood abuse,
    43–46
  etiology of, theory, 36
  versus PTSD, 7–8, 57–78
  suggestibility of patients, 61–62
  theatrical style of patients, 60
Bouchard, T. J., 74
Bouhoutsos, J., 235
boundaries
  in therapy, 108–9, 114–20, 143,
    170–71
  violation of, abuse as, xxi, 174
boundary therapy, 101
Bowker, J., 81
Bradley, R., 94
brain chemistry, changing with SIB,
  88
Brandsma, J. M., 200
Brett, E. A., 214
brief dynamic therapy, meta-analysis,
  15
brief psychotherapy, 10–11
Briere, J., 34, 45–46
Brown, G. R., 45
Brown, J. E., 81
Bryer, J. B., 41, 42, 43, 48
bulimia, and borderline symptoms, 48
Burgess, A. W., 75

Campbell, T. W., 220
caretakers
  abuse by, 51
  disillusion with, 191

mentally ill, abuse by, 197
  role reversal with, 196–98
Carmen, E. H., 37
case examples
  boundaries and affirmation, 114–16
  caring actions, problematic, 131–34
  countertransference, 130, 244
  control and victimization, 164–65
  dependency needs, 138–41
  eroticization of the therapeutic rela-
    tionship, 165–66
  gratification
    of dependency needs, 126–27
    of needs, problematic, 121–25
    of sexual fantasies, 144–47
  interactions
    and power, 161
    levels of meanings in, 227–28
  multiple personality disorder, 215–
    16
  patterns from the past, 223–25
  problems with trust, 220–21
  repetition of destructive behavior,
    223
  replaying old issues
    of betrayal, 169–82
    of victimization, 167–68
  rescue fantasies, 138–41, 141–43
  self-hatred, 218–19
  suicide and dependency needs, 137–
    38
  testing the therapist
    for rejection, 232–34
    for seduction, 237
    for victimization, 238–39
  transference issues, 229
catharsis, xvii, 173
causation, strong and weak influences, 35–36
Centers for Disease Control, 84
central nervous system maturation, 22
change
  in the practice of psychotherapy, 9–
    10
  as the reason for therapy, 137–38

character pathology, 72
Charlton, W., 101
choice, available to adults, 217–18
    see also symptoms, choice of
Christianson, S-A., 66, 154
Christina of St. Trond, 91
chronic disability, and age, 23
Chrousos, G. P., 210
Chu, J. A., 42
Claridge, K., 33
cognitive-behavioral therapies, xix, 10
    drop-out rate, 19
    and parasuicidal behavior, 25
    study of, 15
    for women with eating disorders, 48
collusion between patient and thera-
        pist, 175
    see also complicity
compassion for an abuser, 202–3
complicity, 193
    in abuse, conflict over, 185, 194–
        99
    of the therapist in acting-out, 236
compulsion
    and responsibility, 104
    versus volition, 103, 159, 201
confidentiality, and consultation, 171
conflict in nurturance and caring,
        117
confrontation in therapy, 106
Conn, L. M., 79
consultation, 150
    to avoid problems in transference,
        246
    informal, collegial, 251
    see also peer review; supervision
content, *see* process versus content
context, *see* culture
contracts with patients, 5–6
control
    need for, by males, 221
    and replaying old issues, 174–75
coping styles
    and life stage during abuse, 77
    following trauma, 189

corrective emotional experience, 117
countertransference, 240–47
    in gratification of dependency
        needs, 129–31
Cousins, E. H., 91
Craine, L. S., 39
credibility of abuse reports, 34, 63
    see also false memory syndromes
criticism of patients in therapy, 116–
        17
Crits-Christoph, P., 15
culture
    and adoption of borderline pat-
        terns, 78
    effect on symptom choice, 8, 65,
        213–14
    and SIB, 80–81, 85–86, 95, 96
    condemnation of, 82–83
    meanings of, 86, 89
    social attitudes toward, 94–95
Cunningham, B. B., 200

Davidson, J. R. T., 211
Dawson, D. F., 25, 95
de Cantimpre, T., 92
decision-making for clients, 242
deficit model, 129
De Ganck, R., 90
De Palma, B., 207
dependency, gratification of need for,
        125–38
depersonalization, 189
depression
    and bereavement, 211
    case example, 238–39
    among incest victims, 55
    versus PTSD/borderline disorder,
        131
    and suicide rate, 24, 26–27
    treatment with medication, 10
derealization, 52
determinism versus volition, 222
    see also free will/determinism
developmental psychopathology, 31,
        187

diagnostic group, and hypnotizability, 66
Dialectical Behavior Therapy (DBT), 15
disillusionment, 185, 190–94
dissociation
    child's response to stress, 189
    and PTSD/borderline syndrome, 212–17
    in therapy, 159
dissociative disorders
    and hypnotizability, 66
    and responsibility for SIB, 96
Dissociative Experiences Scale (DES), 42, 68
dissociative scores of patients
    abused in childhood, 40
    with non-borderline symptoms, 42
Dodge, K. A., 75
dominance in a therapeutic setting, 123
double bookkeeping by abused patients, 191–92, 195, 198–99
double vision, therapists', 159
Downie, R. S., 200
Druck, A., 213

early separation experiences, 51
eating disorders, 48
economic factors
    affecting psychotherapy practice, 9–11
    affecting reported abuse, 34
    see also marketing; insurance reimbursement
ecstatic state, 96
emotional overload, 174
emotions, modulation of, 154–55
empirical studies, 36–37
Enright, R. D., 200
entitlement, 28–29, 118, 234
    case example, 126–27
    and forgiveness, 204
    gratification of, 151–52
    and treatment resistance, 112

environment for personality development, 75
ethical issues, 147–48, 166, 235–36
etiology, theory of borderline, xvii, 36
evolutionary biology, 89
    and need for social interaction, 191
expectation, social norms, and SIB, 86
exploitation, testing the therapist for, 238–39
exploratory therapy, 14
expressive therapy, 13

False Memory Syndrome Foundation, 67
false memory syndromes, 64–68, 231, 250
falsification of life stories, 62–64
family relationships, and childhood abuse, 35, 191, 193
Favazza, A. R., 79
fear versus wish, expressions of, 221–22
Finkelhor, D., 37
Flanagan, S., 94
follow-up studies of suicide rates, 7
forgiveness versus irreconcilability, 185, 200–6
Frances, A., 25
Francis of Assisi, 91
free will/determinism, 103–4
    and seduction in therapy, 236
Friedman, L., 107, 153, 160
Frischholz, E. J., 66
Furst, P. T., 88
Fyer, M. R., 26, 136

Gabbard, G. O., 25, 235
Gardner, D. L., 82–83
Garmezy, N., 35
Gartrell, N., 235
gaze aversion, 154
gender, and self-injurious behavior, 95

genetics
  and character pathology, 72
  and schizophrenia, 30
Gibbs, M., 73
goals
  of building trust, 222
  consensus on, in therapy, 102
  of incest oriented psychotherapy,
    194–95
  of patients in therapy, 149–50, 251
  of patients versus therapists, 105–6,
    124–25, 133–34
  of self-injurious behavior, 95
  of therapy, 156
    ideal, 243
  and toleration for self-injurious be-
    havior, 83, 84–85
Goff, D. C., 40
Goldstein, R. B., 24, 135
Goodwin, J. M., 54
gratification
  of dependency needs, 125–38
  of entitlement, 151–52
  problematic, xv, 120–25
  of rescue fantasies, 138–44
  of sexual desires (fantasies), 144–
    51
  from social interactions, 108
  in therapy, 110–53, 119–120, 243
Green, B. L., 72
Green, J., 91
Greenson, R. R., 229
grief
  counseling for, 211
  validation of, 118–20
guilt
  absolution of, 152
  expiation of, in acting-out, 168–69
  patient's belief in, 195
Gunderson, J. G., 14, 19, 51, 212
Gutheil, T. G., 235

Haaken, J., 29, 187
harrassment, sexual, 208–9
Hawton, K., 25

helplessness, and powerlessness, 167
Henderson, J., 81
Herman, J. L., 34, 49, 53, 54, 59, 63,
  71, 73, 75, 86, 87, 188, 235
Hildegard of Bingen, 94
Hill, D., 88
holding environment, 125, 129
  and drop-out rate, 20
Horowitz, M. J., 49, 80
hostility in sexual exploitation, 245
Howard, K. I., 18
Human Development Study Group,
  200
hypnosis, and recovery of memories,
  66–67

iatrogenesis in development of MPD,
  65
Ida of Louvain, 91
idealization/devaluation, 130–31
  in borderlines, 61
  and transference, 243
Impact of Events Scale, 49
incest
  psychotherapy following, 194–95
  reports by psychiatric patients, 39,
    53–55
  risks in therapy for, 29
individual factors in PTSD response,
  71–75
inner life, 154
institutionalization of SIB as communication, 87
insurance reimbursement, 4–5
  effects on types of care, 248
interchange, between patients and
  therapists, 227–28
interpretation in therapy, 106
intervention, and control, 174–75
intrusive process, replaying old issues,
  157
IQ of girls with history of abuse, 52–
  53
irreconcilability versus forgiveness,
  200–206

Jacobson, A., 34, 40, 46
Jenny, C., 72
judgment, therapist's, 247
Julian of Norwich, 94
Juliana of Mont Cornillon, 92

Kallman, F. J., 30
Kashani, J. H., 75
Kernberg, O. F., xi, 20, 212
Kieckhefer, R., 89
King, S., 207
Kisch, J., 18
Koretzky, M. B., 63
Kreitman, N., 136
Kroll, J., 21, 78, 90, 97, 213
Kuhn, T., 55
Kullgren, G., 24, 136

Lambert, M. J., 16
Lawrence, C. H., 90
lawsuits, 5–6
    to express dissatisfaction, 240–41
    and recovery of memories in ther-
        apy, 67
    and responses to acting-out, 115–16
    and responses to threatened suicide,
        135
    following sexual harrassment, 209
Levin, A. P., 83
Lewis, M., 200
licensure, 4
Life Experiences Questionnaire, 42
life experiences theory, 31
life style
    and definition of self-destructive be-
        havior, 83–85
    high-risk, 81, 84
Linehan, M. M., 15, 19, 25
love, and forgiveness, 202, 205
Lutgard of Aywieres, 92
Luthar, S. S., 76

McDonnell, E. W., 90, 91
McGlashan, T. H., 13, 21, 27
managed care programs, 4–5

manic-depressive illness, correlation
    with childhood abuse, 44
Margo, G. M., 43, 44
marketing
    of dissociative disorders, 67–68
    effect on psychotherapy practice,
        208
    of mental disorders, 248
Masson, J. M., 48
mastery through repetition, 168–69
Matas, M., 63
medical-psychiatric model, 175
medications for borderlines, study,
    14–15
medieval ascetics
    opposition to, 91–94
    self-injurious behaviors in, 89–94
Meehl, P. E., 35
memory
    versus reality, 32–33, 59–62
        of incest, 231
    research on, 65–66
    stress, and accuracy of recall, 154
men
    life-time prevalence rate, abuse in
        psychiatric populations, 37
    need for power, 221
mental processing, and psychological
    symptoms, 155–56
Merskey, H., 33, 65
Millon Clinical Multiaxial Inventory,
    41, 68
mistrust, 219–22
MMPI test results
    for discrimination of real and fabri-
        cated PTSD, 63
    methodological problems with, 68
modulation of emotions, 154–55
Mohl, P. C., 14
Morrison, J., 47
multiple personality disorder, 33,
    208
    iatrogenesis in development of, 65
    and suggestibility, 52
    vested interest in diagnosis of, 68

Munchausen's syndrome, parallel in psychiatric patients, 33–34
Murphy, J. G., 200

nature/nurture controversy, 76–77
neediness, 167
needs
   dependency, 125–38
   problematic gratification of, xv, 120–25, 246
negative entitlement, 151–52
negative transference, and anger, 20
neurotic disorders, and childhood abuse, 44
nurturance in therapy, 133, 156

Ogata, S. N., 51, 52, 87
Ornstein, R., 88
outpatient settings, psychiatric patients reporting childhood abuse, 45–47

Palmer, R. L., 44
paradigm defining mental disorders, 10
paradox in treatment of SIB, 97
parasuicidal borderlines, 15
pardon, 202
Paris, J., 21, 26, 79, 136
past
   coming to terms with, 184–206
   control over the present, 207–25
   shaping of transference by, 226–39
patients, goals in therapy, 105–6
peer review, 150, 251
   and countertransference, 246
   research indicating advantage of, 16–17
Perconte, S. T., 63
permission in therapy, 112, 117–18
Perr, I. N., 209

Perry, S., 25
personality
   stress, and development of, 73–74, 77
   traits, versus stylistic adaptations to abuse, 189
personality disorder, correlation with childhood abuse, 44
pharmacological treatment, 9–10
physical abuse, *see* sexual/physical abuse in childhood
Plakun, E. M., 21, 27
Pope, H. G., Jr., 48
Pope, K. S., 235
positive regard, 129, 235
   risks in expression of, 148
post-traumatic stress disorder
   aspects of the past in, 185–90
   versus borderline personality disorder, 7–8, 28–29, 49–51, 57–78
power, 123, 218–19
   of abusive parents, 193–94
   in counseling and in therapy, 232–34, 241–42
   male need for, 221
   and vulnerability, 161–62
Powers, W. K., 81
present, control by the past, 207–25
Pribor, E. F., 55
private experience, linkage with public conduct of SIB, 87–89
problem-solving, process for introducing, 127
process variables
   and content of patient-therapist interchange, 125
   effect on drop-out rates, 19
process versus content, 228–31
   in addressing patients' goals, 148
   in affirmation, 116–17
   in dissociative states, 216
   in successful therapy, 143–44
protest, SIB as, 81, 86
protocol-based therapy, studies of, 16

psychiatric disorders
  non-borderline, and childhood
    abuse, 37–47
  versus normal responses to stress,
    211–12
psychoanalytic psychotherapy, xi–xii,
  229
psychodynamic theory
  of borderline personality disorder,
    31
  organizing principle of, 155–56
  of SIB, 88–89
psychological trauma services, 210
psychology of self, study of, 14–15
psychotherapeutic model, 175
psychotherapy, xvii–xxi
  change in practice of, 9–10
  effectiveness with borderlines, 12,
    13–18, 250–51
  forgiveness in, 200
  labels in, 187
  outline of, for the patient who has
    been abused, 182–83
  technical issues in, 249
  see also technical decisions in ther-
    apy; therapy
public sanction for self-injurious behavior (SIB), 81–82

questionnaires, methodological problems with, 68

reality versus transference, 227–28
regression in therapy, 125–26, 187–
  88
rejection, testing the therapist for,
  232–35
relabeling, 173–74
religion
  and forgiveness, 200
  and self-injurious behavior, 81, 93–
    94
religious organizations, counseling
  sponsored by, 101, 205–6
repetition compulsion, 155–56, 222–
  25

replaying old patterns, 154–75, 243
  of betrayal, 169–73
  constructive, 173–75
  humanness of, 186–87
  in rejection, 233–34
  victimization, 163–69
reporting of abuse, 33
rescue fantasies, 138–44
research
  application of, 6–7
  about treatment of borderlines, 11–
    29
  see also studies
resilience, 75–77
responsibility
  and compulsion, 104
  for self-injurious behavior, 96
  and status as a victim, 209
Rich, C. L., 64
Rigotti, N. A., 84
risk-taking behavior, 142
role modeling, 119, 156, 228
Roy, A., 135
Runeson, B., 24
Rush, B., 212
Russell, D. E. H., 37, 53

sadness
  case example, 224
  in disillusion, 194
Sansone, R. A., 48
Scarr, S., 35, 75
Scheherazade Syndrome, 18
schizoaffective disorder, 40
schizophrenia, 11
  and childhood abuse, 44
    study of, 40
  drop-out rate in therapy, 19
  and genetics, 30
  and hypnotizability, 66
  and suicide rates, 24
Schoener, G. R., 235
Schroeder, S. R., 79
SCL-90R scores, 44
Scull, A., 84
Sederer, L. I., 25

seduction, testing the therapist for, 235–38
selection criteria for studies, 69
self-affirmation, 118
self-blame, case example, 224
self-esteem, 145–46
self-hatred, 217–19
self-image of patients in therapy, 113, 116–17
self-injurious behavior (SIB)
cross-cultural and historical views, 79–97
medieval versus modern, 95–96
publicly sanctioned, 81–82, 96–97
self-mutilative behavior
case example, 140
correlation with suicide, 27, 136
self-pity, management of, 118
self-protection, 118
self-report questionnaire, 41–42
methodological problems with, 68
self-respect, 219
Selzer, M. A., 20
sexual addiction, 62
sexual/physical abuse in childhood, xiv, 30–56, 77
past, coming to terms with, 184–206
rate of, in borderline patients, 12, 27–29
reporting of, 33
and SIB, 87
Shaffer, P., 74
Shay, J. J., 25
Shearer, S. L., 53, 136
Shore, D., 79
Skodal, A. E., 19
Smedes, L. B., 200
smoking, cultural view of, 84
sociocultural components of SIB, 88
Soloff, P. H., 11, 27
Solomon, S. D., 210
somatization disorder
among incest victims, 54
and reported childhood abuse, 47–48

Sparr, L. F., 210
splitting
case example, 231
in inconsistent family relationships, 192
of professionals, case example, 239
by a therapist, case example, 171
Sroufe, L. A., 76
state of consciousness
alteration of, by SIB, 88
disorders of, 214
status of therapists, 101
Stevenson, J., 14, 16
Stone, M. H., 13, 21, 26, 136, 212
Strasburger, L. H., 236
stream of consciousness
ongoing, 155
in PTSD/borderline patients, xv–xxi, 102–3, 185–86
stress
chronic, outcomes of, 189
and psychological problems, 73
stress-response syndrome, 210–11
studies
data from, 9–30
empirical, 36–37
follow-up, importance of, 188
methodology, critique, 68–69
of protocol-based therapy, 16
retrospective, critique, 59–62
see also research
stylistic adaptations to abuse, 189
substance abuse, and childhood abuse, 43, 45
suggestibility of patients, 64, 250
in BPD, 61–62
suicidality, 114–16
and childhood abuse, 45
and dependency needs, 126–27, 132–33, 168
in psychiatric patients abused in childhood, 42
and sadness, 194
and self-worth, 119

suicide rates, 250
    in affective disorders, 135–36
    among borderline patients, 12, 23–26
    disorders associated with, 26–27
supervision, research indicating advantage of, 16–17
    see also consultation; peer review
supportive therapy, 13–14
Surrey, J., 46, 48
surrogate mother role, 196–98
survivors, cultural emphasis on, 71, 207
Swett, C., Jr., 46, 48
symptoms
    choice of, 8, 65, 213–14
    linkage with abuse, 188
    shifting, in borderlines, 17–18
Szasz, T. S., 84

Taube, C., 18
Tavris, C., 248
technical decisions in therapy, 124, 249
    exploration of acting-out, 166
    mistakes in meeting dependency needs, 134
Terr, L. C., 70, 72
therapeutic alliance, 5, 106–7
therapeutic relationship
    acting-out, and eroticization of, 165–66
    changing ethical standards in, 10–11
    integrity of, case example, 116
    normative description of, 153
    standards for, 172
    see also ethical issues
therapists
    goals for therapy, 105–6
    gratification of, 110–11, 153
    interactions with patients, xvii–xviii, 227–28
    judgment of, 171–72, 247
    personal issues of, and therapeutic intervention, 242

prediction of the future by, 134–35
rating of, 13–14
responses of
    ambivalent, to dependency needs, 126–38
    to dissociative episodes, 215–16
    to patients' descriptions, 179–83
    to patients' needs, 120–25, 131–34
responsibility of, 243
self-concepts of, 129–31
status of, 101
tasks of, 107–9
testing for rejection by, 232–35
trust in, 219–20, 222
values of, 205
therapy
    exploratory, 14
    expressive, 13
    failure in, 106
        and interaction style, 235
        and process versus content, 148–49
    goals of, 156
    ideal goals of, 243
    patients' expectations of, 102
    privacy in, 115–16
    real versus theoretical session, 160
    regression in, 125–26, 187–88
    studies
        of drop-outs, first six months, 18–20
        of premature termination, 20–21
        of refusals and drop outs, 14
    supportive, 13–14
    see also psychotherapy; technical decisions in therapy
threshold phenomenon, abuse as, 35–36, 77
time-limited psychotherapy, 19
trance states, self-induced, 216
transference, 153, 157–61
    and idealization/devaluation, 243
    positive, 224–25
        cautious views of, 125
        effect on drop-out rate, 20
    satisfactions of, 110

shaping by the past, 226–39
and victimization, 239, 243
traumas
economic benefits of, 210
reexperiencing of, 189
treatment plans, written, 4–5
treatment resistance
acting-out as, 158
and entitlement, 112
and trust issues, 222
trust in therapists, 219–20, 222

validation, 152
as gratification, 111–12
of grief and anger, 118–20
as permission in therapy, 117–18
validity of abuse data, 34–35
values
affirmation of, in therapy, 116
and healing rituals, 110
and healthy or maladaptive styles,
102
positive, and SIB, 80–81
therapist's, 205
van der Kolk, B. A., 87
Van Gogh, V., 82
verbalization, 173
victimization, 149
passive, 161
replaying, 163–69
testing the therapist for, 238–39
and transference, 239, 243
victims
creation of, 248
patients as, 152, 207

violence
historic cultural perception of, 190–
91
and self-hatred, 218
volition
and blame, 104
versus compulsion, 103, 159, 201
versus determinism, 222
vulnerability, 75–77
of patients in therapy, 111
and power, 161–62
special, of PTSD/borderlines, 246

Waldinger, R. J., 19, 21
Waller, G., 48
Wallerstein, R.S., 13
Weekes, J. R., 65
Weinstein, D., 89
Westen, D., 52
Widom, C. S., 35, 76
Wilson, J. D., 83
Wilson, J. P., 63
Winchel, R. M., 79
women
statistics on abuse prevalence, 35,
37
for psychiatric patients, 43
study of parasuicidal borderlines,
15
world-view of the PTSD/borderline
patient, 105
worthlessness, 112

Zanarini, M. C., 51
Zweig-Frank, H., 72